MYTHS OF THE
Rune Stone

[Viking Martyrs and the
Birthplace of America]

DAVID M. KRUEGER

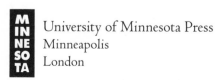

University of Minnesota Press
Minneapolis
London

Portions of chapter 5 were previously published in David Krueger, "Vikings Read with Blood and Dead: Viking Martyrs and the Conquest of the American Frontier," *Claremont Journal of Religion* (January 2012): 159–74.

Published by the University of Minnesota Press
III Third Avenue South, Suite 290
Minneapolis, MN 55401–2520
http://www.upress.umn.edu

Library of Congress Cataloging-in-Publication Data
Krueger, David M.
    Myths of the Rune Stone : Viking martyrs and the birthplace of America / David M. Krueger.
    Includes bibliographical references and index.
    ISBN 978-0-8166-9691-8 (hc)
    ISBN 978-0-8166-9696-3 (pb)
    I. Kensington Rune Stone. 2. Vikings—Minnesota—Legends. 3. Civil religion—Minnesota—History. 4. Community life—Minnesota—History. 5. Group identity—Minnesota—History. 6. Indians of North America—Minnesota—History. 7. Minnesota—Race relations—History. 8. Civil religion—United States. 9. Legends—Political aspects—United States. 10. Ethnicity—Political aspects—United States. I. Title.
    E105.K78 2015
    305.8009776—dc23   2015013268

Printed in the United States of America on acid-free paper

The University of Minnesota is an equal-opportunity educator and employer.

21 20 19 18 17 16 15   IO 9 8 7 6 5 4 3 2 I

This book is dedicated to
John C. Raines
professor, activist, mentor, friend

CONTENTS

PREFACE

Farm kids have a special relationship with land and place. I grew up just a few miles from Alexandria, Minnesota. Encircling my childhood home are endless acres of corn and wheat fields lined by stands of oak and maple trees. As a child, I spent many summer days stacking hay bales on wagons pulled by my dad's old Oliver tractor. On Sundays, my dad and I used to walk through the surrounding fields and woods and he would tell me stories about the hard work that went into tending the land. He told me how his dad had cleared hundreds of trees to make way for farming when he bought the land back in 1915. In the basement of our house, he showed me the yellowed paper deed that contained the record of who had owned the land over the years. At the top of the deed is the record of the first official exchange of land on October 1, 1867. It shifted ownership from the United States General Land Office to a homesteader named John Beaver.

Locals have long been interested in the history of the region prior to white settlement in the mid-nineteenth century, but their curiosity typically had little to do with the earlier inhabitants who were known to have traversed these lands, including the Dakota, the Ojibwe, and the Winnebago. Alexandria, Minnesota, declares itself the birthplace of America—at least that is what it says on the shield of the twenty-eight-foot-tall Viking statue that greets tourists as they come into town. The audacious claim is supported by a Swedish immigrant's discovery in 1898 of a stone tablet with runic letters and the date 1362. By the 1960s, the artifact was widely embraced as proof that Vikings had visited what was to become Minnesota long before the voyages of Christopher Columbus.

By the 1970s and 1980s, when I grew up, confidence in the rune stone as an authentic medieval artifact had waned, but many continued to advocate it as a symbol of Scandinavian pride. Most of my ancestors hail from Sweden and the culinary delicacies of lefse (a potato-based flat bread) and lutefisk (don't ask) made their annual appearance at the Christmas Eve meal. For my family, that was largely the extent of our ethnic devotion. I defined myself primarily in terms of my Christian faith and my American citizenship. Little did I know at the time, but interest in the Kensington Rune Stone during the twentieth century had extended far beyond ethnic concerns. A once-important element of the Kensington Rune Stone story was the notion that the Vikings came to America on a mission to find Norse colonists who had disappeared from Greenland and were feared to have abandoned the Christian faith.

I never took much interest in whether or not the stone was an authentic Norse artifact dating to the fourteenth century. I was, however, fascinated by the ways that people talked about it. While studying American religious history in graduate school, it became evident to me that the story of the Kensington Rune Stone could offer a unique perspective on America's preoccupation with divine blessing and its troubled way of coming to terms with the history of the continent's first residents. The story of the Kensington Rune Stone challenged many of the orthodoxies about America's founders. Although the dominant version of U.S. history highlights stories of English-speaking Protestants in East Coast colonies, the runic myth imagines that the nation began with Catholic Swedes and Norwegians in the heart of continent. It is my hope and prayer that this book will stimulate questions about how Americans tell stories about their past. Who is included in these stories and who is left out? Who is the hero, who is the discoverer, who is the villain, and why?

INTRODUCTION

A Holy Mission to Minnesota

> 8 Swedes and 22 Norwegians on an exploration journey from
> Vinland westward. We had our camp by two rocky islets one
> day's journey north of this stone. We were out fishing one day.
> When we came home we found 10 men red with blood and dead.
> AVM, save us from evil. We have 10 men by the sea to look after
> our ships, 14 days' journey from this island. Year: 1362.
>
> —Translation of the Kensington Rune Stone inscription
> by Erik Wahlgren, *The Kensington Stone: A Mystery Solved*

In the summer of 1962, the Alexandria, Minnesota, Chamber of Commerce sponsored a historical pageant for what they referred to as the six
hundredth anniversary of the Kensington Rune Stone. Although the
stone's existence was unknown until it was unearthed by a local Swedish
American farmer in 1898, its runic inscription told the story of a group
of Swedes and Norwegians who visited what was to become Minnesota
in the fourteenth century. Local residents believed this stone proved that
Europeans traveled to the heart of North America 140 years prior to
the explorations of Christopher Columbus. The Runestone Pageant was
part of a weeklong civic celebration called Viking Days, which included
parades and an appearance by nationally known radio personality Paul
Harvey, who broadcast his show from Alexandria on opening day. A
large Fourth of July fireworks display inaugurated the four-night pageant in an outdoor amphitheater on the shore of the city's Lake Winona.
Civic boosters promoted the event months in advance and hired a community theater professional, Bert Merling, to write the script and direct
the production. Merling cast more than fifty local residents for the roles
of Vikings, Nordic goddesses, and other important characters in the
history of the Kensington Rune Stone.

The opening scene of the pageant takes place in the mid-fourteenth century in the court of Sweden's King Magnus, whom the script refers to as a "defender of Christianity." A chieftain from the western colony of Greenland enters the throne room and reports to the king that the settlers have disappeared and their villages had been raided by "skrælings"—the Norse term for the indigenous people they encountered. The chieftain goes on to say that the settlers have forsaken worship of the Christian God and turned to the worship of pagan gods. King Magnus is distraught over the news and holds a crucifix above his head, proclaiming: "Lord God of Hosts, we commit ourselves to a holy expedition, its undefeatable aim—the reconversion to Christianity of our subjects." King Magnus assembles an expedition team of thirty "Christian Vikings" to find the apostate colonists and return them to the church. To lead this important expedition, Magnus selects his trusted bodyguard, Sir Paul Knutson. While music from Wagner's *Tannhäuser* plays in the background, Knutson declares, "Your Majesties—the crusade begins!"

In another scene, a distinguished-looking man in his mid-fifties and a younger man wearing a University of Minnesota sweatshirt enter the stage and the narrator says

> The great leader, throughout history, is always a lonely
> figure—he ever stands alone, misunderstood, and often slan-
> dered and mocked. And so, too, a scholar-historian who has
> devoted his life to unearthing evidence. That scholar-historian
> is Professor Hjalmar Holand of Wisconsin.

The student was writing his thesis on Norse explorations and appealed to Holand for guidance. "Professor Holand, posterity and the ages will acclaim your lifetime work in uncovering the evidence of the Norse-Swedish penetration to Minnesota in 1362 . . . But frankly, how have you managed to take the slings and arrows of both academical [*sic*] and society's denials, and mockery of your revelations?" Holand responds, "Man's inhumanity to man perhaps . . . I am most happy to say not even the most blinded, biased, prejudiced critic has been able to disprove the Kensington Runestone!" Holand goes on to list the evidence that he claims vindicated his theory: chiseled holes in boulders he called mooring stones that were used to anchor boats along the pathway of the Norsemen to Minnesota, Norse artifacts such as swords and battle-axes found in area farm fields, and the integrity of Olof Ohman, who claimed to have discovered the rune stone in his field.

The next episode dramatizes the arrival of the Norsemen to Minnesota in 1362, which the script describes as "the greatest historical event in American history." The Vikings enter the amphitheater after disembarking from a dragon-shaped Viking ship specially constructed for the pageant. Knutson cautiously leads his men on to the shore and declares: "No hostile skrælings as far as the eye can reach . . . but hidden somewhere in these vast woodlands . . . lurks the enemy." Knutson drops to his knee and gives thanks to God "for His merciful care and protection." Professor Holand and the student return to narrate the ensuing events. The Vikings, Holand explains, were unable to find their missing countrymen. Not seeing any skrælings either, the expedition "was lulled into guardless security." Twenty of the group took a day of leisure to fish on a nearby lake and left ten behind to guard the encampment. As the twenty came home that night, they were greeted with "a ghastly silence," and at that moment "they saw their butchered comrades . . . the scene of which the Runestone froze in stone for all time." "Good God—you mean—10 men Red with Blood and Dead?" exclaimed the student. "The scene on the Kensington Runestone testifies to that . . . No one has ever disproved those runes!" says Holand. The dead Vikings lay sprawled out on the stage while the surviving Vikings wander about the carnage with grief-stricken expressions on their faces. Knutson commands his men to bury the dead, but before they can begin, a scout returns to the camp warning that an army of "savages" had amassed to the west. "Every man to the ship!" exclaims Knutson as the Vikings scurry in hasty retreat. As they depart, Norse goddesses riding real horses rush through the audience and onto the stage to retrieve the slain Viking bodies before they are further "mutilated" by the Indians. This scene is choreographed to Richard Wagner's "Ride of the Valkyries."[1]

In the final episode, Professor Holand stands in front of the stage curtain and declares to the student the veracity of the Kensington Runestone. "Like Gibraltar, the Liberty Bell, or the Pyramids, it attests forever, the historic truth . . . The Norwegians and Swedes were the discoverers of America, and Alexandria's lakelands! Not Christopher Columbus!" The student asks the professor why the history books have not been revised to reflect this truth. Holand answers, "The academicians, in their isolated ivory towers hold back historic truths, [and] often, as in the tragedy of Galileo, even forced him to deny his discovery that the earth moved around the sun, but lad, truth will [win] out." Dazzled by the wisdom of his teacher, the student declares, "[T]o you, Professor Holand, will go the immortal honor of revealing that truth!"

As Holand and the student exit the stage, the curtain opens slowly to reveal a spotlight trained on a solitary Viking carving the inscription onto the slab of stone. Standing behind him is the Goddess Columbia holding an American flag and the Norse Warrior Goddess Brunhilde holding her sword and spear. To their right and left are women holding the flags of Sweden and Norway, both at tilt. The entire cast files onto the stage. The rune master sets down his chisel, turns toward the audience, lifts his hands up, and proclaims, "This eternal monument to you, valiant companions, Swedes and Norwegians, who died in this paradise lakeland wilderness, for Christ, in 1362." The pageant ends with the organist playing, "with all stops out," "America the Beautiful." The stage is bathed in red, white, and blue lights.[2]

An American Rune Stone

The Runestone Pageant Play of 1962 represents the fullest blossoming of the cultural phenomenon first initiated by the charismatic Hjalmar Holand and then embellished by other supporters of the Kensington Rune Stone over six decades. In the years immediately following Ohman's discovery, the stone artifact and its runic inscription were analyzed by geologists, archaeologists, Scandinavian linguists, and historians. Most of them concluded that it was the product of a hoax, created in the late nineteenth century by the immigrant farmer and his neighbors. However, scholarly denunciations did little to dampen the spirits of those who were the stone's ardent defenders.[3] As the script of the Runestone Pageant suggests, there were numerous cultural and religious factors that fueled popular enthusiasm for the artifact. The story it told captured the imagination of western Minnesotans and served as a powerful civic myth of origin.

There was no person more central to the promotion of the Kensington Rune Stone and the construction of its historical narrative than amateur historian and Norwegian immigrant Hjalmar R. Holand. In 1907, Holand acquired the stone from the farmer who discovered it and began a lifelong mission to prove its authenticity. Through dozens of books and articles, Holand constructed a rhetorical fortress in defense of the stone. Much of his argumentation is based on pseudoscience and wild historical conjecture, but in spite of his specious claims, he generated enough publicity for the Kensington Rune Stone that by the 1960s, 60 percent of Minnesotans believed that Vikings were the first European visitors to the state.[4] The artifact was featured at the Smithsonian Institution, the New York World's Fair, and the state's professional football team became known as the Minnesota Vikings.[5] How does one explain the widespread popularity of the rune stone and the theory of pre-Columbian Norse travels to Minnesota considering the lack of credible historical evidence? The key to answering this question begins with understanding Holand's writings as a work of collective memory rather than history.[6] In other words, Holand's pre-Columbian history of Minnesota had contemporary needs in mind.

Holand tells the story of the "birth" of the United States in western Minnesota as marked by the sacrificial deaths of Christian missionaries from Scandinavia. Area residents found great appeal in Holand's theory. Immigrants from Sweden and Norway used the inscribed stone to anchor their presence in the Minnesota landscape and the narrative of American history. They could simultaneously dwell in their new environment while maintaining a mythical connection to their homeland. The immigrants joined other white residents in using Holand's narrative of Viking sacrifice at the hands of Indians to commemorate the deaths of white settlers and justify their violent conquest of the region's first residents.[7] Starting in the 1920s, the rune stone emerged as a sacred civic symbol to unify and empower small-town residents to defend themselves from external cultural critiques, such as those leveled by Sinclair Lewis's novel *Main Street*. Locals came to revere Olof Ohman, discoverer of the stone, as the quintessential "real American," whose humility and common sense exemplified the best of small-town life. Area Catholics were also eager to embrace Holand's story. Archbishop John Ireland gave a ringing endorsement of the stone's authenticity, declaring its inscription to contain a Catholic prayer, the first uttered in North America. This assertion helped church leaders to assert their social power, claim Minnesota as a uniquely Catholic place, and fuel an unsuccessful attempt to proselytize Swedish and Norwegian Americans, who largely adhered to the Lutheran church. As Catholics entered the American mainstream in the mid-twentieth century, they collaborated with Protestants to deploy Holand's narrative to resist the forces of secularism by claiming the United States to be founded as an exclusively Christian nation. Throughout the twentieth century, the "savage skrælings" in Holand's narrative served as a metaphor of external threats to the community and locals used them as a contrast to construct white, Christian, and small-town identities.[8]

In his book *The Kensington Stone: A Mystery Solved*, Erik Wahlgren referred to the artifact as "An American Rune Stone." As he observed, rune stones are not common in the United States, but they are ubiquitous in Scandinavia. Rune stones date to the medieval period and were typically used to commemorate the dead. Less frequently, they were used to commemorate those who died on excursions abroad.[9] As will become clear in chapter 2, this latter meaning was well understood among Scandinavian Americans at the turn of the century.[10] Viewing the Kensington Stone as a product of the late nineteenth century and not the fourteenth, Wahlgren sees the stone and its story as an "episode in the history and development of the American frontier."[11] This book examines the cultural milieu of the late nineteenth century in which the rune stone was likely created, but it also illuminates the myriad ways that the artifact has been interpreted and utilized by Minnesotans subsequently.

The story of the Kensington Rune Stone phenomenon is a helpful lens through which to examine several dimensions of Minnesota culture in particular, and American culture in general. The public debates over the authenticity of stone have been charged with class tension. By "class," I am referring not to group differences based on material conditions, but on cultural distinctions.[12] In this analysis, class distinctions are marked by residence (urban versus rural), region (Midwest versus East Coast), education level (academically trained versus self-taught), and aesthetic preference (the celebration of versus the condemnation of kitsch). Minnesotans variably embraced and condemned the stone with these class distinctions and power differentials in mind.

The quest for an ancient dimension to U.S. history and the desire to prove that one's group "came here first" have been enduring elements of American culture and they were particularly fervent during the nineteenth century. Joseph Smith claimed that the angel Moroni led him to a collection of golden plates buried in a western New York hillside, which told of an ancient American civilization. Smith's "translation" of the golden plates was published in 1830 as the Book of Mormon. The book situated the American landscape in the biblical narrative and inspired a westward migration of his followers. Around the same time period, New England historians and other writers were fascinated with the notion that Norsemen had visited their region prior to Columbus. Norwegian immigrants popularized this notion as a means to bolster their social status, but longtime New Englanders used the claim to address anxieties regarding immigration to the United States.[13] The creation and interpretation of the Kensington Rune Stone will be examined in the context of the widely shared American desire to construct a national prehistory infused with meaning.

The rune stone debates in the twentieth century were inextricably linked to the ways that white Minnesotans talked and thought about the region's first residents. The stone was unearthed during a time period in which there were fervent efforts to commemorate the hundreds of white settlers who died in the Dakota War of 1862. Chapter 2 describes how monuments, memorials, and written accounts of pioneer history flourished in turn-of-the-century Minnesota. In the decades immediately following the traumatic events of the so-called Sioux Uprising, white residents frequently portrayed Indians as irredeemably violent, but by the early decades of the twentieth century, most white Minnesotans portrayed Indians in nostalgic and romantic terms. However, as later chapters will illustrate, many of the rune stone defenders continued to evoke well into the twentieth century images of godless, threatening Indians lurking in the wilderness. This rune stone story exemplifies the enduring legacy of Indian savagery and white martyrdom motifs in American popular culture.

The Cult of the Kensington Rune Stone

Most of what has been written on the Kensington Rune Stone has been preoccupied with questions of authenticity.[14] Was the stone inscribed by Norse explorers in the fourteenth century or by a Swedish immigrant in the nineteenth? Scholars and nonscholars alike have delved into the fields of archaeology, linguistics, runic studies, and Scandinavian history to make their case. Insufficient attention has been given to the reasons for the popular appeal of the Kensington Rune Stone since it was unearthed in 1898. What has been written in this regard has primarily focused on two explanations. The first is that Minnesotans have embraced the rune stone because of its benefits to the local economy. As a book on Minnesota tourism cynically concludes, rune stone enthusiasts were able to overlook scientific evidence against the stone because they "recognized a tourist attraction when they saw it."[15] The second explanation is that Swedish and Norwegian immigrants used the rune stone to justify their place in American society and assert their ethnic pride.[16] Economics and ethnicity play starring roles in the rune stone story, but as the Runestone Pageant suggests, there were multiple factors at play. Religion, in particular, played a feature role in fueling the popular enthusiasm for the artifact and framing the rune stone story as a sacred civic narrative.[17]

Hjalmar Holand's historical narrative became attractive largely because it told the story of heroic Christian sacrifice. However, the Christian motivations of the Norsemen were not at the forefront in Holand's earliest writings about the Kensington Rune Stone. In fact, he posited several other motivating factors for why the Norsemen ventured into the heart of North America. In his first *Harper's Weekly* article published in 1909, he asserted that the Norsemen were on a journey to explore the new continent in hopes of acquiring resources, such as timber, fish, and grapes for Norway.[18] In his second article a year later, Holand said that the Norsemen had ventured westward to fight skrælings who were threatening Norse settlements in Greenland and beyond.[19] It was not until years later that he posited Christian zeal as the central motivation for the medieval Norsemen to embark on their transatlantic journey. As scholarly challenges mounted and ethnic support wavered, Holand baptized his historical narrative to broaden its popular appeal. Thanks to this strategy, a variety of Catholic and Protestant leaders took an interest in the storied artifact who would not have otherwise done so. Although Holand expressed personal disdain for organized religion, he recognized the efficacy of using Christian rhetoric to solicit popular support for his defense of the Kensington Rune Stone.[20]

There is another way that religion factors prominently into the Kensington Rune Stone story. Enthusiasm for Holand's rune stone narrative can be thought of in terms of a cultural religion that transcends the boundaries of traditional denominations and institutions.[21] In other words, belief in the authenticity of the stone can be conceived in terms of a religious expression in and of itself.[22] Religious terms have been frequently used by enthusiasts to describe their endorsement of the artifact.

For example, an Alexandria physician and one of the founders of the Runestone Museum, was highlighted in a 1959 newspaper article titled "Dr. Tanquist's Testimony: Why I Believe in the Runestone." During his speech, Tanquist presented his reasons why he believed the artifact to be authentic to a group of local residents.[23] When Hjalmar Holand released his 1956 book *Explorations in America before Columbus,* Alexandria's Calvary Lutheran Church hosted a "testimonial dinner" to celebrate the book's distribution to public schools across the state. More than three hundred people attended the event and local students were encouraged to read Holand's book in advance of the dinner and write essays about why they believed the Kensington Stone to be true.[24]

Outside observers have also used religious terminology to describe the zeal of Kensington Rune Stone enthusiasts. These characterizations have often been pejorative, implying that the artifact's supporters have abandoned reason. Brian Branston, a British TV producer who spent time in Alexandria researching the rune stone during the 1970s, described the popular enthusiasm in terms of irrational belief:

> Those who believe it bogus rest their case on the arguments of reputable scholars, particularly linguists and runologists who are practically unanimous in declaring the inscription a hoax. Those who believe in the genuineness of the inscription hold on to their beliefs much as one would hold to a religious faith. You cannot reason with faith.[25]

In a subsequent article, Branston addresses a rune stone enthusiast directly: "Holand was a false prophet who has led you and all other ascribers to the Runestone religion astray. You have been literally brought to worship a graven image."[26]

Accusations of idolatry levied toward Kensington Rune Stone supporters have done more to obscure than illuminate the complex cultural and religious dynamics at play. Rather than dismiss the strident devotion to the rune stone narrative as unreasonable, it is necessary to consider what a religious disposition toward the artifact offered its adherents. It has often been argued that science has usurped the authority that science once held.[27] However, it is clear that scientific thinking is limited in its ability to satisfy many human desires.[28] Despite the lack of scientific evidence to authenticate the Kensington Rune Stone, scores of Minnesotans came to its defense because they felt a need for meaning and assurance that the stone's story could provide. The chapters that follow show how belief in the Kensington Rune Stone helped Minnesotans cope with a variety of social challenges in the twentieth century.[29]

Parallels to American Civil and Cultural Religion

Popular devotion to the Kensington Rune Stone and the mythic narrative it symbolizes shares much in common with what has come to be known as American civil religion. In the 1960s, sociologist Robert Bellah observed the overt God language of presidential addresses and founding American documents. He described American civil religion as a "public religious expression" characterized by "a set of beliefs, symbols and rituals" and as "an understanding of the American experience in the light of ultimate and universal reality."[30] Although Bellah, and many scholars who followed him, emphasized civil religious discourse, practices, and symbols at the national level, the present analysis considers how a region appropriated elements of American civil religion for its own purposes.[31] The devotion to the Kensington Rune Stone can be thought of as a local sect of American civil religion that fused national narratives with ethnic, racial, and regional concerns.[32]

The mythic narrative of the Kensington Rune Stone must be understood in the context of several enduring myths in American life.[33] One of the most popular is the notion that the United States is God's "chosen nation" set apart with a special destiny. This trope is frequently appealed to under a secularized guise of "American exceptionalism." The term "manifest destiny," popularized in the mid-nineteenth century, functioned as a divinely ordained ideology to justify westward expansion of white settlement and the displacement of Native Americans. Related to this myth is the notion that the United States is an innocent nation. Such claims are often used by the powerful to disguise their domination over others.[34] Chapter 2 shows how rune stone enthusiasts frequently deployed the language of "innocent domination" and constructed a rigid moral binary between white victim and Indian perpetrator.

Holand's claim that that America was discovered by Christian Norsemen on a journey to save the faith resonated with a popular myth that the United States was founded as a "Christian nation."[35] This claim was particularly fervent during the height of the Cold War, as American leaders contrasted a Christian America with the "godless" Soviet Union.[36] Chapter 5 illustrates how the Runestone Pageant of 1962 and writings produced by rune stone enthusiasts around the same time reveal a degree of anxiety about Minnesotans abandoning the Christian faith. That anxiety was likely fueled by recent Supreme Court decisions and popular media depictions that were perceived as threatening to the Christian faith.[37] Imagining that a Christian nation was birthed in Minnesota gave locals the confidence and hope that the faith would endure.

Holand's rune stone narrative is at its heart a story of American sacrifice. The "ten men red with blood and dead" became martyrs for a variety of causes championed by Minnesotans and had the effect of forging group identity.[38] Immigrant writers in the United States have long endeavored to prove that their group has made sacrifices for the nation. Norwegian immigrants, for example, frequently trumpeted the sacrificial deaths of their peers in the Civil War to prove their commitment to their American home.[39] Scandinavian Americans and other white pioneer residents in Minnesota paralleled their own sacrifices with those of the fourteenth-century Norsemen. Catholic Minnesotans, likewise, upheld the dead Vikings as martyrs for the cause of bringing Christ to the North American wilderness.

Civic myths about the meaning, purpose, and trajectory of a community's history are made all the more powerful when they are made concrete and visible in material form.[40] Americans have considered several objects to be sacred symbols of national identity, including the Liberty Bell, the Statue of Liberty, and the American flag. The American flag in particular has functioned as a sacred, representative emblem of the United States, what Émile Durkheim would call a totem. A totem represents a group's collective identity and has the power to evoke an emotional response when individuals stand in its midst.[41] Identifying with a totem is at its heart an act of worship, or, more specifically, an act of collective self-worship. Thus, in Durkheim's view, society is God.[42] Throughout its history, the Kensington Rune Stone has been handled and conceived in terms of a sacred civic artifact. When on public display, the artifact was often accompanied by armed guards, and local residents frequently expressed concern that it might be desecrated. As chapter 3 demonstrates, defending the Kensington Rune Stone as an authentic artifact became a way to defend the cultural prestige of the region and its residents.

Critical to the symbolic power of the Kensington Rune Stone is its material constitution. Mircea Eliade once observed that "Rock shows the [human] something that transcends the precariousness of his humanity" and therefore conveys power and permanence.[43] In other words, rocks perform cultural work. In the case of the rune stone, it anchored the identity of Minnesotans by claiming an American sacred space.[44] There are numerous stone memorial and monuments that Americans consider to be significant. The Washington Monument in Washington, D.C., and Mount Rushmore in South Dakota are among them. Chapter 3 describes how civic boosters used the Kensington Rune Stone as an inspiration to construct a stone monument dedicated to the nation's true founding fathers: the Norse explorers who memorialized their dead comrades in Ohman's field.

The rune stone discovery site was just one location in a sacred landscape mapped by Hjalmar Holand. Holand identified an imagined pathway of Paul Knutson's expedition as they traveled across the North Atlantic, through Hudson Bay, and up a series of waterways into the heart of North America. Marking this pathway were a series of purported Norse artifacts (battle-axes, swords, fire steels) and mooring stones (boulders with holes used to anchor ships). With the help of area residents who were all too eager to help him find such evidence, Holand claimed that he had found the site of a "Viking massacre" and the site of the first Catholic Mass in North America. By the mid-twentieth century, many white, western Minnesotans accepted it as a given that medieval Norse travelers had left their mark on their region. The following chapters describe the process by which Holand and other rune stone enthusiasts created an American birthplace that bolstered Midwestern identity and erased the claims of the region's first residents.[45]

Sacred places, objects, and stories are often made so through the power of ritual. In American civil religion, reciting the Pledge of Allegiance, making a pilgrimage to sacred civic sites, and celebrating civic holidays such as Memorial Day and Independence Day have the power to arouse patriotic sentiment. In his study of Australia's indigenous population, Émile Durkheim observed that social/religious cohesiveness is created and preserved through sacred rites. Durkheim described how clan assemblies generated feelings of "collective effervescence" where participants experienced "a force external to them" and a sense of grandiosity that united the group members with the symbol that represented them.[46] Enthusiasts of the Kensington Rune Stone also used ritual to foster civic unity and inculcate in the community an authorized historical narrative.[47] The rune stone history pageants dramatized the imagined visit of the medieval Norsemen to Minnesota and community residents could take on the roles of Vikings, Nordic goddesses, skrælings, and even the heroic rune stone defender, Hjalmar Holand. Civic boosters and other community participants often spoke in euphoric terms when discussing these civic events. In addition to analyzing history pageants as sacred civic gatherings, this book will explore the ritualistic dimensions of archaeological excavations, monument fund-raising rallies, and the visits of the Kensington Rune Stone to the Smithsonian Institution and the New York World's Fair.

The chapters of this book follow both a thematic and a chronological order. They are roughly organized by the multiple constituencies that took an interest in the Kensington Rune Stone during the twentieth century. Their interests converge and diverge over time in response to changing historical circumstances and shifting circles of identity. The first chapter traces the early history of the rune stone and the meaning of the artifact for Scandinavian Americans. Chapter 2 illuminates the broader white American interest in the runic inscription and the influence of the Dakota War on its interpretation. Chapter 3 shows how the rune stone emerged as a symbol of regional and civic identity. The Catholic interest in the stone is considered in chapter 4 and chapter 5 situates the artifact in Cold War discourse about Christian identity and national meaning. To reiterate, this book renders visible the construction and evolution of an American myth of origin that Christian Vikings died at the hands of Indians in the Minnesota wilderness prior to Columbus. To begin the process of unveiling the anatomy of this cultural phenomenon, it is necessary to return to Ohman's farm, where the stone hierophany was unearthed.

CHAPTER ONE

Westward from Vinland
An Immigrant Saga by Hjalmar Holand

> Swedes and Norwegians are of the purest Nordic stock and a
> relatively smaller number would have been sufficient to transmit
> the physical peculiarities for which the Mandans were noted
> than if any other nationality had been represented by these early
> culture bearers.
>
> —Hjalmar Holand, *Westward from Vinland*

The events surrounding the unearthing of the Kensington Rune Stone
and its immediate aftermath are contradictory and hotly debated. As
the story is traditionally told by area residents, a Swedish immigrant
farmer named Olof Ohman was hard at work during the late summer
of 1898 cutting down trees on his farm near the town of Kensington,
Minnesota. Ohman and his sons were using a winch to pull tree stumps
out of the ground in order to prepare a new field for cultivation. Tangled
in the roots of one tree was a large, gray slab of stone, which they struggled to pull out of the ground.[1] Ohman's ten-year-old son Edward
noticed strange chiseled markings on two sides of the stone after he had
brushed off some of the dirt with his cap. Ohman called his neighbor,
Nils Flaaten, a Norwegian-American farmer who was working nearby,
to come and view the curiosity. In signed affidavits from 1909, Flaaten
and Ohman testified that the inscription had an ancient and weathered
appearance.[2] They carried the stone back to Ohman's farmyard, thinking it might be of historical importance. Some of Ohman's neighbors
suspected that the stone might be a marker for buried treasure and a
swarm of locals descended upon Ohman's farm with shovels in hand.[3]

Although no treasure was found, numerous area residents viewed the stone with curiosity after Ohman permitted its display in the window of the First State Bank in the nearby village of Kensington.[4] Local residents, primarily of Norwegian and Swedish descent, concluded that the symbols were similar to those found in illustrations of runic inscriptions in Scandinavian history books. Bank cashier and Norwegian immigrant Samuel A. Siverts made a copy of the inscription and sent it to Professor Olaus Breda, a Scandinavian linguist at the University of Minnesota, in January 1899. A month later, the stone was shipped to Professor George Curme, a linguist at Northwestern University in Chicago.

In February 1899, a local newspaper reported that Professor Breda concluded that there were "internal evidences in the inscription that it is not authentic." The chief of these, he says, is that "the inscriptions seem to be a jumble of Swedish and Norwegian in late grammatical forms and here and there English words, but all spelled in runic characters. They are not old Norse."[5] Professor Curme was also skeptical of the runic inscription for similar linguistic reasons. Additionally, copies of the inscription were analyzed by scholars in Oslo, Norway. The conclusions of Christiana University professors Gustav Storm, Sophus Bugge, and Oluf Rugh were published in the *Minneapolis Tribune* in April 1899: "The so-called rune stone is a crude fraud, perpetrated by a Swede with the aid of a chisel and a meager knowledge of runic letters and English."[6] Following the initial scientific assessments and the negative publicity that followed, public opinion of the stone as an authentic medieval artifact quickly faded. To the disappointment of many, it was returned to Ohman's farm, where it sat in obscurity for more than eight years. As one enthusiast described it, the rune stone served as a stepping stone for Ohman's granary and provided "a tolerable place to straighten nails and rivet harness straps."[7]

Leif Eriksson and the "True" Discovery of America

To most observers, it was no coincidence that a rune stone purporting to be from the fourteenth century was unearthed in the field of a Swedish-American farmer in a region heavily populated by recent immigrants from Sweden and Norway. During the late nineteenth and early twentieth century, these immigrants were prolific producers and consumers of historical literature about Viking travels in North America prior to the

The Kensington Rune Stone is thirty-six inches long, fifteen inches wide, about six inches thick, and weighs just over two hundred pounds. Courtesy of the Douglas County Historical Society, Minnesota.

arrival of Christopher Columbus in the West Indies in 1492. The early presence of Vikings in North America demonstrated that Swedes and Norwegians belonged here. Writing in 1900, the Norwegian-American poet Franklin Petersen said, "Because we are reminded of the sagas of old and are proud of the land we forsook. Can it be that the blood of the Vikings still flows in our veins like a still-running brook?"[8] Historian Odd Lovoll uses the moniker "Cult of Leif Eriksson" to describe the widespread enthusiasm for all things Viking.

Rasmus B. Anderson (1846–1936) was the first widely known writer to promote the myth of Viking discovery in his book *America Not Discovered by Columbus* published in 1874.[9] In this book, Anderson attempted to educate both Norwegian immigrants and other Americans about Norwegian literature and mythology, while challenging America's foundation myths by demonstrating that Scandinavians played a vital role in the origins of the United States.[10] According to historian Orm Øverland, immigrant writers have often used "homemaking myths" to convince both fellow immigrants and the dominant society that they belong in America. Immigrants use "foundation myths" to claim that their ancestors were the first or among the first Europeans to explore and settle in North America. "Blood sacrifice myths" are used to demonstrate that an immigrant group has made sacrifices for the host nation in some way, especially in times of national crisis. Ideological homemaking myths describe how a particular ethnic group had already embodied certain central components of American ideals before arriving in the United States. All three of these myths can be found in the writings of Rasmus B. Anderson.[11]

Born in Wisconsin to Norwegian-born parents, Anderson was a professor of Scandinavian languages at the University of Wisconsin–Madison. He reinforced the widely shared notion among some New England historians of his day that Vikings had explored North America and even settled as far south as New England.[12] Using the Vinland sagas as his primary source material and writings by nineteenth-century New England historians interested in Viking history, Anderson argued that the Vinland spoken of in the Norse sagas was located off Narragansett Bay in modern-day Massachusetts and Rhode Island. Anderson offered two pieces of archaeological evidence to support his claim: the Dighton Rock, a large boulder with a number of supposed runic markings inscribed on its surface near Fall River, Massachusetts, and a stone

Stone tower in Newport, Rhode Island, circa 1899. Library of Congress Prints and Photographs Division, Detroit Publishing Company Photograph Collection.

tower near Newport, Rhode Island, purported to have been built by medieval Norsemen.[13] The dominant historiography of the day identified New England as the geographic birthplace of the future United States. If Norwegian Americans were to have a place in the founding narrative of America, the presence of their ancestors had to be inscribed into this landscape.

Anderson made his case that contemporary Norwegian Americans deserved a measure of gratitude because their ancestors made numerous sacrifices in founding America. He portrayed the Norsemen as preparing the way for the Pilgrims by bringing Christianity to the Indians and argued that Leif Eriksson's brother Thorwald died at the hands of Indians in a self-sacrificial attempt to settle Cape Cod.[14] Anderson also argued that the Norse spirit of sacrifice was still alive in the nineteenth century, as evidenced by his fellow Norwegian immigrants' willingness to give their lives in the Union army during the Civil War.

Anderson appealed to the American elite by arguing that Scandinavians were the source of America's democratic ideals. He noted that one of England's most significant rulers, William the Conqueror, had descended from Norsemen who invaded Normandy in 912.[15] When William invaded England in 1066, he brought with him the democratic ideals of Norse culture that would come to have a major influence on English society. Anderson claimed that the Puritans of seventeenth-century Massachusetts came from parts of England that had been colonized by Norsemen. According to Anderson, the Puritans brought the "Norwegian plant of liberty" with them on the Mayflower to New England, where it took root and thrived in American soil:[16]

> Yes, the Norsemen were truly a great people! Their spirit found its way into the Magna Carta of England and into the Declaration of Independence in America. The spirit of the Vikings still survives in the bosoms of Englishmen, Americans and Norsemen, extending their commerce, taking bold positions against tyranny, and producing wonderful internal improvements in these countries.[17]

Anderson demonstrated that American society owed a great deal to Scandinavians for their contribution to the most sacred of American institutional ideals.

Playing into the racial politics of the nineteenth century, Anderson argued that Norwegian Americans and Anglo-Saxon Americans shared a common heritage. His writings are likely affected by the anti-immigrant rhetoric of the Know-Nothing movement during this period. Know-Nothingism promoted the superiority of the Anglo-Saxon race, which had as its source Teutonic or Germanic blood. As one historian observes, Anderson was not content to have Scandinavian Americans just be accepted as white; he believed they were true Anglo-Saxons as differentiated from immigrants originating in other parts of Europe.[18] Anderson did not challenge notions of Anglo-Saxon superiority; he wanted Norwegians to be included with them and share their privileges.[19]

Anderson's writings produced a Norwegian-American mythology that both glorified the virtues of Norwegian-American immigrants and praised the cherished values of the host country. His aim was to get Anglo-Americans to recognize Scandinavian immigrants as close family members who could share the exclusive privileges that belonged to a people of a superior race. Considering the contributions of Norwegians to American history, Anderson argued for the inclusion of Norse history in public education and hoped for a day when the great Viking explorers Leif Eriksson and Thorwald would become household names.[20] Anderson experienced some success in this regard. Working with a handful of New England historians, he initiated a movement that created a monument to Leif Eriksson in Boston in 1887. In later years, statues of Erikson were installed in prominent public spaces in Chicago, Seattle, and Duluth, and in front of the Minnesota state capitol in St. Paul. As a historian, Anderson was criticized by his peers. Scholarly reviews in both Europe and the United States of *America Not Discovered by Columbus* were generally negative. Most of them characterized his work as ethnic propaganda devoid of academic merit.[21] Not surprisingly, Anderson was praised in the Norwegian-American press and his work was widely read by Scandinavian Americans in Minnesota.[22]

Building an Immigrant "Sacred Canopy"

Myths about pre-Columbian Viking visitors to North America not only helped bolster immigrant social power, they also served to satisfy a variety of cultural longings for immigrants. New arrivals from Sweden and Norway came from countries where the Lutheran church largely monopolized religious and social life. Every citizen was registered by the government through the local parish church. Parishes were the means through which civic life, cultural life, and religious life were held together. Sociologist of religion Peter Berger would describe this as a "sacred canopy" that maintained social cohesion and provided a shared system of meaning.[23]

Upon their arrival in Minnesota and other parts of America, the immigrants had to come to terms with living in a much more diverse religious marketplace.[24] The Lutheran church was no longer the dominant religious institution, and immigrants were subjected to recruitment by Baptists, Methodists, Episcopalians, Evangelicals, Mormons, and Catholics. In such a pluralistic environment, Scandinavian immigrants lost the overarching system of meaning that had once framed their lives. The immigrants were now faced with a bewildering array of religious options that divided their fellow countrymen not by a local parish, but by denominational preference. Even within a denomination like the Lutheran church, there was no guarantee of unity. Norwegian Lutheran churches, in particular, were split into multiple factions divided by differing views on doctrine, worship preferences, polity, and the minister's leadership style. This exemplifies what historian Odd Lovoll describes as Norwegian Lutheranism's "tradition of disharmony." [25]

There were other sources of social fragmentation for immigrants in Minnesota. Norwegians often came from rural villages and towns that were both physically and culturally isolated from one other. [26] The geographic isolation of Norway's fjords and valleys shaped communities with a strong sense of local identity. When Norwegians came to Minnesota, they settled in areas represented by persons from a variety of local districts or *bygds*. For the first time, they encountered Norwegians with different dialects and customs. For many Swedes and Norwegians, the disorientation of immigration and the ensuing religious and social fragmentation stimulated a need to construct a new sacred cosmos. [27] Through the dissemination of Viking discovery narratives, ethnic boosters such as Rasmus B. Anderson constructed what can be called an ethnoreligion, which met the various social and psychological needs of his immigrant peers.

Ole Rølvaag, in his 1927 novel *Giants in the Earth: A Saga of the Prairie*, tells the story of a Norwegian immigrant family struggling to establish a homestead in Dakota Territory during the 1870s. Rølvaag uses the novel's main characters, Per Hansa and his wife Beret, as contrasting figures of how immigrants experienced their new life in America. Per was a boundless optimist who thrives in the face of pioneer life's numerous challenges. He dreams of building his own kingdom on the prairie by providing a prosperous future for his family. Beret, by contrast, is overwhelmed by homesickness and desperately wants to return to her native Norway. The isolation of pioneer life drives Beret into a state of depression and, later, madness. Her only solace is a small chest containing various artifacts that reminded her of home.

The contrasting immigrant desires to establish roots in America while retaining symbolic connection to the home country resonates well with Thomas Tweed's characterization of immigrant religion as "dwelling" and "crossing." [28] An ethnoreligion based on the myth of pre-Columbian Viking visitors to North America addressed the twin immigrant concerns embodied by Per Hansa and Beret Hansa. In terms of dwelling, Rasmus B. Anderson's promotion of the Dighton Rock and

Cover of O. E. Rølvaag's 1927 novel, *Giants in the Earth.* Courtesy of Special
Collections and Rare Books, University of Minnesota Libraries.

the Newport Tower can be seen as a strategy to establish a sacred ethnic map, which situated Norwegian immigrants prominently in the larger American narratives about the history of the nation.[29] Viking enthusiasm also draws upon human and suprahuman forces to overcome obstacles and cross boundaries. Vikings became exemplars of a heroic way of life and provided immigrants with "an irresistible symbol of pioneer boldness."[30] The possibility that the ancestors of Swedish and Norwegian immigrants had the fortitude and strength to traverse oceans that other Europeans could not boosted the confidence of Minnesota farmers who faced market fluctuations, drought, and grasshopper plagues. Viking enthusiasm enabled Scandinavian immigrants to build a symbolic bridge to their heritage and homeland. It helped them to alleviate feelings of isolation and homesickness, knowing that other Swedes and Norwegians had long ago traversed the American landscape. In short, myths about Viking forebears tempered loneliness, alienation, and social fragmentation by providing an imagined community.

Fertile Ground for a Midwestern Viking Hoax

Rasmus B. Anderson's mythologized landscape had one limitation. Anderson's Norsemen had only left their mark on New England. Most Swedish and Norwegian immigrants had established their homes and farms more than a thousand miles to the west.[31] In Douglas County, where the Kensington Rune Stone was unearthed, Swedes and Norwegians were by far the dominant ethnic groups, although Germans also had a sizable presence. The counties to the west were more heavily Norwegian and the counties to the east were dominated by German Catholics.

In the late nineteenth century, it is evident that Scandinavian immigrants in this region were seeking signs that their ancestors had prepared the way for their new life in the upper Midwest. In 1887, Danish historian Gustav Storm took Anderson's writings to task, claiming that Norsemen "in the eleventh century had never been within the present boundaries of the United States." As Wahlgren observed, "such an assertion created tremendous ill-will in Scandinavian-American circles."[32] Several scholars have argued that a particular word used in Storm's text directly inspired an immigrant or immigrants to produce the inscribed stone in Ohman's field. The word *opdagelse* or "discovery," used multiple times in his text and also in press accounts, is also a key word in the Kensington Rune Stone inscription. In the context of this potent ethnoreligious milieu, inscribing the runic message would be a way to reassert Nordic pride in the face of academic attacks on the historicity of Viking discovery narratives.

Chicago's World's Columbian Exposition of 1893 served as another possible inspiration for the Kensington Rune Stone inscription. In 1880, a Viking Age ship called the *Gokstad* was unearthed in Norway. This archaeological find provided a model for the construction of a replica ship called the *Viking*. Norwegian crew members sailed the *Viking* from Bergen, Norway, to the Chicago lakefront via Newfoundland, the Hudson River, the Erie Canal, and the chain of Great Lakes.[33] The ship arrived in mid-July 1893 to the Exposition, which commemorated the four hundredth anniversary of Christopher Columbus's "discovery" of North America. The sailing expedition was a demonstration that Norwegians had the ability to sail across the Atlantic many years before Columbus. Replicas of Columbus's ships were also part of the celebration but they were plagued with mechanical problems. As Iver Kjaer observes, "they had been unable to cross the Atlantic on their own, and they even experienced difficulty in sailing on Lake Michigan."[34] The superior performance of the *Viking* was a source of great pride to Scandinavians and Scandinavian Americans. Details about the voyage reveal peculiar similarities to the story told in the Kensington Rune Stone inscription. One scholar observes that the Viking ship had to be towed from New York City to Chicago. The length of time was fourteen days, which could have a connection to the reference to fourteen days in the runic inscription.[35] Also, there were thirty-two men on the ship. Thirty men are mentioned on the Kensington Stone.

As noted in the introduction, the nineteenth century was a popular period for "discoveries" that illuminated an ancient American history.[36] Joseph Smith's discovery of the golden plates in western New York inspired a westward movement of pioneers to settle the American West. Starting in the 1850s, Mormon missionaries recruited new settlers from Europe to join their kingdom-building efforts in Utah. Mormons experienced their greatest success in Scandinavia and some thirty thousand converts from Denmark, Sweden, and Norway emigrated to the United States between 1850 and 1900.[37] It is quite possible that Mormons, or at least former Mormons, settled the region where the Kensington Rune Stone was unearthed. Whether Mormons were present or not, the story of Joseph Smith's unearthing an inscribed artifact from a primordial era was widely known by Swedish and Norwegian immigrants.[38]

In addition to the multiple sources of inspiration for creating a myth about pre-Columbian Vikings, Swedish and Norwegian immigrants in the late nineteenth century were quite familiar with rune stones and runic writing. In medieval Scandinavia, rune stones were typically used to commemorate dead family members. As Christian practices spread in Scandinavia, bodies were buried in churchyards rather than near homes. However, rune stones continued to offer family members a way to commemorate loved ones in a traditional pre-Christian way.[39] Additionally, rune stones were sometimes erected to commemorate heroic Vikings who died on excursions abroad. Although the latter would account for a small percentage of rune stones, this purpose has most often been emphasized in Scandinavian-American popular culture.[40] As historian Theodore Blegen observed, there was widespread popular interest in runic writing in Minnesota. Within days after a facsimile of the runic inscription appeared in local newspapers, three individuals submitted relatively accurate translations.[41]

"The Stone Is Resurrected": Hjalmar Holand's Rediscovery

Even though scholars quickly dismissed the artifact as an immigrant hoax, the Norwegian-American writer Hjalmar Holand dedicated his life to proving its authenticity. The historian and traveling book salesman "resurrected" the symbolic power of the stone that was all but dead.[42] Holand had studied under Rasmus B. Anderson at the University of Wisconsin–Madison and developed a strong interest in pre-Columbian Norse explorations of North America. In 1907, Holand visited Douglas County as part of a research project for the Norwegian Society of Minneapolis. The Norwegian-born Holand had been commissioned by the organization to gather oral histories of pioneer immigrant communities from throughout the upper Midwest.

Although Holand claimed in his later writings that he knew nothing of the Kensington Stone prior to his visit to the Ohman farm, the evidence indicates that he first heard of the stone in 1899 and had long endeavored to see it.[43] In his autobiography, he gives an account of his first encounter with the rune stone.[44] He maintains that he stumbled on

Hjalmar Holand, circa 1900. Library of Congress Prints and Photographs Division, George Grantham Bain Collection.

the artifact while questioning locals about "things of historical interest," and claims that he was told a farmer named Olof Ohman had discovered a stone "with some writing on it," but no one knew what it said. His curiosity was piqued and he went out to visit Ohman. Holand described his first meeting with the farmer: "I found him to be a tall, well-built man of about fifty years with a frank and rugged countenance and quiet dignity." Holand notes that Ohman was from a province of northern Sweden, where students completed less than a year of schooling.[45] He asked to see the artifact and Ohman escorted him to his granary, where the stone lay facedown as a step into the small building. After turning it over, Ohman took a broom and swept off the dirt. "To my amazement I saw that more than half of the face of the stone was covered with very neatly carved characters."[46] Ohman proceeded to tell Holand about how he found the stone clutched in the roots of a tree several years earlier. Holand asked Ohman if he still had the stump of the tree. "No," said Ohman, "I kept it for several years, and I finally burnt it up. It was no use keeping it seeing the inscription was a fraud." "Why was the inscription rejected?" asked Holand. "I don't know," responded Ohman. "It was something about the language."

As Holand stood there "gazing at the strange and mystic characters on the stone," he considered the circumstances behind its discovery and concluded it was not a fraud. "I recognized them as runic signs, because I had pondered over many runic inscriptions in my favorite study of Norse antiquities." He then told Ohman that he would like to study the stone and asked how much he would accept for it. In Holand's telling of the story, Ohman asked him how much he was willing to pay and Holand reached into his "nearly empty wallet" and pulled out a five-dollar bill. Ohman responded, "Hm. It ought to be worth ten anyhow." Holand then told Ohman that this artifact was quite possibly priceless and that he wished to subject it to "a thorough study and that may give you some satisfaction. I would be willing to meet your price, but at present five dollars is all I have." "Well," said Ohman, "I think you're just as poor as I am, so you can have the stone for nothing."

Most observers agree that Ohman gave Holand permission to take the stone and study it, but it is unclear if ownership was actually transferred to Holand or if Ohman merely lent it to him. In Holand's mind, there was no ambiguity.[47] Just three years later, Holand tried to sell the stone to the Minnesota Historical Society (MHS) for five thousand dollars. According to MHS documents, Holand delivered "an impassioned sales pitch about the merits of the stone" and tried to persuade the MHS of the stone's "rightful place in history and the appropriateness of having it permanently housed at the Society." Despite what he described as the priceless quality of the stone, Holand conceded, "I have, however, decided that I would not avail myself of my position as owner of the stone to ask a higher price."[48] Holand, ever a salesman, was trying to persuade the MHS that the five-thousand-dollar price tag was a bargain. The historical society grew suspicious about his claim of ownership and sent a representative to Kensington to speak with Ohman. The MHS concluded that the stone was not Holand's to sell and Ohman, soon after, asked the society to keep it until Holand had "settled this question of disposing the same with me."[49] The MHS voted against purchasing the Kensington Stone owing to the controversy over ownership and Holand's high asking price.[50] Although we don't know the true details of what transpired during the summer of 1907, we do know that Holand then took possession of the rune stone and began a tireless, lifelong struggle to prove its authenticity.

Holand's Rune Stone Crusade

Holand was well prepared to promote the story of the Kensington Rune Stone through his writings about Norwegian immigrant pioneers in the Midwest. He first introduced the artifact to a public audience in *De Norske Settlementers Historie (History of Norwegian Settlements)* published the year after his visit to Ohman's farm. He opened his volume with a prologue titled "Vinland Expeditions," which frames his immigrant peers as heroic men and women who made sacrifices to build a nation. Building on Rasmus B. Anderson's theme of transatlantic Viking travel, Holand juxtaposes the Norsemen's need to move west during the medieval era with that of Norwegian pioneers of the nineteenth century. In this westward sojourn, Holand also applied Anderson's theme of sacrifice. When read in the context of his historical writings about the Norwegian settlement of the upper Midwest, Holand's narrative about Norsemen killed by Indians in the distant past is clearly a way to magnify the sacrifices of his immigrant peers. He boasted that Norwegians in the United States had brought an estimated 22 million acres of land under cultivation and, in doing so, lost many lives. He describes in vivid detail the experience of Norwegian settlers who were massacred by Indians at the Norway Lake settlement near Willmar, Minnesota, in 1862: "Without the slightest warning, the storm struck. It made this smiling and friendly plain the bloody stage setting for murder, fire, violence, rape and desperate flight."[51] According to Holand, both the Norwegian Americans and the medieval Norsemen struggled to build peaceful settlements in the midst of hostile "skrælings," be they Indians in Minnesota or Inuit in Greenland. Holand emphasizes the innocent motivations of the Norwegian pioneers with their plows and axes: "They were not out to assault humans, but the savagery of nature."[52] His portrayal of Knutson's men as the "first white martyrs of the West" was a public assertion that persons of Scandinavian descent in the United States were truly Americans.[53]

The Norwegian Society took a keen interest in Holand's rune stone research and commissioned an investigation in 1908 by a medical doctor named Knut Hoegh, who interviewed Kensington-area residents. Hoegh and Holand worked together to collect signed and notarized affidavits from Ohman, his son, and other neighbors. These affidavits testify that Ohman had indeed unearthed the stone from his field and

that he did not manipulate the evidence. At the conclusion of his investigation, Hoegh published his report in a Norwegian-American peri-
odical. He praised the integrity of local residents, describing one as "a
faithful example of trustworthy, wise, Norwegian farmer."[54]

Although Holand had successfully gained the endorsement of Norwegian cultural organizations, he had mixed success in the academic
and scientific communities. In 1909, he persuaded Professor George T.
Flom, a Scandinavian linguist from the University of Illinois, to analyze
the runic inscription. Flom concluded that the stone "must be adjudged
a fake" because the linguistic forms on the inscription were "a mixture
of nineteenth century Norwegian and Swedish, with a few antiquated
words modified further by an evident antiquarian effort in orthography,
which, however, the modern rune-master not possessing a knowledge of
Old Swedish, fails to harmonize with the orthography and pronuncia-
tion of the time."[55]

Unable to persuade linguists of the authenticity of his rune stone,
Holand turned to a geologist, Newton Winchell, who chaired the Department of Archaeology at the Minnesota Historical Society. From 1909
to 1910, Winchell investigated the geological conditions of Ohman's
farm and interviewed Ohman and his neighbors about the discovery of
the stone. He also studied the physical properties of the stone and its
inscription. He concluded that that the age of the inscription was "at
least 50 to 100 years" because he found no evidence of a residue of white
stone powder in the crevices of the inscription indicating a recent carving.[56] The historical society issued a report in the spring of 1910 that
stated that the authenticity of the Kensington Rune Stone could not be
proven with certainty, but that the weight of the evidence indicated that
it *could* be authentic.[57] The committee decided to withhold its tentative
endorsement of the stone until it could be subjected to further analysis
by linguists.[58]

Holand was unable to get the full endorsement by scholars in the
United States, so in the summer of 1911 he turned to Europe. He traveled with the rune stone to Rouen, France, and gave a presentation at a
history conference. Later, he went to Sweden, where he was able to display the Minnesota artifact in the Stockholm Museum. Despite these
efforts, he had little success in persuading European scholars of the
stone's authenticity. University of Christiana runic scholar Alexander
Bugge declared the Kensington inscription to be a hoax in a Norwegian

newspaper.[59] While speaking at the University of Christiana, Holand was challenged by another runic specialist, Professor Marius Haegstad, who also concluded that the Kensington Rune Stone was a nineteenth-century creation.

Westward from Vinland: The Saga of Paul Knutson

Undeterred, Holand continued to write prolifically over the coming decades. He self-published a first book-length treatment, *The Kensington Stone*, in 1932. This book was slightly revised and retitled *Westward from Vinland: An Account of Norse Discoveries and Explorations in America 982–1362*, which was released by a New York publisher in 1940. In these volumes, Holand advanced several forms of evidence to support his belief in the rune stone's authenticity. He embeds this evidence in a lively narrative, dedicating the first third of his books to early Norse explorations in Iceland, Greenland, and, finally, Vinland. He shares Anderson's assumption that Vinland is the eastern shore of North America.

The bulk of the book, however, deviates from Anderson's interpretation of pre-Columbian history. While Anderson would depend almost exclusively on the Vinland Saga texts for his historical narrative, Holand would, in essence, produce his own saga by consolidating disparate historical and archaeological evidences.[60] The title of his book *Westward from Vinland* asserts that medieval Norsemen's travels did not end in New England; they penetrated deep into the heart of the continent. In doing so, Holand challenged one of the great orthodoxies of historiography about the United States: the nation's origins were on the East Coast.

Holand asserted that the party of Norse explorers who had carved the rune stone inscription was on an expedition commissioned by the king of Sweden. He cites Gustav Storm's 1887 text *Studier over Vinlandsreiserne*, which reprints an obscure sixteenth-century Danish copy of a decree that King Magnus had written in 1354. In this decree, the king expressed his concern upon hearing that some Norse residents in Greenland had fallen away from the Christian faith. In response, the king commissioned an expedition led by Paul Knutson to search out the missing Norsemen and bring them back to the church. Holand argued that members of this expedition traveled west of Greenland, found their way through Hudson Bay, and traveled up the Nelson and Red rivers, eventually making their way to what is now Kensington, Minnesota, in 1362. Holand theorized that ten members of the expedition were killed by Indians. Before returning to Norway in 1364, the survivors commemorated the tragic event by carving a memorial rune stone.

Holand argued that the Knutson expedition left evidence behind on its journey through the North American landscape. For example, the path from Hudson Bay to Minnesota is strewn with a number of large stones with clearly demarcated holes, which Holand declared to be "mooring stones." According to Holand, these so-called mooring stone holes were chiseled for the purpose of holding a ringbolt to secure a boat to the shore. He declared that the Norse explorers had brought large, thousand-pound boats that could carry twenty men. These boats were so heavy, he reasoned, that they would have needed a solid place to secure them. He claimed to have identified thirteen mooring stones, each of them seventy-five miles from the other in western Minnesota. The number of mooring stones conveniently fit with the rune stone passage indicating that it is located fourteen days' journey from where the ships were left behind.

Along Holand's trail of mooring stones, he identified several artifacts that he attributed to the presence of medieval Norsemen. Inspired by Holand's writings, immigrant farmers from throughout the upper Midwest sent him artifacts they hoped would help prove the authenticity of the Kensington Stone and validate the early presence of their ancestors in the region. In 1910, Holand wrote that Ole Skaalrud presented him with an ax head that he had found next to Norway Lake. In 1911, a Clay County man, Hans O. Hanson Strand, showed Ohman a sword he had found in his field. Another farmer from Polk County, Ole Jevning, reported that he had found an iron fire-starting tool known as a firesteel while digging posthole for a fence back in the 1870s. To the delight of area residents, Holand declared these items to be Norse artifacts dating to the medieval era.

Most of Holand's "Nordic" tools and weapons would be debunked as fraudulent in later decades. Some of the so-called Viking battle-axes had actually been discovered throughout the United States. They were tobacco cutters manufactured by an iron company in Ohio and distributed as part of a promotional campaign by the Battle Ax Tobacco Company.[61] Additionally, the chiseled boulders of Holand's "mooring stone" theory would later be identified variously as receptacles for blasting dynamite, markings for surveyors, and anchors for fish traps.[62]

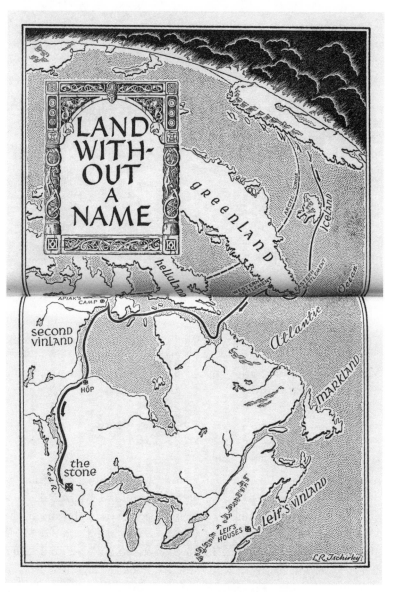

LAND WITH-OUT A NAME

greenLand

Iceland

ARCTIC CIRCLE

WESTERN SETTLEMENT

EASTERN SETTLEMENT

ocean

helluland

APIAK'S CAMP

SECOND VINLAND

HÓP

the stone

Red R.

Atlantic

markland

LEIF'S HOUSES

Leif's vinland

L.R.Tschirley

A map showing the Vikings' route as they traveled from Norway to near Alexandria, Minnesota, printed in *Door to the North: A Saga of Fourteenth-Century America,* by Elizabeth Coatsworth, 1950.

One of Holand's alleged mooring stones located near the rune stone discovery site. Photograph by the author.

Nonetheless, this material evidence, Holand argued, marked the western Minnesota landscape with signposts of "one of the greatest exploring trips in the world's history."[63]

Purest Nordic Stock: Viking Survivors and the Blond, Blue-Eyed Mandans

In addition to the material evidence allegedly left behind, Holand identified what he believed to be biological and cultural evidence of Nordic explorers in North America. Holand theorized what became of the Viking survivors who were not found "red with blood and dead." He ultimately concluded that they had been captured by American Indians and eventually intermarried with them. As proof, he cited the European characteristics observed among the Mandan Indians.

Since the eighteenth century, historians had speculated about pre-Columbian contact between the Mandan Indians and Europeans. The French explorer and trader Captain Pierre Gaultier de Varennes, Sieur de La Vérendrye was the first known European to encounter the Mandan

Indians in 1738. At the time, they were living in the upper Missouri River Valley in what is now North and South Dakota. Holand noted that La Vérendrye's journals revealed that he had encountered Mandan Indians with blond hair and light skin who lived in spacious homes kept clean and well supplied, a fact that La Vérendrye claimed to be different from other tribes.[64] Additionally, La Vérendrye observed that they sustained themselves through settled agriculture rather than nomadic hunting. Holand also referred to the writings of nineteenth-century traveling artist George Catlin, who claimed to have found evidence that the Mandan had incorporated a number of biblical stories into their belief system.[65]

Holand concluded from La Vérendrye's and Catlin's observations that the "superior intelligence and ability" of the Mandan could only be attributed to their partial descent from Scandinavians.[66] "Swedes and Norwegians are of the purest Nordic stock and a relatively smaller number would have been sufficient to transmit the physical peculiarities for which the Mandans were noted than if any other nationality had been represented by these early culture bearers." The members of Paul Knutson's expedition not only possessed a vastly potent and superior biological makeup; they possessed superior cultural and moral traits. Holand argued that if the Mandan in the eighteenth century still exhibited cultural traits they had absorbed from the Norse nearly four hundred years earlier, it is proof that these early white strangers had "great tact, intelligence and force of character."[67] In Holand's mind, the "ardent" religiosity of the remnant members of the Knutson expedition had left an indelible mark on the culture of the Mandan people. For Holand, it is only the presence of Nordic blood and Nordic Christian virtue that could have enabled the Mandan people to be "the most intelligent, well-mannered and hospitable of all the tribes of the north." Their "superior civilization" and "peaceful disposition" were for many centuries an "oasis of comfort and gentleness in a desert of savage and warring Indians."[68]

Similar to his mentor Rasmus B. Anderson, Holand appealed to notions of Scandinavian pride in this narrative. While Anderson simply argued that Scandinavians should be accepted as Anglo-Saxons because of their similar origins, Holand used North American Indians as a foil in order to praise Scandinavian virtue and racial superiority. As Michlovic and Hughey have observed in their reading of Holand, "the self-esteeming mythology of one's group often feeds off the excoriation of another."[69]

Rune Stone Rejection: Constructing
Modern Scandinavian-American Identity

Despite Holand's best efforts, Scandinavian Americans were never unified in their endorsement of the Kensington Rune Stone. Many of them were simply not persuaded by his rhetorical defense, and some were embarrassed and even angered by his pseudoscientific, filiopietistic writings.[70] Some saw the dubious artifact as a potential threat to the social status of Scandinavian Americans, and by declaring it a hoax they were able to produce, or at least preserve, accumulated social capital for their groups. Thus, the rune stone enthusiast became a useful foil against which to define modern, Scandinavian-American identity.

One of the first and most persistent critics of the artifact's authenticity and the theories of Holand was Johan A. Holvik, a professor of Norse Studies at the Norwegian Lutheran Concordia College in Moorhead, Minnesota. Holvik focused his research on the circumstances of the stone's discovery. He pointed to discrepancies in the affidavits signed by Ohman and his neighbors in 1909 regarding exactly *where* the stone was discovered (either five hundred feet or five hundred yards from Nils Flaaten's house) and *when* the stone was discovered (either in August or in November). Holvik also noted the varying estimates among Ohman and his neighbors about the age of the tree whose roots had held the slab of stone (ranging from ten to seventy years).[71] Holvik concluded that these inconsistent testimonies indicate deception, and he took direct aim at Olof Ohman's character. He obtained a letter from the local postmaster, who said that Ohman had once told him that "he would like to figure out something that would bother the brains of the learned."[72] The postmaster said that Ohman's neighbor Sven Fogelblad was known for similar resentment toward intellectuals and likely worked with Ohman to produce a practical joke. Holvik offered the following hypothesis: the discrepancy in the dates of discovery indicated that the stone had been unearthed two times: first when Ohman discovered a blank stone tangled in the roots of a tree, and the second time after an inscription had been carved into it. Holvik maintains that Ohman and his neighbors had dug the stone up, carved the inscription, reburied it, and later unearthed it a second time in November 1898.[73]

Holvik's outspoken opposition to the Kensington Rune Stone has been described as an "obsession."[74] Holvik opposed the controversial

Site of the discovery of the Kensington Rune Stone, circa 1910. From left to right: Edwin Bjorklund, Nils (Olaf) Flaaten, and Olof Ohman. Courtesy of the Minnesota Historical Society.

artifact on the grounds that it had the potential to be an embarrassment to his people. His fear was that it might one day be proved a hoax, thereby making Norwegian Americans to look like fools.[75] Holvik had strong credentials as an advocate for Norwegian-American culture. Born in South Dakota in 1880 to parents who had recently arrived from Norway, he was educated at Norwegian schools in the United States and Norway. He later played an important role in organizing the Norwegian-American Centennial celebration in 1925, an event that commemorated the arrival of the first Norwegian immigrants to the United States. The Norwegian Centennial celebrated Leif Eriksson as the true discoverer of America but made no mention of the Kensington Rune Stone. Holvik likely played an important role in keeping references to Holand's stone out of the event materials. The rejection of the controversial artifact by Holvik and other Centennial boosters does not mean that they abandoned their desire to integrate their ethnic brethren into America's sacred myth of origin; it simply means that they endeavored to craft an image of modern Norwegian Americans as sophisticated and intelligent enough to resist what they saw as pseudoscientific hucksterism.

Theodore Blegen was another early and vocal critic of Holand and his rune stone. A major figure in the field of Minnesota history during the middle of the twentieth century, he was also an important Norwegian-American historian. Born in Minneapolis to Norwegian immigrant parents, Blegen became one of the founders of the Norwegian-American Historical Association (NAHA) in 1925.[76] One of NAHA's main goals was to replace myths about Norwegian Americans with verifiable history. They endeavored to use historical methods that were considered credible among the leading American historians of the day. Blegen and other young Norwegian-American historians challenged the filiopietist writing of the older generation. These scholars saw themselves as descendants not of Leif Eriksson, but of nineteenth-century immigrants from Norway. In 1931, Blegen published his own version of immigrant history, *Norwegian Migration to America, 1825–1860.* Unlike Holand's *De Norske Settlementers Historie,* Blegen wrote in English, used proper historical methodology, and avoided uncritical veneration of his ethnic peers.[77]

Soon after founding the Norwegian-American Historical Association, Blegen took direct aim at one of Holand's historical claims about the Kensington Stone. A few years earlier, Holand had written that there were no white settlers in Douglas County prior to 1865. In making this claim, Holand attempted to show that the tree under which the slab of stone was found had existed prior to the arrival of Scandinavian immigrants. In his 1925 article, Blegen challenged Holand's claim by citing census data indicating that there were 195 residents in Douglas County in 1860 and more than 1,300 persons of Scandinavian descent living there by 1870.[78] This would be the first of many efforts by Blegen to challenge Holand's inaccurate and often deceitful historical methods.

Even the great Norwegian-American booster Rasmus B. Anderson refused to endorse his former student's rune stone. In a 1910 article titled "The Kensington Runestone Is Fake" published in a Norwegian-language newspaper, Anderson argued that the inscription did not match the runic language used in the fourteenth century. Later that year, he published another article in the *Minneapolis Journal* where he gave an account of a conversation he had with Andrew Anderson, brother-in-law to Olof

Ohman. He described Ohman's relative as a man of "great intelligence and education" who had extensive knowledge of runic writing. After their conversation, he claimed that Andrew Anderson had strongly implied, but not directly stated, that he had something to do with creating the inscription.[79] Rune stone enthusiasts did not take kindly to Anderson's rejection of the stone's authenticity and Holand accused him of being the first to "tarnish the names of Ohman and Fogelblad by . . . accusing them of having perpetrated a fraud."[80] Who are we to believe? Holand is not the only one with something at stake in the Kensington Rune Stone debates. Anderson built his career on developing a historical narrative of Viking discovery that centered on the presence of Norsemen in New England. Perhaps he saw the Minnesota artifact as deviating from his well-established script, which appealed to America's cultural elite. Anderson seemed especially troubled that the runic inscription stated that both Goths and Swedes accompanied the exploration, given, as he claimed, that only men from Norway went on voyages of exploration.[81] Anderson may have seen the rune stone as a threat to the Norwegian–Swedish rivalry from which he benefited.

The Kensington Rune Stone: Beyond Ethnicity

Although there were lingering anxieties among some Swedish and Norwegian Americans in the 1920s about their place in American society, most enjoyed the privileges of political and cultural power in Minnesota, especially in comparison to immigrants from Southern and Eastern Europe. Lovoll says that Norwegian immigrants were typically characterized by native-born white Americans as "hardworking, thrifty and law-abiding," and there were "few examples of direct discrimination" against them.[82] Immigrants from Sweden and Norway enjoyed more immediate acceptance via immigration policies because they were better able to fit the mold of what looked to be "American" in the eyes of those who held power.[83]

This cultural privilege helps explain the early political success of Scandinavian Americans. By 1892, Norwegian immigrants could boast that one of their own, Knute Nelson, had become governor of Minnesota. Just a few years later, Nelson was elected to the U.S. Senate, where he served until 1923. By the 1920s, it is evident that Norwegian Americans wielded significant influence over national politics. Of the numerous speeches given during the Norwegian-American Centennial celebration, none was more anticipated than that by newly elected President Calvin Coolidge. Addressing a crowd of more than eighty thousand people, Coolidge acknowledged their claim that the Norwegian explorer Leif Eriksson had discovered America many years prior to Christopher Columbus. A local journalist characterized the response of the crowd: "The great roar that rose from Nordic throats to Thor and Odin above the lowering gray clouds told that the pride of the race had been touched."[84] Coolidge had won the 1924 election with the support of Minnesota, and he took this opportunity to praise Norwegian-American voters as "good and trustworthy citizens."[85]

Just as Norwegian Americans reached this pinnacle of social status, appeals to ethnic identity began to weaken. Lovoll argues that the Norwegian-American Centennial of 1925 marked the "final mustering of strong Norwegian ethnic forces."[86] He tracks the decline of participation in the *bygdelag* movement following the event and the decline of Norwegian-language publications during this decade.[87] Fewer Swedes and Norwegians emigrated to the United States. As a consequence, the percentage of foreign-born in Douglas County, Minnesota, dropped from around 29 percent in 1905 to approximately 15 percent in 1930.[88] National crises such as the Great Depression and the world wars fueled the trend away from ethnic self-identification. By 1946, many churches, such as the Norwegian Lutheran Church in America, had dropped the term "Norwegian" because "it was no longer felt to be a natural qualifier for its members."[89]

Although the need for Scandinavian immigrants to prove their "Americanness" declined in the first decades of the twentieth century, the popular appeal of the Kensington Rune Stone continued to surge.[90] However, the continued devotion to Viking discovery narratives had little to do with the need to bolster ethnic virility or soothe immigrant dislocation anxieties. Like other white Minnesotans in the early twentieth century, these children of Sweden and Norway were haunted by a violent past. The landscape on which they had made their home was once occupied by someone else. The rune stone inscription spoke directly to this concern.

CHAPTER TWO

Knutson's Last Stand

Fabricating the First White Martyrs
of the American West

{ "This vast stretch of beautiful land was to be his—yes his—and no ghost of a dead Indian would drive him away!" }

—Per Hansa in Ole Rølvaag's novel *Giants in the Earth*

Although the inscription on the Kensington Rune Stone makes no reference to how the ten Norse travelers ended up "red with blood and dead," to Holand and other white Minnesotans at the turn of the twentieth century the answer is obvious: they were killed by Indians. In an article in *Harper's Weekly* in 1909, Holand claimed that the reason for their deaths "is so plain that it scarcely needs an explanation," yet he offered a rich, dramatic narrative to do just that. As Holand told the story, the Norsemen camped near a fishing lake in Minnesota. Some members of the expedition went across the lake to go fishing. Those who remained at the campsite were suddenly "attacked by a ferocious band of savages." In a "desperate" struggle of hand-to-hand combat, "the whites are overcome one by one." The fishing party returned later in the day and "they discover, to their horror, the mutilated bodies of their comrades now stiffened in death." Holand went on to describe the reaction of the surviving Norsemen: "Breathing a fervent prayer to the Virgin Mary to save them from this unknown enemy, and throwing a rough burial mound over their friends, they hastily leave the sad spot. They take refuge upon an island in a lake a day's journey away. Here they find this stone, suited by nature for an inscription, and amid the ominous silence of a savage wilderness, they carve their tragic story upon it."[1]

With the *Harper's Weekly* article, the Kensington Rune Stone extended far beyond the Norwegian-speaking audience Holand addressed in his first publication, *De Norske Settlementers Historie*. As noted earlier, Holand used the story of the dead Norsemen to show that nineteenth-century Scandinavian Americans were not alone in the sacrifices they made to settle the American West. Their ancestors from the fourteenth century had done the same. The *Harper's Weekly* editors recognized that the Kensington Rune Stone was not merely an ethnic curiosity of interest to a minority immigrant group. A story of primeval Viking sacrifices at the hands of Indians appealed to a broad American readership.

Pre-Columbian Norsemen in the Yankee Imagination

Interest in the notion of pre-Columbian Nordic visitors to the north-eastern United States flourished during the mid-nineteenth century, and not just among Norwegian-American immigrants like Rasmus B. Anderson.[2] Henry Wheaton's *History of the Norsemen* (1831), Carl Christian Rafn's *Antiquitates Americanae* (1837), and recent English translations of the Norse sagas found large audiences in New England. By the 1850s, new historiographies about New England began to include Nordic history.[3] As noted earlier, a statue of Leif Eriksson was installed in Boston in 1887 and the Viking explorer became known as the city's "other founding father."[4] Viking history found its way into popular writings. Henry Wadsworth Longfellow's poem "The Skelton in Armor" (1841) was inspired by the discovery of a supposed "Viking grave" in Massachusetts during the 1830s.[5] In a series of letters known as the *Biglow Papers* published in the spring of 1862, Massachusetts poet James Russell Lowell tells the fictional story of a minister who discovers a rune stone outside the mythical town of North Jalaam.[6] Reverend Homer Wilbur sent copies of the runic inscription to "learned men" for translation, but he later discovered that he could read the runes if he turned them upside down. The runes told a story about a character in the medieval Norse literature named Bjarna who had been lost at sea but stopped in New England to smoke tobacco with the Indians. It is apparent that Lowell is poking fun at rune stone enthusiasts, but it is an indication of the degree to which "Viking mania" captivated the imaginations of white New Englanders in the mid-nineteenth century.[7]

Viking discovery narratives satisfied several cultural desires of New Englanders. First of all, they played an important role in soothing anxieties caused by shifting trends in immigration. Historian J. M. Mancini observes that New England's cultural elites of the late nineteenth century embraced a trend of "racialized history":

> At a moment of increasing fear that the nation was committing race suicide, the thought of Viking ghosts roaming the streets of a city increasingly filled with Irish, Italian, and Jewish hordes must have been comforting to an Anglo-Saxon elite whose political power, at least, was decidedly on the wane.[8]

Second, Mancini observes that Viking myths conveyed regret over the plight of Indians in the nineteenth century. Rasmus B. Anderson portrayed Vikings as the first Europeans who sacrificed their lives in an attempt to Christianize New England. Crafting a narrative of white innocence, Anderson implied that Christianity in the Americas

> had been born not in the brutal conversion and decimation of Aboriginal peoples but in blood spilled by European Vikings upon the shores of Massachusetts. In thus offering victimized Vikings as the true colonizers of New England, Anderson offered a salve to Americans' . . . increasingly guilty conscience about "the future of the Indian," whose degradation and disappearance were becoming causes célèbres . . . and whose fate was frequently pondered by defenders of the Viking theory of New World discovery.[9]

The notion of a pre-Columbian presence in North America by Norse or other exotic visitors appealed to white, English-speaking Americans for other reasons. In 1773, Boston minister Samuel Mather wrote a book called *An Attempt to Shew, That America Must Be Known to the Ancients,* which claimed that America was first settled following the worldwide flood described in the book of Genesis. These first settlers were followed by Northern Europeans and, later, Phoenicians, who were among the many people who greeted Columbus and other explorers. In effect, Mather crafted a "providential history" that placed America in "a biblical past and redeemed future."[10] Mather shared his writings with Benjamin Franklin, who became persuaded that Swedes, among others, had reached America prior to Columbus. This alternative origin story had the effect of decentering Britain's role in American history and shaped a new national narrative as Americans tried to sever ties with their colonizers.[11]

As explorers and settlers ventured west in the early decades of the nineteenth century, white Americans found additional appeal in establishing a primordial history for a young nation. Joseph Smith claimed that an angel named Moroni led him to a collection of golden plates buried in a western New York hillside that told the story of a lost tribe of ancient Israel reaching the Americas in the sixth century BCE. Smith's "translation" of the golden plates was published in 1830 as the Book of Mormon. When the amateur archaeologist Caleb Atwater encountered massive burial mounds and inscribed copper artifacts in southern Ohio, he imagined them to be the creation of a superior civilization from "Hindoostan." The ethnologist and geographer Henry Schoolcraft also interpreted a number of artifacts he found as evidence of non-Indian, pre-Columbian visitors from Phoenicia, Gaul, Britain, and, particularly, Scandinavia.[12] Politicians such as Governor DeWitt Clinton of New York argued that such advanced peoples had been overwhelmed and "exterminated" by Indian "barbarians." President Andrew Jackson used this martyrdom narrative to argue for the Indian Removal Act of 1830 to displace nations such as the Creek and the Cherokee and move them west of the Mississippi River.[13]

The Dakota War of 1862:
Inspiration for a Violent Myth of Origin

Most Minnesotans in the late nineteenth century had little sympathy for North America's first residents. Memories of violent encounters with Indians still haunted the memories of living pioneers. During the Dakota War of 1862, hundreds of white settlers and soldiers died at the hands of Dakota warriors following a skirmish with reservation agents. In just a few weeks, vast swaths of Minnesota were virtually depopulated by white settlers fleeing in fear. In all likelihood, the traumatic events of 1862 directly inspired the creation of the Kensington Rune Stone inscription in the nineteenth century, and they influenced the stone's interpretation in the twentieth.

The tragedy of the Dakota War has often obscured the nearly two-hundred-year history of reciprocal interaction between Indians and European Americans prior to 1862. French fur traders maintained their networks through the cultivation of kinship relationships with the Ojibwe and the Dakota.[14] A wholly distinct culture emerged known as Métis, which was neither Indian nor European. The region during this period should not be viewed as a "site of conquest," says one historian, but instead "a meeting ground of civilizations, a place where geographic and cultural borders were blurred and unfixed."[15] There was even a short period of peaceful interaction between Presbyterian missionaries and Dakota Indians during the 1830s.[16] These cross-cultural relationships would be strained severely as white settlers began to migrate in large numbers.

When the Minnesota Territory was organized in 1849, the U.S. government increased pressure on Indian tribes to vacate their land. In 1851, Dakota chiefs signed treaties that surrendered some 21 million acres of prime farmland for a mere pittance.[17] As a result of the treaties, the Sisseton, Wahpeton, Mdewakanton, and Wahpekute bands of Dakota Indians were relegated to a twenty-mile-wide strip of land along the Minnesota River. It is well documented that these treaties were essentially political theater and that the United States would have forcibly removed the Dakota even without a treaty.[18] In 1858, Dakota chiefs were pressured to concede even more land and they signed away the ten-mile strip on the north side of river. To make matters worse, the chiefs signed a document promising that the tribes would reimburse fur traders for debts owed by individual Indians. Reservation land quickly became depleted of wildlife, and nearby white traders were said to have "hovered around them like buzzards around the carcasses of slaughtered buffalo, systematically cheating them out of the greater part of the promised annuities."[19] Many Indians were forced to turn to these traders for credit.

In August 1862, smoldering tensions between the Dakota and the white settlers ignited a conflagration of violence that swept across the prairies of southern Minnesota. Payments from the federal government were late to arrive at the reservation headquarters and the rumor among the Dakota was that the U.S. government had exhausted its treasury fighting the Civil War. Facing starvation, some Mdewakanton men descended on the Redwood Agency to demand food. One storekeeper, Andrew Myrick, famously refused to extend credit and arrogantly told the men to "eat grass." A few days later, four frustrated and hungry Wahpeton braves killed a family of seven white settlers near the town of Acton. On August 18, Taoyateduta or "Little Crow," a longtime mediator between Indians and whites, was persuaded to lead a group of warriors in an attack on the Redwood Agency. They killed twenty agency employees and traders, including Andrew Myrick, whose body was found with his mouth stuffed with grass. Over the next few weeks, the Dakota warriors spread throughout the countryside, killing many white settlers in their homes, including unarmed women and children. In the words of one historian, "survivors hid in the woods or crawled on their knees through the tall prairie grasses, quaking at every sound as they struggled toward the relative safety of Fort Ridgely." An estimated four hundred civilians were killed and many died of thirst and exposure while fleeing. This was the largest mass killing of civilians in the history of the United States to that point, and the number would not be surpassed until the attack on the World Trade Center in 2001.[20]

In coming weeks, soldiers were dispatched from Fort Snelling, and by the end of September, Dakota forces were militarily defeated. Hastily organized military tribunals tried four hundred Dakota prisoners and sentenced 303 of them to death. Some of the court cases lasted as little as five minutes. The generals overseeing the tribunals had every intention of carrying out the executions immediately, largely because of the fear of vigilante violence. This fear was not unwarranted as newspaper headlines from across the state called for the "extermination" of Dakota people. As U.S. troops forcibly relocated a group 1,700 Dakota men, women, and children who were not convicted of a crime to a prison encampment at Fort Snelling, angry white settlers threw rocks and shouted insults at them. In one graphic story, a white woman grabbed a nursing Dakota child from its mother's arms and threw it to the ground. The baby died a few hours later.[21]

The executions could not be carried out immediately because death-penalty cases required presidential review. Upon reading the initial tribunal report, President Lincoln and his cabinet were struck by the "irregularity of the proceedings" and the president ordered a stay of execution until he could personally read the trial transcripts. Lincoln had recently been visited by Episcopal missionary Bishop Henry Whipple, who argued that government policies toward the Dakota were to blame for the violence unleashed in the summer of 1862. In a published letter, Whipple wrote: *"Who is guilty of the causes which desolated our border: At whose door is the blood of these innocent victims?* I believe that God will hold the nation guilty."[22] Few

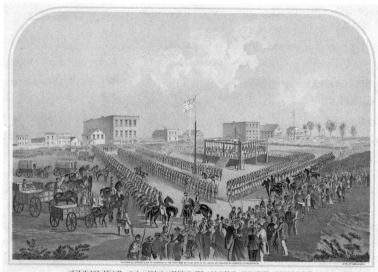

EXECUTION OF THE THIRTY-EIGHT SIOUX INDIANS
AT MANKATO MINNESOTA DECEMBER 26,1862.

The hanging of thirty-eight Dakota men in Mankato, Minnesota, on
December 26, 1862. Library of Congress Prints and Photographs Division.

Minnesotans shared Whipple's sympathy for the Dakota, and Lincoln
faced intense pressure to exact vengeance. In the end, Lincoln agreed
to commute most of the death sentences, reserving the penalty for only
those charged with killing unarmed civilians.[23]

On the day after Christmas in 1862, thirty-eight Dakota men were
hanged in a public square in Mankato, Minnesota. As many as four
thousand spectators traveled to Mankato to witness the event. When
the thirty-eight were dropped from the gallows and the ropes tightened
around their necks, the crowd fell silent for a moment, then released a
"loud, drawn-out cheer in approbation."[24] The bodies of the men were
buried in a mass grave next to the river, but they did not stay there long.
In the middle of the night, local medical doctors opened the grave and
divided up the corpses for medical research.[25]

The execution of the thirty-eight men did not entirely satisfy most
Minnesotans, and a campaign of vengeance against the Dakota would
continue. Many Minnesotans were unwilling to distinguish between
Indians who committed murder and the overwhelming majority who
were innocent. All Indians were lumped together as a distinct and guilty

race incapable of living among whites. The state government offered bounties for Dakota scalps. During a special legislative session, Governor Alexander Ramsey declared, "If any shall escape extinction, the wretched remnant must be driven beyond our borders."[26] A forced exile of Dakota people from the state of Minnesota began in the spring of 1863. Some 1,300 Dakota, mostly women, children, and the elderly, were loaded on overcrowded steamships to take them down the Mississippi River and up the Missouri River to the Crow Creek Reservation. More than three hundred died of disease and starvation along the way, and upon their arrival at the remote site in Dakota Territory, they discovered nearly desolate prairie wasteland with few resources on which to subsist. The Dakota clung to survival in virtual concentration-camp conditions for three years before the U.S. government moved them to a slightly better reservation in northern Nebraska. Within a short time after the 1862 conflict, the Dakota population in Minnesota declined from seven thousand to less than two hundred.[27]

Although thousands of pioneer settlers abandoned their claims, never to return, waves of new white settlers poured into southern and western Minnesota following the Civil War. The population of the state mushroomed from 172,023 in 1860 to 439,706 in 1870.[28] Many, no doubt, were drawn by the federal government's offer of 160 acres at little or no cost through the Homestead Act of 1862. Despite the apparent triumph of white civilization over "Indian savagery," the events of 1862 made an indelible imprint on the social psyche of Minnesotans. Myriad cultural expressions of the event flourished in the decades following the war. Artist John Stevens created a series of tableau paintings representing Minnesota's "Indian Massacre" of 1862. A panorama exhibit circulated throughout the region, particularly in small towns, through the 1870s.[29] In the 1890s, Bohemian-born artist Anton Gág created a large, painted panorama that vividly depicted several scenes of Indians brutalizing white settlers. The panorama was first displayed in New Ulm and later at the 1893 World's Columbian Exposition in Chicago.[30] Minnesotans were also avid consumers of memorabilia from the mass execution in Mankato. In 1902, the Standard Brewing Company produced a commemorative beer tray that depicted U.S. soldiers relaxing round a table drinking beer while the gallows dropped on the thirty-eight Dakota men.[31] Ignatius Donnelly's 1883 novel *Ragnarok: The Age of Fire and Gravel* referenced the events of the Dakota War. The story describes the discovery of golden tablets with runic writing in a grassy field, an ancient civilization based in the Midwest, and a cataclysmic comet strike in Minnesota in August 1862.[32]

In his famous speech at the 1893 Columbian Exposition in Chicago, historian Frederick Jackson Turner pondered the consequences of the demographic reality that the United States no longer had a frontier line. For Turner, the frontier was the place where pioneer settlers, many of them immigrants, learned the quintessential American virtues of strength, individualism, and creativity.[33] The "closing" of the frontier evoked widespread anxiety about a perceived decline of masculinity.[34] At the first Old Settlers' reunion in Alexandria, Minnesota, in 1900, there was a pervasive theme of nostalgia for the hard work of the pioneers. Settlers were asked to share their remembrances of a time when the "region was being subdued from its primeval state" and became transformed into an "abode of civilized men."[35] One speaker warned the younger generation against pursuing education in order to avoid hard work: "Nothing could spoil a boy sooner . . . The successful man is the one who is not afraid of hard work."[36] At the turn of the century, many Minnesotans were fearful that stories of frontier life would not survive the deaths of their aging pioneers. Local historians endeavored to collect memories of these settlers and convey their stories of sacrifice to successive generations.[37]

The stories of pioneers were inscribed on civic monuments and memorials throughout the state. In the town of New Ulm, for example, one of the key battle sites of the 1862 war, a state monument called Guardians of the Frontier was dedicated in 1891. Monuments were also dedicated at the Birch Coulee battlefield in 1894, Fort Ridgely in 1896, the Guri Endreson gravesite near Willmar in 1907, and several other locations.[38] A painting commemorating the Dakota attack on New Ulm was hung in the state's new capitol building completed in 1905. Gravestones were also an important means of commemorating the white settlers who died in the Dakota War. A group grave marker for five white settlers near Litchfield was dedicated in 1878. One observer identified and documented two hundred such grave sites, noting that a high number of them specify how each person died. "Probably nowhere else in the nation will one find so many gravestones declaring, 'Killed by Indians' or 'Massacred by Indians.'"[39]

The proliferation of gravestones and memorials following the Dakota

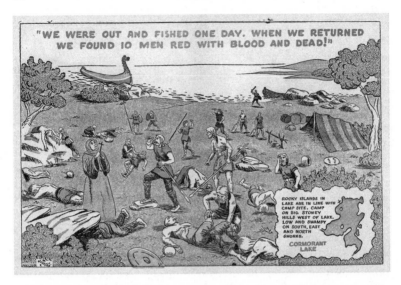

Viking massacre scene from Margaret Leuthner's *Mystery of the Runestone* comic book, 1962.

War should be understood in light of how attitudes about commemorating the dead shifted as a result of the American Civil War. As historian Drew Gilpin Faust has observed, fallen soldiers were no longer considered to be the concern of family and friends, they were thought to be part of a larger "imagined community." Their memory was evoked for the benefit of the larger society and to provide "meaning for the war and its costs."[40] In his Gettysburg Address, President Lincoln interpreted the deaths of the tens of thousands of soldiers as a sacrifice for the nation to be reborn. In a similar fashion, the Dakota War grave sites and other commemorations in Minnesota incorporated dead pioneer settlers into a larger narrative of sacrifice for American progress and westward expansion.[41]

In this potent civil religious milieu of paintings, memorials, monuments, gravestones, and memorabilia, it is easy to see how a Minnesotan could have been inspired to produce a memorial inscription that commemorated a primeval story of American sacrifice. Observers of the Kensington Rune Stone phenomenon have frequently noted the curious five-hundred-year gap between the dates on the stone's inscription (1362) and the year of Minnesota's "most dramatic event" (1862).

Although we can only speculate about the motives of those who created the runic inscription, we know that many Minnesotans in the early twentieth century interpreted the artifact as a monument to white pioneer sacrifice. Holand's mythic narrative about slain Norsemen in the fourteenth century magnified the imagined savagery of "precivilized" Minnesota serving to make the achievements of pioneer settlers in the nineteenth century all the more exceptional. Furthermore, Holand used the rune stone and other purported Viking artifacts to naturalize and justify white claims to the landscape.

Remember Lake Cormorant!
Manufacturing the Site of the Viking Massacre

Myths carry more power when they are made concrete and visible by occupying a physical space. There is no debate among historians as to the locations of various sites of violence during the Dakota War of 1862. The Battle of New Ulm took place in New Ulm, the Battle of Fort Ridgely took place at Fort Ridgely, and so on. When it came to the imagined Viking massacre in 1362, however, there was no consensus on its location. The rune stone inscription indicates that the location of the fated camp was "by two rocky islets one day's journey north of this stone." Holand, the tireless researcher, dedicated himself to solving this mystery and he was confident that he could determine the location of the event with certainty. His aim was to ensure that one day a "fitting monument may be erected over the grave of these first white martyrs of the West."[42] His efforts to identify the "massacre" site reveal the strategies he used to make it appear self-evident to Minnesotans that Norseman had once visited their state and lost their lives at the hands of the region's first residents.

In an article published in 1920, Holand said that he had recently investigated several lakes located approximately eighty miles north of the site where the Kensington stone had been discovered. According to Holand, "one day's journey" refers to a measurement of eighty miles, as understood by Scandinavian sailors in the Middle Ages. He found what he was looking for when he discovered Lake Cormorant in Becker County, where he noticed a large hill rising one hundred feet above the lakeshore. From the top, he could view two rocky outcroppings or "skerries" that he understood to be the same features mentioned in the

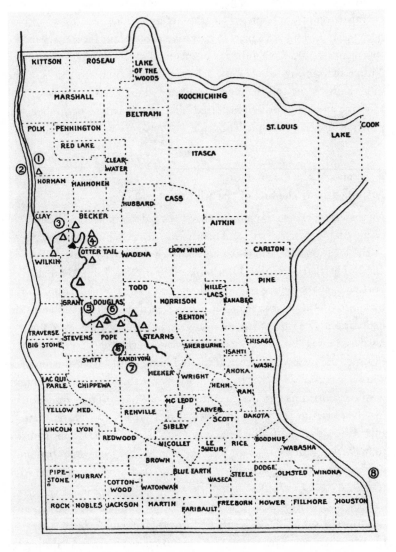

Minnesota's sacred Viking sites anchored by mooring stones. Included on this map are locations pertaining to the imagined Viking massacre, the place where the memorial stone was inscribed, and the location of a supposed Viking Catholic Mass service printed in *A Pre-Columbian Crusade to America*, by Hjalmar Holand, 1962.

inscription. Holand claimed to have been accompanied by local farmer John Johnson, who owned land along the lake. While inspecting the site, they identified two boulders with triangular-shaped holes above the shoreline and determined them to be mooring stones. Holand proclaimed with certainty that this was the site of the massacre: "No one who has stood upon the high hill on the northwestern shore of the lake and has seen these two remarkable skerries lying in a straight line before him can doubt that these are the right skerries."[43]

Through "serious deductive reasoning," Holand described the background to the massacre that he said took place at this site. He claimed that the Norse explorers would have approached this location on their journey that began in Hudson Bay and continued up the Red River. "After a long and wearisome march over the Red River Valley prairie, where game would be scarce and hard to approach, the wooded hills and beautiful expanse of Cormorant Lake would look very pleasant to them and invite them to a long stay."[44] The need for food prompted the men to build a raft in order to go out fishing on the lake. Holand concluded that the raft had to be large enough to accommodate the ten men who were out fishing during the massacre, but it was too big to be pulled onto the shore of the lake, hence the need for the mooring stones he discovered at the site.

The position of the boulders posed a problem for Holand's theory. If they were truly mooring stones, they would have been much lower than several feet above the lake level where they were found. In his 1940 account, Holand presents a letter from a county surveyor who determined that the lake level had once been approximately nine feet higher, before it was drained. He also measured the stone holes to be at a level of approximately nine feet. But this leads him to recognize a problem: the "skerries" would have been covered in water and therefore not visible to Knutson and his men in 1362. The answer to this conundrum is simple, says Holand: it is evident that these "skerries" were once much higher. Shifting ice on the lake had eroded them by several feet over the years.

Holand spared no opportunity to bend the evidence to fit his theory and his experiences at Lake Cormorant were embellished and often altered with each retelling. The 1920 article mentioned only one other person accompanying him on his visit in October 1919. In his 1940 account, his first visit to the lake was in the summer of 1919 and he returned the following autumn with "several other men."[45] In his autobiography,

written in 1957, the numbers swelled substantially. He claimed to have
been accompanied to the site by forty men after he spoke to a congregation located near the lake: "When reported that the place of massacre
of these explorers 600 years ago was only a few miles from the church, a
large number of men asked me to show them this historic spot."[46] In the
face of growing criticism of his theories during the 1940s and 1950s,
Holand often felt compelled to multiply the number of witnesses to his
discoveries.[47] In 1948, his perennial critic, Johannes Holvik, publicized a
testimonial from a local farmer, who said he had chiseled one of the boulders that Holand claimed was a Norse mooring stone.[48]

There are other examples of Holand's attempt to twist the facts.
In his writings after 1920, he fails to divulge that the shore of Lake
Cormorant was not the first location where he was certain that the
Norsemen had been killed. Writing in 1910, he had first declared that
the site was on the southwestern shore of Pelican Lake just over twenty
miles northwest from where the Kensington Rune Stone had been
unearthed on Ohman's farm. In a 1909 newspaper article, a Lutheran
minister traveling with Holand shared his certitude and waxed eloquent
about how the two rocky islets visible from shore had for centuries
"stood as sentinels to a very sad story."[49] However, the Pelican Lake location later proved incompatible to how Holand mapped the Norsemen's
larger sojourn through North America. The rune stone inscription
indicates that the expedition had left ten men by the sea fourteen days'
journey from where it was located. The sea, for Holand, is Hudson
Bay, located, by his measurement, 1,120 miles to the north. Dividing
that number by fourteen days, Holand determines the length of a day's
journey to be eighty miles. As a later critic of Holand would point out,
the claim that eighty miles was a standard measurement of Nordic travel
was an inaccurate "manipulation" of another scholar's claim.[50]

Despite the inconsistencies of his claims about Lake Cormorant,
Holand's promotional efforts inspired rune stone enthusiasts to descend
upon the site in search of Viking graves. During the 1950s, an Iowa man,
John Colby, and his three teenage sons, armed with a metal detector and
a Geiger counter, embarked on a summer-long search for Viking relics
and graves.[51] It appears that Colby family expedition was unsuccessful,
because a decade later officials from Alexandria's Runestone Museum
sponsored another search for Viking graves at Lake Cormorant. The
working theory for this expedition was that the Norsemen would have

sunk the bodies of their ten dead comrades to the bottom of the lake in a Viking ship filled with heavy stones in order "to prevent the Indians from getting to the bodies of their friends." Viking enthusiast Marion Dahm led several scuba divers on a three-hour search scouring the lake bottom. The only items they were able to retrieve were "fishing gear, parts of motors, modern anchors, one golf ball, a pair of lawn clippers, and a pirate flag with skull and cross bones drawn in white."[52] With the exception of a short residential street named "Viking Bay Road," there are no markers to indicate that a Viking massacre occurred at Lake Cormorant. Although Holand was unsuccessful in erecting a physical memorial at the site where he thought that the Knutson expedition met its demise, he was successful in producing an imaginary sacred space around which Minnesotans oriented themselves to establish order out of chaotic memories of frontier conquest.[53]

Save Us from Evil! Prayerful Vigilance against Savagery Past and Present

Writing in 1916, rune stone enthusiast and Douglas County historian Constant Larson wondered why the Kensington artifact had been found in Olof Ohman's field with the inscription facedown. Larson theorized that the Norsemen would have originally positioned the stone in an upright position like a gravestone. Because of the beveled cut of the stone, Larson reasoned, gravity would have eventually pulled the stone backward so that the inscribed surface would have been faceup. Therefore, at some point in history, he deduced, somebody pushed the stone over to face the ground. Larson concluded that this was done by the Indians who carried out the massacre because they feared its power, seeing it as a "retributive, threatening reminder of their pale-face victims."[54] If Larson interpreted the rune stone as having the power to threaten savages of the fourteenth century, he and other white Minnesotans believed it had the power to do the same in more recent times. For twentieth-century rune stone enthusiasts like Larson, and quite possibly the inscription's author(s) in the nineteenth century, the Kensington stone symbolized protection against vulnerability and evoked notions of immortality.[55]

Despite the mass expulsion of Dakota people from Minnesota in 1863, Minnesotans experienced periodic episodes of panic that Indians would once again rise up in mass revolt. One such episode occurred not far from where the Kensington Rune Stone was unearthed. Local historian Helen Joos Cichy gives an account of what she calls "the final Indian scare of 1876." According to Cichy, "a party of Chippewa Indian men" from a nearby reservation stopped at a saloon on the way back from a trip to purchase horses. After indulging in too much alcohol, they began to "help themselves to whatever appealed to them." Their horses ended up trampling the garden and the wheat field of a local farmer. Cichy said that the custom of the day among white settlers was not to resist Indians for fear of escalating violence, but "the news of an Indian raid spread as fast as a prairie fire on a hot autumn day. Each retelling improved it until it was full-fledged massacre."[56] She noted that rumors about "the Great Custer Massacre" had likely fueled the panic. Many farm families gathered their possessions and fled to the town of Alexandria in hope of finding protection.

One of the last military conflicts between an Indian tribe and the U.S. government occurred in Minnesota during the same year that the Kensington Rune Stone was unearthed from Ohman's field. Just months before Minnesota troops would struggle to suppress an insurrection in their newly acquired empire in the Philippines, they battled Ojibwe Indians in northern Minnesota.[57] Tensions on the Leech Lake reservation in the 1890s were high because tribal members resented logging companies who were illegally harvesting timber from their land.[58] In late September 1898, two Ojibwe men were arrested by U.S. marshals and held as witnesses for a bootlegging trial. One of them was a tribal elder named Bagone-giizhig or Hole-in-the-Day. As an outspoken critic of U.S. Indian policies, Hole-in-the-Day had been arrested before and falsely accused of bootlegging. He was determined to avoid arrest and called on onlookers to help him. After a short skirmish, the two captives fled the custody of the marshals and took refuge in a cabin across the lake.

After an unsuccessful attempt to get Hole-in-the-Day and his men to surrender, local authorities requested reinforcements from Fort Snelling. On the morning of October 5, several marshals and seventy-seven soldiers of the Third Regiment boarded steamboats to cross the lake to Hole-in-the-Day's cabin on Sugar Point. Upon arrival, they could not find him and prepared for a lunch break in a lakeside clearing. Reports differ on what happened next, but one of the soldiers discharged his gun.

This led to a volley of gunfire from armed Indians in the nearby woods. In the end, six U.S. soldiers were killed, including the commanding officer.

In white communities throughout the region, "hysteria mounted" and many feared a widespread Indian uprising. Newspaper headlines from towns as far as sixty miles away warned of imminent attacks and even the front page of the *New York Times* carried the sensational and inaccurate headlines "Rumored Massacre of One Hundred Soldiers" and "Fierce Fight with Bear Lake Savages in Minnesota."[59] Residents of Bemidji barricaded themselves in the courthouse and many communities formed citizen militias. A regiment of 214 men and a Gatling gun were dispatched to the Leech Lake town of Walker. By mid-October the commissioner of Indian affairs negotiated a truce with the Ojibwe leaders and it became clear that they were not intending to mount an insurrection.[60]

As the preceding events indicate, many rural, white Minnesotans were still fearful of Indians and saw them as a threat as late as the turn of the century. Even in Alexandria, more than a hundred miles away from the nearest reservation, a newspaper headline from 1900 declared "No Indian Uprising" after a "raucous powwow" near the Canadian border was determined not to be a preparation for war.[61] It is not surprising that most Minnesotans understood the nebulous runic inscription to describe an Indian massacre. Even the circumstances of the Leech Lake incident resembled the events of Holand's imagined Viking massacre at Lake Cormorant. Both serve as reminders of human mortality. However, despite the fear of death, commemorating white sacrifices, both in the distant past and in the more recent past, functions as a form of symbolic immortality.[62] The Kensington Rune Stone helped to temper the death anxiety by offering hope that sacrificial deaths will be remembered.

Even if flesh-and-blood Indians posed a decreasing physical threat to the larger white society, retelling and even reenacting the rune stone story, or other stories of Indian violence, became ways to vicariously participate in past battles and still come out alive. As noted earlier, late-nineteenth-century Minnesotans consumed several forms of media that centered on the violence of the Dakota War. However, fascination with the history of conflict with the region's first residents persisted well into the twentieth century. Buffalo Bill's traveling Wild West show, which dramatized battles between Indians and pioneer settlers, was wildly popular at the turn of the century. The dime novel *Indian Jim: A Tale of the Minnesota Massacre,* first printed in 1864, was rereleased in 1908. The scalp and skull of the Dakota leader Little Crow were publicly displayed at the Minnesota Historical Society until 1915. Holand's narrative about primordial Viking martyrs can be understood as another spectacle of violence that satiated a contemporary desire for vicarious heroism.

Scapegoat Skrælings

Social scientists have shown that when humans are reminded of their own mortality, they tend to be more aggressive toward people who are different from them.[63] In the early twentieth century, the skrælings in Holand's history emerged as a scapegoat on which to project contemporary social anxieties and frustrations. In his book *History of Douglas and Grant Counties,* local historian Constant Larson used the motif of primeval Indian savagery to blame nineteenth-century Indians for western Minnesota's lack of growth and prosperity in the early twentieth century.[64]

Larson's historical account, written in 1916, asserts that Douglas County had two beginnings: the first in 1858 with the arrival of the Kinkaid brothers, and the second after the first settlement was abandoned because of the "Sioux Outbreak of 1862."[65] William and Alexander Kinkaid first came to the area in 1858 and built a cabin on the shore of Lake Agnes. By 1860, the population of white settlers numbered 187 and roads and farms were appearing throughout the county.[66] Larson waxed eloquent about the first settlers' hopes for the continued development of the "Park Region." The area promised to become "one of the most desirable points of settlement in the western part of the state . . . all seemed well with Douglas County, with a bright future—full of promise, when the dread event occurred."[67]

When the news arrived in the isolated outpost of Alexandria in August 1862 that the "Indians had declared war," most residents abandoned their homesteads in panic, leaving behind all of their belongings. They escaped on foot or by oxcart to military stockades far to the east.[68] Upon hearing that two pioneers had been found dead in Douglas County, the settlers became so fearful that they refused to return to their farms until the U.S. Army built a stockade in Alexandria later that autumn.[69] Even then, only a few chose to come back; many never

Fort Alexandria was built to protect area settlers in the aftermath of the Dakota War of 1862. This painting from 1962 is by Ada Johnson and is now in the Runestone Museum in Alexandria. Photograph by the author.

returned. In Larson's words, the "Sioux Outbreak" had proved "a setback for all of western Minnesota." The "Indian massacre" had "interrupted the course of empire in Douglas County." Larson laments that it was not until 1874 that all of the tillable land had finally been claimed. It was only then, he said, that "the white man came into undisputed possession of this fair region and no longer stood in terror of the relentless fury of the savages."[70]

Larson makes a clear delineation between white victim and Indian aggressor. Of the Indians, he said, "The fiends of hell could not invent more fearful atrocities than were perpetrated by the savages upon their victims." The only ones spared were the "young and comely women, to minister to the brutal lusts of their captors." For rhetorical effect, he goes on to make an exaggerated claim that eight hundred whites were killed in a period of thirty-six hours.[71] Regarding the legal outcome for the Sioux, Larson insisted that each of the condemned received a "fair and impartial hearing." According to him, President Lincoln was wrong to give in to the pressures of "sentimental persons in the East."[72]

Just prior to Larson's chapters on early white settlement and the "Sioux Outbreak" is the chapter "The Kensington Rune Stone: An Ancient Tragedy," which opens as follows:

> If the conclusions of eminent archeologists be correct, the
> one outstanding, paramount fact in the history of Douglas
> County is that one hundred and thirty years before the voyage
> of Columbus to America, white men—Europeans—had trod
> the soil of that section of Minnesota now comprised within the
> boundaries of Douglas County and left here a record of their
> travels and of their perilous adventures and the death of ten of
> their number at the hands of savages.[73]

Larson refers to the rune stone as both a gravestone and a monument
to commemorate the dead Norsemen, and arguing for its authenticity is
clearly a high priority for him.[74] At fifty pages, this chapter is the longest
of his book *History of Douglas and Grant Counties*. He offers a detailed
account of the discovery of the stone, an analysis of the inscription, an
assessment of the geological evidences, and a defense of the integrity of
Ohman and his neighbors. Although his defense of the rune stone relies
heavily on Holand's writings, it is clear that he has invested a significant
amount of effort in analyzing his own sources, nearly sixty of which he
cites in an annotated bibliography at the conclusion of the chapter. In
Larson's mind, there is a direct correlation between the "ancient tragedy" as witnessed in the rune stone inscription and the modern tragedy of "The Sioux Outbreak of 1862": Indians were responsible for
both. The terms "massacre" and "massacred" are used multiple times to
describe both the death of the Norsemen and also the white settlers in
1862. In both cases, the terms "savage" or "savages" describe the Indian
perpetrators.

Given the anxieties about the decline of masculinity in the post-
pioneer age, Larson's emphasis on the savagery of the skrælings is likely
a strategy to magnify the prowess of his fourteenth-century forefathers,
and hence his fellow Scandinavian Americans in the early twentieth
century. However, his strategic use of the Kensington Rune Stone story
in relaying the recent history of his community should be recognized
as an example of a scapegoat mechanism, evoking René Girard's classic
theory of religion and violence. In Girard's "mimetic model," individuals and groups imitate one another in their desire for objects. When
multiple groups or individuals are competing for the same thing or
things, competitive violence can result and escalate to an endless cycle of
attack and revenge. Societal conflict rises to such a point that it becomes

intolerable. For Girard, this crisis is only resolved through a religious ritual where a scapegoat is identified and sacrificed for the good of the society. According to Girard, this sacrifice has the ability to safely purge violence from the society so that social stability can be restored. The sacrifice has the result of bringing peace, even if temporary. Social groups will develop religious rituals systems that reenact the sacrifice in order prevent further violence.[75] Historian Jon Pahl summarizes this process: "For the 'illegitimate' violence of unchecked rivalry, attack and vengeance, religion substitutes a 'legitimate' violence, as enacted in the practices of ritual and encoded in the discourse of myth."[76]

Girard's theory is often seen as applying only to the analysis of premodern tribal societies, but it is also relevant to large, modern societies.[77] The public execution at Mankato in 1862 can be thought of in terms of a Girardian ritual of sacrifice carried out by the U.S. government. The intention of the executions was to channel the lust for revenge through the mechanisms of the state. However, neither the execution nor the forced exile of Dakota people could adequately purge the collective anger of Minnesotan settlers. White residents used the Kensington Rune Stone story to channel their residual rage. Each retelling of the story of the Knutson expedition becomes a way to ritually commemorate the sacrifice of white pioneers of the nineteenth century and excoriate those who killed them. This scapegoat mechanism would have an enduring afterlife. As later chapters will show, western Minnesotans continued to invoke the notion of a primordial Viking massacre at the hands of savage Indians to face a variety of social and religious threats in the twentieth century.[78]

Rocky Revelations and the Anxieties of Conquest

Larson's and Holand's integration of the Kensington Rune Stone narrative into their historical accounts provided Minnesotans with what Max Weber would call "the psychological reassurance of legitimacy."[79] In other words, the artifact bolstered the conviction that their success, happiness, and prosperity were deserved and were bestowed on them by the providence of God.[80] According to the way the story is typically told, the immigrant farmer Olaf Ohman "discovers" the Viking relic while clearing trees from his land in order to prepare it for cultivation. Therefore, the rune stone becomes a sign that God has blessed the farmer's efforts

The Great Seal of the State of Minnesota.

to reclaim the land from its wild state.[81] Because the stone emerges from ground that is already claimed by European Americans, it is interpreted as a revelation that God considered their ownership of the land justified.[82]

Evoking memories of Indian savagery would be one attempt to demonstrate that white residents had a rightful claim to the landscape, but nostalgic renderings did the same. Henry W. Longfellow's poem *The Song of Hiawatha* became a template for the construction of a modern, peace-loving Indian far more palatable to white Minnesotans than the "savages" of the Dakota War and the flesh-and-blood Ojibwe Indians who continued to live in Minnesota.[83] The poem popularized the notion that Indians were a people who had disappeared, or at the least had come to terms with the triumph of white civilization. One of the poem's female characters, Minnehaha, is the namesake of a Minneapolis park dedicated in 1889. "Noble Indians" became the centerpiece of numerous advertising campaigns in the early to mid-twentieth century, including Hamm's beer and Land O'Lakes butter. Starting in the 1940s, civic leaders in Pipestone, Minnesota, held an annual historical pageant based on Longfellow's poem. The pageant romanticized tribal cultures as "noble and heroic" but ultimately "destined to vanish with the perceived advance of American society."[84] The notion of vanished Indians was also evident on one of the most sacred of civic symbols: the state seal of Minnesota, which depicted a farmer with his hands to the plow next to a stump with a rifle leaning on it. The farmer's eyes were fixed on an Indian on horseback riding off into the setting sun.[85] A 1944 poem by Gertrude E. Anderson interprets the meaning of the seal.

> An Indian, mounted on his pony, Rides full speed toward the setting sun; Behind him, the white man, bending, plowing, Visions the glory of work to be done. His ax sunk deep in a near-by tree stump, His heavy rifle, lying low . . . Galloping, galloping goes the pony . . . "White man here now; Indian must go." Fainter, fainter, the pony's hoofbeats . . . Almost vanished, the Indian horde . . . Freedom! Freedom! The white man's struggle still goes on. L'etoile du nord![86]

Despite the fact that Minnesotans were comforted by the notion of "vanished Indians," they continued to include living Indians in civic events to commemorate the sacrifices of white settlers. For the fiftieth anniversary of the Battle of New Ulm in 1912, "a peace delegation" of local Dakota Indians was invited to march in the town parade. Formerly imagined as "savages," contemporary Indians were imagined to be "agents of wisdom and peace."[87] In 1938, Alexandria civic leaders hosted a "Runestone Remembrance Days" celebration in which Ojibwe Indians from the Leech Lake Reservation played an important role. Tribal members were among the actors in a historical pageant dramatizing the rune stone story and were also part of a "life-like Indian camp" staged for a film crew documenting the week's events.[88] Local papers noted that Chief Chibiaboos, a "full-blood Chippewa," was a featured performer and "one of the most popular personages of the celebration."[89] It is likely that the presence of real, live Indians at their history pageant helped

This photograph depicts a reenactment of one of the rune stone pageant scenes from 1938. It is unclear if the "Indians" in this particular scene are white residents dressing up in stereotypical costumes, but it is known that Ojibwe tribal members from Cass Lake were present during the week's celebrations. Courtesy of the Douglas County Historical Society.

local white residents reassure themselves that the skrælings, once so savage, had now happily embraced their Nordic conquerors.[90]

It is evident that some early-twentieth-century Minnesotans expressed a degree of moral ambiguity about the violent expulsion of Indians from Minnesota during the nineteenth century. For some, these anxieties morphed into feelings of regret and guilt regarding the plight of Native Americans. At times, even Holand conveys regret for the plight of Indians in the face of white settlement: "The saddest memories in America's history are those in connection with the displacement and extermination of the Indians."[91] Ole Rølvaag's widely read novel *Giants in the Earth* suggests that many Norwegian Americans in the region felt anxiety about claiming and settling a land that was not necessarily empty. In one scene, Per Hansa walked with his neighbors to the top of a hill overlooking his newly acquired plot of land and "stopped beside a small depression in the ground, and stood gazing at it intently for quite a while; then he said quietly: 'There are people buried here . . . That is a grave.'" Rølvaag portrays Per Hansa and his Norwegian neighbors as somewhat disturbed by this discovery, but ultimately callous to the claims of others: "This vast stretch of beautiful land was to be his—yes his—and no ghost of a dead Indian would drive him away!"[92]

One of the strategies to justify the conquest of one group over another is to construct and perpetuate a legitimating myth framed by the notion of "innocent domination," which Jon Pahl defines as "patterns or systems of domination, hegemony, or power over others that are largely absent of malice on the part of the perpetrators."[93] Producing this type of myth requires a number of rhetorical devices, one of which is to demonstrate that one's own group is more innocent than other dominating groups. Holand portrayed medieval Norsemen as morally superior to other explorers, such as the Spaniards, because the former "placed a much higher view on America's importance." Christopher Columbus and his ilk, claimed Holand, came with "thieves' eyes" valuing America only as a place from which to extract wealth.[94] The noble intentions of the Knutson expedition are likened to those of modern Norwegians who came not "to establish new kingdoms like the Mormons, or to dig for gold, or with force and intrigue to gain political power." To the contrary, the aim of the pioneer immigrants "was to establish peaceful communities and build roads, to till the soil and the wilderness to bloom."[95] With such rhetoric, Holand disguises the complicity of Norwegian Americans in the violent conquest of Native Americans. Although most Norwegian settlers were not directly involved in the removal of Indians from Minnesota, the U.S. Army did it on their behalf.[96]

The innocence of one's group is enhanced by appeals to divine blessing. When writing about the history of Norwegian immigrant settlement, Holand asserted his group's innocence in the conquest of the frontier by situating the endeavor in a biblical framework: "It was as if we were transported back to remotest antiquity, when man heard the first divine command to replenish the earth and subdue it. The greatest contribution the Norwegians have made to America is their obedience to this ancient command."[97] Holand implies that the experience of frontier life is what made Norwegian Americans so much more religious than those they left behind in Norway: "There is no more gratifying challenge . . . than to transform a wilderness into flourishing fields . . . It is as if one identifies himself with the Creator as he converts a chaos into a cosmos."[98] In Holand's logic, it is God who has initiated the campaign of conquest; Norwegian Americans could not be held culpable for the violence they perpetrated. It was not only the Norwegian immigrants who understood God to be on their side. Many Christian missionaries viewed the Dakota conflict as a war of religions. Blaming traditional Dakota religion for instigating the conflict, they interpreted the victory of white civilization as divine affirmation that Christianity was superior.[99]

Another component of a myth of innocent domination is to portray the dominated as needing to be thus. They are either irrepressibly savage or unable to manage themselves or their environment in a proper manner. Through their portrayals of Indians as the savage "other," Holand and Larson also make it appear that Indians by nature are unable to relate peaceably to European Americans. Therefore, their need to be conquered is both natural and divinely ordained.[100] Holand also emphasized that white settlers had a greater claim to the land because they made better use of it than did the Indians. He portrays the work ethic of white settlers as superior to that of the Indians:

> But one day the white man came to these parts—the energetic Yankee and the strong serious Norseman. For him, life is not long, and carefree, but short and filled with responsibility . . . He digs himself a hole in the side of a hill for a house . . . He chops and saws the hard oak trees and builds strong fences around his property, sows his corn, digs a well, drains and irrigates, plows and digs. Soon a small church appears where he can beseech a God he more fears than loves. For him, life is serious.[101]

The theme of divinely ordained white supersession is evident in Holand's story of Norwegian settler Søren Bache who made his pioneer home in an Indian mound: "Bache excavated a roomy tunnel through this mound . . . in this way he acquired a fairly cozy place to live." Capitalizing on an opportunity to expand local commerce, Bache later transformed his dwelling into what Holand calls "the first Norwegian grocery store in America." In later years, Holand says that "this same Indian mound was to become the first Norwegian-Lutheran parsonage in

America."[102] Finally, in 1844, the Indian mound was leveled and the first Norwegian Lutheran Church was built on top of it.[103] In this vignette, Holand charts a clear path of "progress" from Indian savagery to a white, prosperous, Christian civilization.[104] Holand's rune stone functions as a primordial land claim foreshadowing this divine destiny.

The mythology enshrouding the Kensington Rune Stone became a repository for settler anger over the events of the "Indian Massacre of 1862." Far from removing violence from the culture of Minnesotans, the mythic narrative and the ritualized evocations of Viking martyrdom perpetuated ongoing notions of both Scandinavian immigrant and Anglo-American innocence in the genocide and exile of Native Americans. This civic myth with violence at its center yielded an enduring and elastic symbol, the skræling, which could be rhetorically applied to a variety of threats in the twentieth century. In short, the Kensington Rune Stone became a tool in a "cosmic war" between the forces of savagery and civilization that used a mythic past to justify the policies of the present.[105] As part of Minnesota's sacred civic landscape, Holand's Viking trail served to further reify white claims to the land. If God's blessing of the American nation extended so far back in to the past, it would surely extend into the future.

CHAPTER THREE

In Defense of Main Street
The Kensington Rune Stone
as a Midwestern Plymouth Rock

> [Small-town life] is an unimaginatively standardized background, a sluggishness of speech and manners, a rigid ruling of the spirit by the desire to appear respectable. It is contentment . . . the contentment of the quiet dead, who are scornful of the living for their restless walking. It is negation canonized as the one positive virtue. It is the prohibition of happiness. It is slavery self-sought and self-defended. It is dullness made God.
>
> —Sinclair Lewis, *Main Street*

Despite the enduring appeal of the Kensington Rune Stone narrative for addressing external enemies and defending military campaigns of the past and present, it was also used to confront enemies closer to home. By the 1920s, there was more at stake in the promotion of the rune stone than justifying white claims to the landscape or bolstering ethnic power. Memories of the Dakota War of 1862 were fading and Swedish and Norwegian Americans no longer required homemaking myths to prove that they were loyal Americans. Residents of rural and small-town Minnesota during this period faced new and immediate threats to their economic well-being and sense of identity. Despite the rapid economic growth in urban, industrial areas during the 1920s, Minnesota farmers were suffering from an economic downturn. Grain prices had dropped sharply after the wartime demand for grain collapsed. Rural areas suffered population loss during the decade as younger residents migrated to cities for employment.[1] And just as the material prosperity of rural Minnesota was eroding, its cultural prestige was under attack.

Sinclair Lewis and the Marginalization of "Main Street"

Sinclair Lewis's depiction of small-town American life in his novel *Main Street* was in stark contrast to typical portrayals from the era. In the first two decades of the twentieth century, American literature and popular culture depicted small towns as the source of American virtue.[2] The Norman Rockwell cover art on the *Saturday Evening Post* during this time frequently depicted sentimental scenes nostalgic for a small-town past.[3] The accelerating forces of industrialization and urbanization left many Americans yearning for small-town life and its values. However, Lewis's *Main Street* took aim at small-town boosterism and the idealizing of rural life. Released in 1920, it was wildly successful, selling more than 2 million copies within a few years. The success of *Main Street* has been described as "the most sensational event in twentieth-century American publishing history," and its impact on popular depictions of small town life in the 1920s was profound.[4] In the aftermath of its publication, "[t]he term Main Streeter became a pejorative for someone who was gauche and provincial."[5] The public spectacle of *Main Street* identified a fault line in American culture between Middle America and the cultural elites of the East Coast.[6]

Lewis's mythical town of Gopher Prairie, the setting of his novel, was based largely on his hometown experience in Sauk Centre, Minnesota. Lewis spent his childhood in Sauk Centre, but moved to Greenwich Village in New York in 1910 and lived among artists, authors, and left-wing political activists. Sauk Centre residents were not pleased with Lewis's depiction of their town as parochial, gossipy, and narrow-minded. The local newspaper refused to acknowledge the book until six months after it was released, and its initial coverage was defensive: "A perusal of the book makes it possible for one to picture in his mind's eyes local characters having been injected bodily into the story."[7] Local residents feared that they had become "the butt of a national joke."[8] The local outrage, however, was short-lived. Within two years, Sauk Centre came to embrace Lewis as a local boy who made good. Local business entrepreneurs capitalized on the publicity of his book. In 1923, a billboard was placed at the entrance to town describing Sauk Centre as America's "Original Main Street." In following years, a hotel opened with the name Gopher Prairie Inn and a local restaurant was named Main Street Diner.

Sociologists Amy Campion and Gary Alan Fine asked how and

why the town of Sauk Centre came to embrace the one who attacked them the most harshly. Because of *Main Street's* immense success, Sauk Centre residents had to find a way to embrace it; to reject Lewis's novel would demonstrate that they actually were Gopher Prairie. Campion and Fine remind us that external criticism often has the effect of making a community aware of itself: "Such a community may have some sense of group identity, but until that identity is questioned, it remains largely undefined and unarticulated."[9] They describe the town's civic leaders as "reputational entrepreneurs" who were able to foster collective identity by challenging, incorporating, and reinterpreting criticisms of small-town life in *Main Street*. These community boosters or image makers utilized "neutralization" techniques to address the attacks. First, they "revalued" the message of the critic by making it "to mean the opposite of what was intended."[10] Civic leaders claimed that Lewis had neglected to describe the "other side of Main Street." This was the "true" Sauk Centre that locals experience as a "haven of warmth and virtue" in contrast to cities like Minneapolis, which they described as a place of "corruption and hostility."[11] In promoting their town, civic boosters used only the few quotations from Lewis's novel that spoke of the town in a positive light; they ignored the many quotes that critiqued the town. Additionally, they portrayed the author as a person who really loved his town despite his criticisms. In short, the reputational entrepreneurs of Sauk Centre seized control of the town's identity by reinterpreting *Main Street* for their own purposes. By embracing Lewis, they promoted Sauk Centre "as the original, quintessential small town." Lewis's novel emerged as what sociologist Émile Durkheim would refer to as a "totem," which represented the aspirations and identity of the community.[12]

Main Street evoked an emotional response among residents of Alexandria, just twenty-four miles to the west of Sauk Centre. In September 1921, several newspapers throughout the country reported that Lewis's novel had been banned from Alexandria's public library. The articles attributed this to a rumor that Alexandria residents were concerned that the novel had their town in mind when he wrote about Gopher Prairie. An article in the *Kansas City Star* stated:

> *Main Street's* expulsion was a highly secretive affair. Those
> who asked at the library had been told for some time that the
> book was not in favor among the best people because it wasn't

altogether fair to the small town. But the demand was insistent and the library board finally authorized the purchase of a few copies. Then one dark night the copies disappeared.[13]

Many of these articles accused the people of Alexandria of taking Lewis's novel "too seriously."[14] Not even Alexandria's neighbor, Sauk Centre, refrained from heaping ridicule. An article in the *Sauk Centre Herald* stated that Alexandria was simply "jealous" of all the publicity that Sauk Centre had received. Alexandria's public library director, Gustav A. Kortsch, publicly denied that Lewis's book had been banned; he maintained that the library had received a defective copy and had returned it to the publisher.[15] The damage, however, had already been done. Alexandria appeared to outsiders as having lived up to Lewis's depiction of small-town residents as defensive and paranoid. Unfortunately, unlike Sauk Centre, Alexandria and other small towns in western Minnesota were not able to turn Lewis's critique of small-town and rural life into a cultural benefit. They had little to gain from endorsing his book because they could not claim Lewis as a native son. These communities would have to find other means to rehabilitate their civic image and boost the local economy.

Bjorklund's Dream: Erecting a Monument to America's True Founders

American civil religion has been inscribed into the American landscape through the construction of monuments, museums, and war memorials. Although the largest concentration of the nation's sacred monuments and sites is in eastern cities such as Washington and Philadelphia, civic leaders from across the country integrated their own spaces into American narratives. On July 4, 1927, Gen. John J. Pershing laid the cornerstone for the Indiana War Memorial in Indianapolis, "consecrating the edifice as a patriotic shrine."[16] In 1927, carving began on a South Dakota mountainside that was to be transformed into a monument dedicated to U.S. presidents. Dubbed "America's Shrine of Democracy," Mount Rushmore became a sacred civic site accessible to millions of Americans in the middle of the country.[17]

Also in 1927, a group of western Minnesotans started their own campaign to construct a monument of national significance. In the spring of that year, a local pharmacist named Edwin T. Bjorklund awoke from a dream in which he saw a tall monument to the Kensington Rune Stone surrounded by a large crowd marveling at its enormity. The monument rose so high that it could be seen from towns throughout western Minnesota, as far as sixty miles away. Bjorklund said he also heard "an eloquent speech" given by a defender of the historical authenticity of the rune stone. According to local accounts, Bjorklund got out of bed in the middle of the night and went directly to his drugstore to begin work on making the dream a reality.[18] Soon after, on a local radio broadcast, Bjorklund shared his vision for erecting his monument, which would measure more than two hundred feet tall. Following his radio appearance, the Alexandria paper reported that "great excitability and enthusiasm has prevailed among the people of Kensington and throughout Douglas County."[19]

In May 1927, Bjorklund marshaled this collective zeal into a rally to promote the monument's construction. The June rally was held at the Nils Fahlin farm, located just two miles to the east of the rune stone "discovery" site, to officially kick off the fund-raising campaign.[20] Bjorklund opened the event by leading the crowd estimated at five thousand in the singing of the patriotic hymn "America the Beautiful." Throughout the day, several speakers addressed the crowd, emphatically connecting the sacred value of the artifact to the identity of local residents. Congressman Ole J. Kvale "paid a glowing tribute to the Scandinavian people who developed the northwestern United States." Playing up the theme of ethnic nostalgia, he stated that "observing the traditions of the forefathers was not a distraction to being good Americans." To the contrary, he argued, it actually intensifies their patriotism and makes them better citizens.[21]

Hjalmar Holand was a central figure at the rally and delivered a speech in defense of the historical authenticity of the Kensington Rune Stone. Holand at first refused to allow his beloved artifact to be displayed at the rally for fear that it might be stolen. His fears were assuaged when two World War I veterans dressed in full battle gear and carrying rifles agreed to guard the stone throughout the day's festivities. Local papers noted that the two veterans, Gilbert Hanson and John Ecklund, were from the "Lost Battalion" of the First World War, a U.S. military unit caught behind German lines that suffered heavy casualties. Hanson and Ecklund were among the survivors. Their presence next to the stone may have been intended to evoke the image of the Norse travelers as also

having been "behind enemy lines" while they suffered Indian attacks.[22]
Rally attendees were able to file past the guarded rune stone, which was
mounted on a platform. The enthusiastic speeches and the dramatic
method of display had the effect of raising the sacred value of the stone
in the eyes of many attendees, as evidenced by an essay written by a local
seventh grader:

> The Kensington Runestone is undoubtedly of much more
> importance than the Plymouth Rock, which hundreds of
> thousands of people go to see yearly just because it is the
> rock on which the Pilgrims stepped when they landed on the
> Atlantic coast three hundred years after the Norsemen left
> the Runestone. The stone itself is an object of great impor-
> tance . . . I think everything possible should be done to promote
> the building of the Runestone Monument.[23]

In short, the Oscar Lake rally marks the beginning of when the Kensington Rune Stone became widely recognized as a sacred regional symbol.
    Civic promoters built on the momentum of the rally by forming the
Runestone Foundation.[24] Board members included residents from nearly
a dozen small towns scattered across western Minnesota. Boosters of
this civic project boasted of the project's significance:

> This Runestone Park and monument project is said to be the
> biggest undertaking launched by any Scandinavian body in
> the United States of America, and the Runestone state park
> and tower when completed will be one of the rarest and most
> uncommon architectural constructions in the state, and thou-
> sands upon thousands of tourists will visit the historical site
> yearly. It will point a gateway to the beautiful lake region dis-
> trict of Minnesota and Douglas County, where future genera-
> tions will see this fitting memorial to commemorate the sturdy
> Vikings who left this evidence, the Kensington Runestone in
> the visit to Minnesota in 1362.[25]

That summer, plans for the monument from a Minneapolis-based archi-
tectural firm were unveiled in the local newspapers. The monument was
to include a two-hundred-foot square shaft with a circular foundation

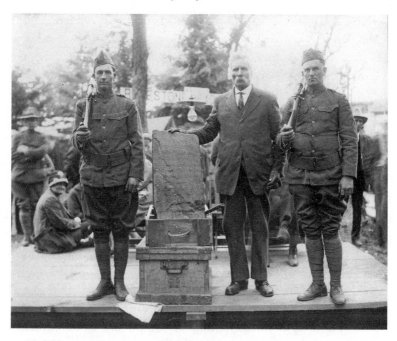

Olof Ohman and war veterans stand next to the Kensington Rune Stone display at a monument fund-raising rally near Oscar Lake in 1927. Courtesy of Douglas County Historical Society.

of columns to be constructed at its base. The interior of the foundation would include a room, forty-six feet in diameter, to provide a permanent home for the Kensington Rune Stone and "other articles of ancient origin."[26] With the construction projected to cost an estimated three hundred thousand dollars, newspaper articles assured readers that letters had already been received offering donations: "Enthusiasm is in great evidence not only in Minnesota but in adjoining states."[27] The committee planned to start the following September with an effort to approach "every Scandinavian in four states" to make a contribution of one dollar per family member.[28]

The peculiar design of the monument gives a clue to its symbolic intentions. The square shaft is an obelisk and the design bears striking resemblance to one of Robert Mills's design proposals for the Washington Monument from 1845.[29] It is not known why this particular design was chosen for the Runestone Monument, but there are some possible explanations. The Washington Monument commemorates the founding father of the United States. So the choice of the obelisk design for the Kensington Rune Stone monument likely demonstrated that the fourteenth-century Norsemen were the real founders of America.[30] The monument design also resembled the plans for a new skyscraper called the Foshay Tower, which was being constructed in Minneapolis that same year. Civic boosters like Bjorklund may have hoped the monument would help their rural hometown to be associated with the prestige of Minnesota's largest urban center.[31]

Many of the persons associated with this monument project, including Bjorklund, were members of Masonic lodges. The man behind the Foshay Tower was also a prominent Freemason, as were most businessmen of this era. One early rune stone observer argued that the "AVM" in the Kensington inscription is actually "AUM" and would indicate the markings of a Masonic symbol.[32] As Wahlgren observed, the term "AUM" is familiar among Freemasons because it is noted in their manuals as a reference to "God" in the religions of India.[33] Whether or not Freemasons recognized the Kensington Rune Stone as a particularly Masonic symbol is not known. However, fraternal organizations such as the Freemasons have been characterized as "a form of institutionalized civil religion" with the aim of cultivating morality among their members. Masonic literature has frequent references to God as transcendent over the nation and the source of civic virtue. The preoccupation with the nation's founders is well documented. Masonic doctrine upholds George Washington as a moral exemplar of "devotion to God and country" and the revolutionary period is characterized as a golden age of U.S. history.[34]

Masonic themes occur in the monument promotion rhetoric in the months following the summer rally near Ohman's farm. At an Alexandria gathering in late 1927, orations delivered by several dignitaries extolled the sacred role that the rune stone should play in the identity of the region's residents. The governor of North Dakota, Arthur G. Sorlie, maintained that the monument should not be viewed as a cost but as an investment to build a Midwestern tourist destination that would rival the historic sites in eastern cities like Philadelphia and Boston.[35] Together with South Dakota's Mount Rushmore, the monument to America's Norse founders in Minnesota could draw visitors to a region often overlooked by tourists traveling to national parks in Wyoming and Colorado.

One civic promoter said that the view from on top of the new monument would be as "interesting to the eye as the Rocky Mountain scenery to the west."[36]

A well-known Norwegian-American Lutheran minister from Minneapolis, Rev. J. A. O. Stub, gave a speech arguing for the cultural and religious importance of the Kensington Stone. The inscription, said Stub, commemorated the first time that Swedes and Norwegians had been brought together for a common purpose. Even if the artifact eventually proved to be a hoax, he said, bringing modern Scandinavians together to work on a common civic goal was a worthy endeavor. He pointed to Leif Eriksson and other Norseman of the Middle Ages as exemplars of the "industry, thrift, bravery and a willingness to sacrifice" that help the immigrants to become American.[37] He implored the crowd to consider the "higher things of life," such as maintaining their cultural traditions, and warned his listeners not to become preoccupied with the pursuit of wealth.[38]

Holand followed the moral exhortations of the minister with some of his own. In his afternoon speech, he repeated his standard linguistic and archaeological arguments for the authenticity of his beloved artifact, but he particularly emphasized noble purposes behind the Norse explorations of North America. Whereas Christopher Columbus was motivated by selfish commercialism, he said, Paul Knutson was a Christian missionary motivated to seek a new home and explore undiscovered lands. Holand argued that the Kensington Rune Stone was the most significant historical artifact in the United States, far more valuable than Plymouth Rock.[39]

The Runestone Rally in Alexandria must have made quite an impression on local business leaders, because in February 1928, a group of ten businessmen, led by the Alexandria attorney and local historian Constant Larson, paid $2,500 to Hjalmar Holand to take possession of the rune stone. The Commercial Club of Alexandria soon announced that it had purchased an old bank building on Broadway to house its offices and to become "a real civic center where public meetings of all sorts can be held." Club members said that the building would be an appropriate place to display Holand's artifacts and Indian relics that, at the time, were stored at the library.[40] Over the next few years, the rune stone traveled to towns throughout western Minnesota accompanied by Constant

Larson and his daughter Lorayne. The stone was also brought to the Minnesota State Fair to represent Douglas County at its display booth.[41]

Following the purchase of the stone by the Alexandria businessmen, it was generally thought that it would remain in Alexandria until there was enough money to construct the monument on the Ohman farm. The details of the fund-raising campaign are not clear, but the monument was never built. Contemporary observers attribute this to a loss of project funds during the bank defaults of the Great Depression.[42] However, the Alexandria Chamber of Commerce had already made plans to keep the stone in the city of Alexandria prior to the start of the Great Depression. An August 1929 news article announces the installation of a custom-made six-foot-high iron-and-glass display case for the rune stone in the Chamber of Commerce building.[43]

Bjorklund clearly wanted the artifact to return to the Ohman farm near Kensington. He was quoted as promising Olaf Ohman's wife: "Mother, you are going to see this stone once more and a high monument shall be erected on your farm to your honor."[44] Holand did not share this commitment to keep the artifact at the Ohman farm. His primary interest was to generate funds to further his research, and the businessmen of Alexandria were the people with the money at the right time and place.[45]

The list of people who invested in the purchase of the Kensington Rune Stone demonstrates that by 1928 it was no longer an artifact of significance to Scandinavian Americans alone. A newspaper article noted that the first person to put up money was Philip J. Noonan, "an Irishman." Also in the list of names are persons evidently of German and English descent.[46] Thus, by 1928, the Kensington Rune Stone had become valuable to a diverse cross section of the community.[47] This is also reflected in the shift from the use of the term "Kensington Rune Stone" to "Kensington Runestone." The melding together of "rune" and "stone" reflects an Anglicizing of the term and indicates a shift away from the exclusively ethnic connation of the artifact.

However, the purchase of the stone by a group of businessmen should not lead observers to conclude that these men were only concerned with economic profit. The rhetoric at the fund-raising rallies indicates that monument promoters recognized that the artifact would bestow prestige on the region. The rhetorical juxtaposition of Plymouth Rock with the Kensington Rune Stone was not only a strategy to promote tourism; it was a claim of national origins. The date on the rune stone inscription proved that American history began not on the East Coast, but in Minnesota, the heart of the continent. In the same issue of the local newspaper that announced the sale of the stone, there was an editorial that spoke to issues of civic identity among Alexandria residents:

> We frequently hear the complaint voiced by younger residents of Alexandria that they are fed up with the small town and that they long to get out into the world and do things and enjoy life to the fullest. We suppose that only experience can teach them the disappointments the outside world holds in store for many of them. Those of us who have gone through the same thing can sympathize with the boy who isn't satisfied with his hometown. But we know that opportunities in it are far greater than they were a generation ago and happiness and contentment are greater than in the places into which they want to drift. We have the auto, the radio, the picture show the same as the large cities and along with them we have something that the big city is short on, and that is genuine sociability and the friendship of those about us. We may not live as "fast" as they do in the big cities but we are due to live a little longer.[48]

The editorial goes on to acknowledge that not all of the town's young people can be expected to find successful careers there, but "those who do take advantage of opportunities and find a life-work here are not going to regret it in later years. There's still a chance to amount to something in the old home town."[49] The editorial reflects lingering resentment over the impact of Lewis's novel on the image of small-town life.[50] However, civic leaders creatively responded to external criticism of their community by articulating a new sacred regional identity. No matter what outsiders said, the Kensington Rune Stone inspired a new public narrative that asserted the significance of the small town in the American story.

Even though the monument was never built, the promotional efforts during this time period facilitated the apotheosis of the Kensington Rune Stone. The campaign events functioned as civic religious rituals that generated feelings that Émile Durkheim might refer to as "collective effervescence":

Swept away, the participants experience a force external to them, which seems to be moving them, and by which their very nature is transformed. They experience themselves as grander than at ordinary times; they do things they would not do at other times; they feel, and at the moment really are, joined with each other and with the totemic being.[51]

Local residents embraced the rune stone as their totem, projecting their aspirations and vulnerabilities onto it. The sacred value of the artifact is further illustrated by the civic leaders' concerns about leaving the stone unattended. One local resident expressed fear that the relic would be defaced or destroyed unless it was guarded continually.[52] After the stone was purchased by the Alexandria businessmen, some suggested that it be put on display in front of the Alexandria city hall where it could be seen by the public. However, they also argued that it would have to be installed behind an iron fence so it would not be "harmed by souvenir-hunters and vandals."[53] Finally, Chamber of Commerce officials decided on an even more secure approach: to store it in the old bank vault in the basement of their building. The stone resided primarily in this inner sanctum for the next two decades, an indication of the fragility of the civic self-esteem it generated.

Ritualizing the Birth of a Nation:
The Runestone History Pageant

Although the Ohman farm never became the national tourist Mecca that early civic boosters had dreamed of, the story of pre-Columbian Viking visitors became a cornerstone of a new effort to attract visitors to Alexandria. In 1933, a popular travel guide sponsored by the Continental Oil Company included Alexandria as an important roadside destination. Even in the midst of the Great Depression, locals began to express optimism about the local tourist economy: "Alexandria will be prominently mentioned in the booklet and because of the importance of the famous stone . . . hundreds of people driving through will stop and see the stone."[54]

For the fortieth anniversary of the unearthing of the rune stone, the Alexandria Chamber of Commerce announced that it was sponsoring the first "Runestone Remembrance Days" celebration during the height of the tourist season in June 1938. In the months prior, weekly front-page articles informed the public of the progress of the festival preparations. The event was to include several speakers and a performance by the Odin Male Chorus from Concordia College, but the highlight of the celebration was to be the Runestone Pageant. Directed by local resident Lorayne Larson, the pageant would be a "historical drama of the first visit of white men to Minnesota."[55] Event promoters sought the support of local residents by putting out an appeal to purchase ten-dollar certificates in order to finance the advertising and decorations.[56] Local residents were even asked to open up their homes to accommodate out-of-town guests.

Local historical pageants were popular throughout the United States in the early twentieth century. Besides the economic benefits they yielded for local communities, historical pageants also generated a number of cultural benefits. They fostered community loyalty through the affirmation of a common history. They also served to "express local interpretations of and participation in the drama of national history."[57] Civic boosters often saw history pageants as having the power to transform a local community. In the words of one historian, pageant promoters of the early twentieth century operated with "the belief that history could be made into a dramatic public ritual through which the residents of a town, by acting out the right version of their past, could bring about some kind of future social and political transformation."[58]

Newspaper articles in the weeks leading up to the rune stone celebration conveyed a giddy enthusiasm and locals hoped the event would bring the community widespread acclaim. One article said the celebration promised to be "the most pretentious ever attempted in Alexandria."[59] Another article maintained that the historical pageant "will be generally conceded to be the finest outdoor historical drama ever presented in Minnesota."[60] More than 150 actors were to participate in the event, which promised to be "much more than an ordinary pageant." Larson wrote the script herself and said that she "spent several months reading up on Norse sagas and the history of the Middle Ages in order to get a correct historical background for the scenes in the play and for the proper costuming of the players."[61] Event promoters anticipated large crowds; seating was made to accommodate five thousand people for each of the four nights of the pageant. Several dignitaries were scheduled to address the crowds, including a congressman, the state treasurer, the dean of St. Olaf College, and a U.S. senator. In the days leading up to the festival, banners with Viking shields and flag bunting in the colors of Norway, Sweden, and Denmark adorned the lampposts along city streets. The Chamber of Commerce distributed small replicas of the rune stone that could be displayed in homes and offices.[62] The Alexandria Boat Works constructed a fourteenth-century replica Viking ship on wheels that was used to promote the rune stone celebration; it also played a starring role in the pageant.

The Runestone Pageant was divided into three episodes. The first scene took place in the court of King Magnus and dramatized the moment that Paul Knutson received his orders to lead an expedition to search for his fellow Norsemen who had "lost their Christian ways." The second scene depicted the moment when the traveling Norsemen discovered their companions "red with blood and dead." The final scene took place in the town hall of Rouen, France, where Holand presented the Minnesota artifact to the World Congress of Historians in 1911. In this scene, "The Runestone is brought in to the meeting by a guard of honor and noted English, Swedish, and Norwegian scientists give their opinion that the stone is authentic history." According to pageant promoters, "Every effort has been made to give an exact historical picture to the unfolding of the interesting drama of a band of Vikings penetrating to the center of the continent hundreds of years ago."[63]

Despite the enthusiastic promotional efforts, the Runestone Remembrance was nowhere near as successful as civic boosters had hoped. Newspaper articles in the days and months following the civic celebration reflect a deep disappointment over the attendance at the pageant. One article questioned how it could be "that in our city of Alexandria, with a population of 4,265, only 1,700 persons took advantage of the opportunity to see the show."[64] Another article lamented that rain "ruined" the Friday night show, but other nights were not well attended either. The state treasurer could not speak because of the rain and both the senator and the congressman were inexplicably unable to make it from Washington. Event promoters failed to raise enough money to cover expenses as had been planned.

Citizen participation in Runestone Remembrance Days became a barometer by which community leaders measured the durability of the civic religious identity of the region. As a sacred civic event reminiscent of Durkheim's notion of a clan assembly, Alexandrians experienced several moments of "collective effervescence" and event preparations were highly charged with emotion. Civic boosters saw the success of celebratory events as tied to the long-term success of the community. This is why they interpreted the lack of attendance at the civic event as an indication that Alexandria's citizens did not truly embrace their community. From the opportunity to host out-of-town guests to the chance to purchase loan certificates in small denominations, the civic religious leaders made a strong effort to elicit broad participation among the citizenry. Both pre-festival and post-festival rhetoric suggests that civic leaders expected that virtually everyone would attend the community ritual. Full participation in group ritual might occur in small tribal societies as conceived by Durkheim, but it rarely if ever happens in modern differentiated societies—even in small towns.

Eastward Ho! The Kensington Rune Stone Goes to Washington

During the Second World War, the Kensington Rune Stone received little press coverage. Yet, Hjalmar Holand was hard at work writing and publishing two volumes, *Westward from Vinland* (1940) and *America, 1355–1364: A New Chapter in Pre-Columbian History* (1946).[65] By 1947, Holand's tireless promotional efforts had caught the attention of the nation's premier historical institution, the Smithsonian. In December of that year, museum officials sent a representative to Alexandria to examine the rune stone. A few weeks later, the Alexandria Chamber of Commerce, the organization in possession of the rune stone, received a letter from the Smithsonian stating: "[W]e feel that the Runestone will make an excellent exhibit specimen and is worthy of display among our national collections."[66] The artifact was promptly shipped to the Smithsonian, where it remained on display for a little over a year—February 17, 1948, to February 25, 1949.

The September 1948 article in *National Geographic* gave the Kensington Rune Stone a favorable endorsement, greatly expanding the artifact's nationwide recognition. The head of the Smithsonian department of American ethnology, M. W. Stirling, is quoted as saying that the Kensington Rune Stone was "probably the most important archaeological object yet found in North America."[67] In the fall of that year, the stone had attracted the attention of another prominent scholar, Professor Johannes Bronsted, an archaeologist from Denmark. Bronsted joined

Holand on a tour of several rock formations in the Alexandria area that Holand claimed were mooring stones to anchor Norse ships.[68] After three months of research, the local newspaper triumphantly reported that Professor Bronsted had officially "verified" the rune stone.[69]

The Kensington Rune Stone's yearlong stay at the Smithsonian Institution was a cause for celebration among western Minnesotans. Recognition of the artifact meant recognition of their community: "The stone may have lain in relative obscurity for many years but it certainly is receiving a lot of publicity at this time, putting Alexandria and Kensington in the national and international spotlight."[70] Alexandria newspapers noted the favorable coverage in Minneapolis newspapers, *Newsweek* magazine, the *Saturday Evening Post*, and a national ABC radio broadcast. An Alexandria resident who visited the Smithsonian exhibit spent a few days observing visitors and reported that "well over 60 percent of visitors inspected the Runestone before they looked at any other historical item." He went on to assure Alexandrians that "a very large percentage" of the people he spoke to saw the rune stone as authentic and recognized it as "one of the most important historical items in the museum."[71] The artifact was welcomed home from the Smithsonian as a celebrity. In March 1949, it was put on display at the Minnesota Historical Society, commemorating Minnesota's Territorial Centennial. Later that summer it was featured at the state fair, where more than sixty thousand visitors viewed the exhibit over a ten-day period.[72]

Surely, the Smithsonian exhibit and the endorsements of Bronsted and Stirling must have been a high point for Holand and other rune stone enthusiasts. As historians Rhoda Gilman and James Smith observe, "Holand and his supporters were quick to claim that the question was at last settled."[73] Yet it is important to note that the stone's supporters had incorrectly concluded that the Smithsonian had endorsed the artifact.[74] In a response to an inquiry by a rune stone critic, the Smithsonian acknowledged that none of its staff had the expertise to properly analyze the runic inscriptions. Therefore, "the institution has not issued any formal statement or belief as to the authenticity of the Kensington Stone." As to the conclusions of Sterling, "our staff members as individuals have their own personal opinions."[75] By 1955, even Professor Bronsted had revised his early assessments of the artifact, concluding that the inscription "leaves some question of deliberate fraud."[76] That same year,

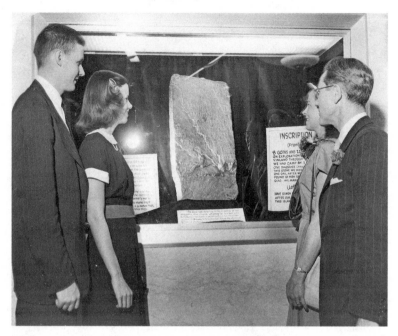

Visitors marvel at the Kensington Rune Stone display at the Alexandria Chamber of Commerce in the 1950s. Courtesy of the Douglas County Historical Society.

the Smithsonian Institution also clarified its position and endorsed the updated conclusion of Professor Bronsted.

The most vigorous attacks levied against Alexandria's adopted civic artifact came from Moorhead resident Johannes A. Holvik. In December 1948, the Alexandria newspaper reported that the city's sacred artifact had suffered "a derogatory blast from a professor of Norwegian at Concordia College in Moorhead." This article outlined Holvik's recently publicized arguments against the authenticity of the rune stone. Holvik announced that he possessed a letter signed by a farmer who claimed in 1908 to have drilled holes in the boulders near Lake Cormorant that Holand claimed were Norse mooring stones. Holvik repeated the Masonic observation from the early twentieth century that the letters "AVM" on the runic inscription referred not to a Catholic prayer to the Virgin Mary but to "AUM" or "the supreme God" in Eastern religions. Holvik later discovered AUM written prominently in an article in a scrapbook owned by the Ohman family.

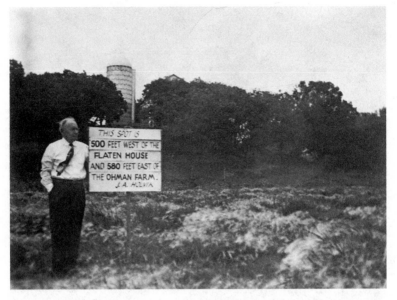

Johan A. Holvik stands near the supposed site of the rune stone discovery, circa 1950. Courtesy of the Minnesota Historical Society.

To acquire the scrapbook and other research materials from the Ohman family, Holvik visited the Ohman farm in the fall of 1949 to speak with Amanda, Ohman's daughter. Amanda showed Holvik a copy of a book by Carl Rosander, *The Well-Informed Schoolmaster (Den Kunskapsrike Skolmästaren)*. The volume was not noticed by earlier researchers but was inscribed by Ohman in 1891, seven years before the rune stone was unearthed. According to Holvik, this Swedish text yielded sufficient information for Olof to create the runic inscription and the book also contained the phrase "save us from evil." This new piece of evidence formed the linchpin of Holvik's argument and he concluded that Olof's ability to carry out the rune stone hoax was "evidence of genius."[77] Ohman's daughter found no consolation in her deceased father being portrayed as a brilliant deceiver. Although a direct connection cannot be proven, Amanda took her own life just over a year later, the second of the Ohman children to do so.[78]

Not surprisingly, Holvik's assertions gave no solace to Alexandria's citizens either. Holvik maintained that the Kensington Rune Stone was nothing more than a tool to generate tourist publicity.[79] One local article characterized his words in terms of a military assault, stating that he had "let loose his second barrage of criticism directed at the Kensington Runestone's authenticity."[80] Local hostility took the form of personal attacks directed toward Holvik. One article took aim at his credentials by claiming that he was a member of a "small" department of Norse at Concordia and that he had only taken a "few short courses" from the University of Oslo "during summer recess." The article also stated: "Just why he persists in lambasting the stone's authenticity is not known as many of the items he disputes are clearly outlined with substantiating evidence in books written by H. R. Holand."[81]

Despite these protests, the Alexandria boosters were relatively unfazed by the mounting criticism of the rune stone. They took full advantage of the publicity surge to use the stone as a totemic emblem for promoting the local economy. In 1950, the Alexandria Electric Company changed its name to the Runestone Electric Association. In following years, local businesses also began to use the words *runestone* or *Viking* in their names. One of the first was the Runestone Turkey Ranch. By the end of the decade, the local business directory included the Viking Beverage Company, Viking Oil Company, and Viking Reinforced Plastics.[82] The Kiwanis Club of Alexandria raised $6,500 to construct a twenty-two-ton replica of the Kensington Rune Stone. The massive stone, quarried in central Minnesota, is twelve times the size of the original. In 1951, it was installed in a small roadside park at the eastern entrance to the city on what was then State Highway 52. Tourists from the urban locales to the east typically approached Alexandria from this direction. The massive icon of Alexandria's founding myth quickly became a popular site for family photos and visitors.

Civic leaders used other forms of visual display to evoke the power of America's true discoverers. During the 1950s, two Viking murals were painted in prominent city buildings, one in the Runestone Electric Association headquarters and another in the lobby of the Farmers National Bank. The latter, eight by eighteen feet, depicted a scene of the fourteenth-century Norsemen at the site where the rune stone inscription was carved. One member of the Viking expedition holds a hammer and chisel to memorialize his fallen comrades on a slab of stone. Others carefully scan the horizon with weapons at hand, perhaps contemplating how to respond to imminent danger. Yet others stand in various postures of defense: some holding swords and some scanning the horizon, as if

Alexandria businessmen designated the region as "Viking-Land, USA" to promote local tourism. Courtesy of the Douglas County Historical Society.

A painted mural depicting the creation of the rune stone hangs in the Runestone Museum of Alexandria. Courtesy of Edward "Mike" Wick.

on the lookout for lurking skrælings. The tools they carry look primitive, but their lean and muscular bodies wield them with purpose and precision. The Viking men are depicted as strong, muscular, virile, and capable of overcoming seemingly insurmountable odds. In an era when more and more men were leaving behind farmwork and other forms of manual labor for desk jobs and managerial positions in town, this visual display of primeval masculinity likely helped assuage anxieties about modern men going soft.[83] As civic religious iconography, these murals depict the Vikings as godlike figures with the symbolic power to overcome economic challenges and defend against threats to civic pride.[84]

Olof Ohman as the "Real American"

Although Olof Ohman died in 1935, he continued to live on as a symbol of rural Minnesota virtue. Arguments for the authenticity of the Kensington Rune Stone have been the most strident when defending the character of the stone's discoverer. In nearly all of his volumes arguing for the artifact, Holand dedicated considerable space to defending Ohman from those who accused him of carving the inscription as a practical joke.[85] Holand gave two primary reasons why Ohman was not responsible for creating a hoax. First, Ohman was not intellectually capable of fabricating the inscription, and second, his exemplary moral character and work ethic did not incline him to perpetrate a fraud. Holand asserted that Ohman "had only nine months of schooling in his life, and though he could sign his name, he had to ask for help when it was necessary to write a letter."[86] What little education he had, claimed Holand, was almost exclusively religious in content and had the purpose of preparing students for confirmation in the Lutheran church. History and geography were barely considered and "runic writing was not even mentioned."[87] Holand also emphasized Ohman's industriousness as a farmer. Ohman was so busy transforming his hardscrabble piece of land into a productive farm, Holand argued, that he would never have had time for practical jokes. Finally, Holand claimed that anyone who had met Ohman testified to his honesty and candor, and even quoted one investigator who said that he would make "an excellent witness in a court of law."[88]

Holand did more than attempt to exonerate Ohman from accusations of malfeasance. Ohman emerged as an important literary figure in Holand's defense of the rune stone. Referring to Ohman as "the scapegoat of the Kensington inscription," Holand holds him up as a superhuman figure, describing him as "a large and powerful man" who stood as a "representative of the stalwart pioneers who laid the foundation for America's prosperity."[89] With Holand's help, Ohman came to embody the quintessential Minnesota farmer: hardworking, honest, and pragmatic. Challenges to Ohman's testimony were often received by western Minnesotans as an attack on their civic identity. In 1955, *Minneapolis Star* reporter George Rice wrote a series of articles to "explore the controversy concerning the Kensington rune stone."[90] Rice became interested in the rune stone after he read Holand's 1940 book *Westward from Vinland* and was at first persuaded that the artifact was authentic. However, after his study of Holvik's writings, Rice abandoned his faith in the rune stone. In his articles, Rice provided a survey of Holvik's arguments against Holand's theories. In general, Rice took a respectful tone toward rune stone enthusiasts, but he argued that many of them lacked basic investigative skills: "some are learned and some are simply enthusiastic about Minnesota history."[91] Rice focused on Holand's oft-repeated claim that Ohman was incapable of faking the stone: "[t]his is, in fact, a very cornerstone of the temple of faith that has been built up around the stone."[92] Although many rune stone supporters claimed that Ohman was illiterate, he was, in fact, an avid reader, according to the testimony of his two sons. He had a small library with some books of "a high literary caliber."[93] Rice also noted that Ohman's family had presented Holvik with books on Swedish history and runic language that would have been helpful in producing the inscription.[94]

About a month after Rice's articles appeared, the *Minneapolis Star* published additional articles written by supporters of the Kensington Rune Stone. Ralph Thornton, an Alexandria attorney and local historian, accused Rice of resurrecting the "once-dead" hypothesis that Ohman was responsible for the hoax. In doing so, Rice had "cast aspersions" on Ohman, who Thornton described as a "hardworking, kindly, well thought of, and painfully honest Swedish immigrant." Regarding Rice's and Holvik's claim that Ohman endeavored to come up with something to "puzzle the brains of the learned," Thornton argued that this is not sufficient evidence to prove a hoax. More likely, he said, it was "simply the guileless and understandable remark of a man who, like many others in his day, found himself frustrated by the lack of formal education which so often cramped expression of his native intelligence."[95]

Thornton defended Ohman's integrity by maintaining that it was unreasonable to think that Ohman could have kept such a powerful secret for more than thirty-seven years. Furthermore, it was illogical to assume that Ohman would have been knowledgeable enough to produce a hoax as complicated as the Kensington Rune Stone: "Was Olof Ohman a stump grubbing, stone picking Swedish immigrant who worked count-less hours each day eking out a living from reluctant soil a 19th century dual personality? Was he, unbeknownst to his family and neighbors, also a Latin scholar and philologist years ahead of his time?"[96]

Residents of western Minnesota braced themselves in advance of the articles in the *Minneapolis Star*, which were "not expected to be favor-able."[97] A *Park Region Echo* article criticized Rice for assuming that he could make a definitive statement about the authenticity of the stone inscription:

> Just how a reporter could make an intensive study of the stone without delving into considerable ancient history he does not state. Professor Holand has spent years studying the stone and still has merely scratched the surface in uncovering all the evi-dence, much of which is buried in Scandinavian records.[98]

The author goes on to say that Rice has done nothing more than write "a fascinating story" and assures his fellow Alexandria residents "that nothing new will be uncovered that has not already been thoroughly checked by historians." A few days after the appearance of the Rice articles, the local Kiwanis Club chapter hosted a meeting with Edward J. Tanquist and Thornton as speakers. Tanquist was quoted as criticizing the Minneapolis paper, stating that it was "spending a lot of money to question the intelligence of Minnesota citizens."[99]

In his articles in the *Minneapolis Star*, Thornton took a respectful tone in addressing his interlocutors. He stated that Rice had argued "ably" and "colorfully" but that he "failed to deliver a knockout punch." Thornton was even willing to extend deference to Holvik by giving "due credit" to his sincerity. Thornton's tone shifted when he spoke before his fellow Alexandria residents and exhibited little patience for former believers in the Kensington Stone. In this venue, he argued that "the

Minneapolis Star story was not impressive to intelligent people as it showed many mistakes." According to Thornton, Rice had wrongly accused everybody associated with the discovery of the stone as being "liars and perjurers."[100] He expressed the frustration of many Alexandria area residents regarding the growing attacks on the city's civic totem: "Those who reside in Minnesota at times become discouraged with unfavorable publicity given the Runestone and Hjalmar Holand's devoted study."[101]

When local residents claimed that Olof Ohman had been slandered, they were asserting that residents of western Minnesota had been as well. It is certainly true that various academics and reporters in the urban-based news media had accused rune stone enthusiasts of being anti-intellectual and opportunistic hucksters. However, it would not be accurate to characterize them as victims. Kensington Rune Stone enthusiasts used external critiques of the rune stone and their community to their material and symbolic advantage. Despite Thornton's claim that "nobody has made a cent of profit from the Runestone," it is clear that it was a keystone to the local tourist economy. His statement is particularly odd considering that he was a representative of the Chamber of Commerce speaking to a group of businessmen. Similar to Sauk Centre's civic leaders in the 1920s, Alexandria's "reputational entrepreneurs" deployed the motif of victimhood to portray rural and small-town Minnesotans as industrious, honest, and morally superior.[102] By the 1950s, the by-then-deceased Olof Ohman had emerged as a martyr for rural virtue and united white, western Minnesotans around a story that defined their region as significant in American history and culture. However, the source of that rural virtue was not often articulated in the early twentieth century. It seemed so obvious that it need not be mentioned. By the 1950s, Minnesotans had come to embrace the Christian motivations of the Knutson expedition as outlined by Holand. As will be explained in chapter 5, the needs of the Cold War era required more explicit assertions of religiosity. However, it is first necessary to describe how Catholics took the lead in embracing the symbolic power of a story of medieval adventurers to Minnesota.

CHAPTER FOUR

Our Lady of the Runestone and America's Baptism with Catholic Blood

No doubt you have heard about Our Lady of Lourdes. And
Our Lady of Fatima, too. Perhaps you've even heard about Our
Lady of Guadalupe. But I'm sure you haven't heard about Our
Lady of the Runestone . . . I'd like to think of her under another
title, Our Lady of North America.

—Father Vincent A. Yzermans, "Special Title of Bl.
Mother Is Our Lady of the Runestone" (1954)

In the aftermath of the national publicity generated by the visit of the
Kensington Rune Stone to the Smithsonian Institution in 1948, Minnesota's Catholics leaders voiced their opinion about the controversial
stone. Editors of the St. Cloud diocesan newspaper argued that the artifact should be permanently displayed at the Smithsonian Institution in
Washington "rather than remain a local tourist curiosity in Alexandria."
Because of "the Catholic historical implications" of the Kensington
Rune Stone, it would best "advance the cause of history and the Catholic Church in a much more practical way in Washington rather than
in Alexandria."[1] By the mid-twentieth century, the famous artifact had
become more than a symbol of ethnic, racial, and civic identity. Local
Catholic leaders used the rune stone to claim Minnesota as a uniquely
Catholic place and to demonstrate that Catholics were true Americans.

As noted in the introduction, Holand gradually revised his narrative to explicitly emphasize the Christian motivations of the Norse
explorers. As academic critiques mounted and ethnic support wavered
in the 1920s, this new emphasis extended the popular appeal of the
rune stone to those who would not otherwise be interested. Anchoring

Holand's claim is an obscure royal document from 1354 that describes an expedition commissioned by King Magnus of Sweden. According to the document, Magnus received word in 1348 that the Norse Christian settlement in western Greenland had been abandoned. The king was troubled by this news, but was unable to respond at the time because he was preoccupied with a campaign to seek converts in Russia. In 1354, the king received additional information that the Greenlanders had given up the Christian faith and had become "idolaters." According to Holand, Magnus was "greatly disturbed" and decided to take action. He appointed Paul Knutson, "a good Catholic," to lead an expedition to search for the lost Greenlanders, who, Holand theorized, had sought refuge on the North American continent. King Magnus addressed Knutson and his men before they departed:

> We ask that you accept this, our command with a right good
> will for the cause, inasmuch as we do it for the honor of God
> and for the sake of our predecessors who in Greenland estab-
> lished Christianity and have maintained it to this time, and
> we will not let it perish in our day.[2]

Holand summarizes what he saw as the true reason for this expedition: it was an endeavor motivated "not by greed of gold, but born of brotherly love and hope of saving human souls."[3]

Although there is no evidence that this expedition was ever carried out, King Magnus and Knutson's men were Catholic. The Protestant Reformation, ignited by Martin Luther and others, did not reach Scandinavia until the mid-sixteenth century. The Catholicism of pre-Columbian Nordic explorers in North America was either deemphasized or ignored by most Americans, particularly Swedish- and Norwegian-American Lutherans. Rasmus B. Anderson makes no reference to the Catholic identity of Leif Eriksson in *America Not Discovered by Columbus* and cites the death of Leif's brother Thorwald as the "first Christian" to die in America.[4] Such omissions were not merely accidental. There is a long tradition of anti-Catholic rhetoric among Norwegian- and Swedish-American writers who touted Leif Eriksson as the true discoverer of America. In his 1892 book *Nordmannen i Amerika*, the Swedish-American journalist Johan Enander said that Leif Eriksson's contributions to American history had not been recognized owing to

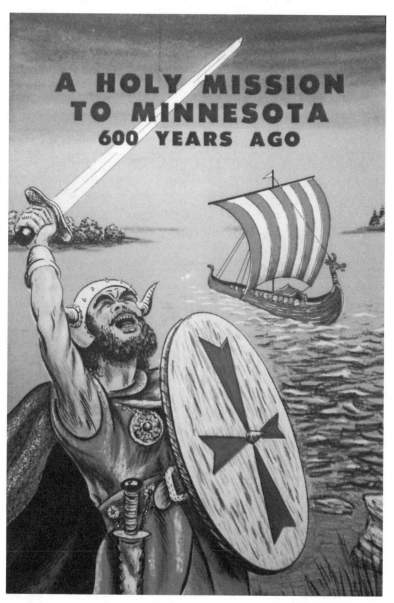

Hjalmar Holand produced this booklet in 1959 for the Runestone Museum of Alexandria. Copies were distributed to museum visitors and other tourists visiting the area.

the influence of Italian Americans and the pope. According to Enander, they had created a cultural environment in the United States where it is "considered High Treason" to question the historical orthodoxy that Christopher Columbus had discovered America.[5] As one historian observes, writers such as Anderson and Enander "had tapped into a powerful vein of anti-Catholicism" that aimed to fortify the Protestant origins of the United States.[6]

The Catholic identity of Viking explorers was not ignored by Catholic historians such as John Gilmary Shea, who starts his 1855 volume on Catholic missionaries in the United States with the chapter "Norwegian Missions in New England." Shea claimed that the Catholic church was the first European institution in what was to become the United States, and this argument would be further bolstered by Holand's rune stone.[7] In contrast to the Lutherans Anderson and Enander, Holand often noted the Catholic faith of his Norsemen, and Minnesota's Catholics took notice. Although Minnesota's Catholics were largely of German and Irish ethnicity, it did not stop Catholic bishops, priests, and laity from becoming some of Holand's strongest allies in promoting the authenticity of the Scandinavian stone.

Claiming the Rune Stone as a Catholic American Artifact

The first and most prominent Catholic to endorse the Kensington Rune Stone was the St. Paul Archdiocese bishop, John Ireland. Ireland attended a Minnesota Historical Society meeting in December 1909 where Holand and other rune stone supporters gave presentations in favor of its authenticity. The archbishop was quoted in the next day's *St. Paul Dispatch* stating that he believed the Kensington Rune Stone to be an authentic medieval artifact because its inscription contained a phrase that was "characteristically Catholic."[8] Ireland was referring to the inscription "AVM save [us] from evil." He interpreted these letters to indicate the phrase "Ave Virgo Maria," which is the first part of the "Hail Mary" prayer and the last part of the "Our Father" prayer.[9]

It is significant that Archbishop Ireland took the time to attend the Minnesota Historical Society meeting given his other commitments at the time. A week after the meeting, Ireland wrote an apologetic letter to diocese churches for not fulfilling his promise to administer confirmation in their parishes owing to the many and "burthensome" issues

St. Paul Archdiocese Bishop John Ireland, 1908. Photograph by Golling
Studio. Courtesy of the Minnesota Historical Society.

that had occupied him in recent months.[10] It is not explicitly clear why
Ireland made it a priority to learn more about Holand's rune stone, but
there are reasonable possibilities considering the history of Catholics in
Minnesota and Ireland's vision for American Catholicism.

Although Minnesota has a reputation for being predominately
Scandinavian and Protestant, Catholics have had a long and significant
presence in the state. In 1660, French Catholics were the first Europeans to explore the region that became Minnesota. Many of Minnesota's
most prominent place-names are associated with early Catholic missionaries such as Jacques Marquette, Lucien Galtier, and Louis Hennepin,
who named the famous Minneapolis waterfall after his patron saint,
St. Anthony. French-speaking missionaries and traders were drawn to
the area in search of Indian converts and animal skins. Jesuit priests
had some success converting Ojibwe, Dakota, and Métis (persons of
mixed Indian and French ancestry) to the faith. Catholicism was virtually the only expression of Christianity in the region until Protestant
missionaries and settlers began to arrive in the mid-nineteenth century.[11]

In addition to the many Norwegian, Swedish, and old-stock American Protestants who settled the vast tracts of land the U.S. government
acquired from the Dakota in 1851, Catholic pioneers also had a strong
presence in early Minnesota. Irish-born Catholics numbered more than
20 percent of the state's foreign-born population in 1860.[12] German-
speaking immigrants made up the largest number of Catholics in Minnesota. Although Germany is known as a birthplace of the Protestant
Reformation, immigrants from Catholic regions such as Bavaria and the
Rhineland settled in large numbers in central and southern Minnesota.
By 1905, Stearns County, just to the south and east of where the rune
stone was unearthed, could boast that 67 percent of its foreign-born
immigrants came from Germany, and around 86 percent of the county
residents who claimed a religious affiliation identified as Catholic.[13] Germans were the largest foreign-born group in Minnesota between 1860
and 1905, when Swedes took over that distinction.[14] By the beginning of
the twentieth century, Irish immigration had slowed significantly. The
masses of Italian Catholics arriving in the United States at the turn of
the century did not venture to Minnesota in large numbers. In 1909,
Archbishop Ireland was likely concerned that Scandinavian Protestant
churches would outpace the growth of the local Catholic church.

Archbishop Ireland had long expressed interest in converting Scandinavians in Minnesota despite their widespread rejection of the Catholic church.[15] Given the similarity between Lutheran and Catholic views on dogma and sacraments, Ireland considered Scandinavians to be "fruit ripe for the Catholic picking."[16] In a letter to Baltimore's Cardinal James Gibbons in 1889, Ireland requested help in recruiting Scandinavian priests for his diocese. He told Cardinal Gibbons that the St. Paul diocese had made "serious efforts" to recruit Scandinavian priests, but it could point to only one Norwegian convert, George A. Arctander. Ordained to the priesthood in 1896, Arctander served St. Paul-area parishes up until his sudden death in September 1909. Following the loss of his lone Scandinavian priest, it is possible that Ireland attended the December meeting because he hoped the Kensington Stone could ground a new strategy to persuade Lutherans and other Protestants to return to the pre-Reformation church.

Archbishop Ireland was keenly aware of the long history of anti-Catholicism in the United States and he aimed to prove to the nation's Protestant majority that Catholics were patriotic Americans.[17] The mid- to late-nineteenth-century influx of Catholic immigrants into eastern cities ignited fears among many Americans that the dominant Anglo-Saxon Protestant culture was at risk. Protestants feared that Catholics were a threat to American democracy and they often accused Catholics of having primary allegiance to the pope rather than to the U.S. government. During the 1840s, Protestant nativists rioted, burning Catholic churches and killing residents of Irish neighborhoods in urban centers such as Philadelphia. Anti-Catholicism framed the platform of the Know-Nothing political party of the 1850s and was evident in the rhetoric of the 1884 presidential campaign, where one Protestant minister warned voters of the threat of "rum, Romanism, and rebellion."[18] Anti-Catholic sentiment was institutionalized in organizations such as the American Protective Association, which sought to place limits on non-Protestant immigration. Based in Clinton, Iowa, this organization had particular appeal among Scandinavian immigrants in the Midwest and reached the peak of popularity during the 1890s.[19]

Although it would not be fair to say that Catholics were actively persecuted in Minnesota, they were in the cultural and political minority. It appears that Catholics had limited political success, at least at the state level, until later in the twentieth century. Just a few months before Ireland attended the rune stone meeting, a Swedish-born Lutheran,

Adolph Olson Eberhart, had been elected as governor. The first Catholic governor, Rudy Perpich, would not be elected until the 1980s.[20] This suggests that Catholics were still somewhat at the margins of statewide political power in the early twentieth century.[21] Under Ireland's leadership, however, Minnesota's Catholics were gaining in social status. In 1909, Ireland oversaw the construction of two cathedrals in St. Paul and Minneapolis and he could boast there were two Catholic seminaries and two Catholic colleges in his diocese. He also oversaw the Catholic Truth Society, which sought to educate the public about the basic teachings of Catholicism through the distribution of literature, to deliver "prompt and systemic correction of misstatements or slanders against the Church," and to publish "reliable news about Catholic events." Catholic leaders counted the organization successful in "breaking down anti-Catholic prejudices."[22] Despite these accomplishments, there was one area of Catholic ideological work that needed attention: establishing a Catholic presence in the discourse of American history and, especially, Minnesota history.

As Robert Orsi observes, there was a "rise of U.S. Catholic historical consciousness at the turn of the twentieth century."[23] Ireland's endorsement of the Minnesota rune stone can be seen as an effort to bolster the social status of his fellow Catholics by integrating them into the American collective memory. The runic inscription demonstrates the presence of Catholic missionaries five hundred years before Minnesota became a state. When Ireland spoke of Scandinavian Americans, he remarked that they were "always largely represented in the legislature and in various state and municipal offices."[24] By declaring the Kensington Rune Stone to be Catholic in origin, he was able to tap into its power as a symbol of ethnic pride for Protestant Scandinavian Americans. If Swedes and Norwegians could prove their loyalty by claiming a foundational role in the origins of the United States, so too could Catholics.[25] Ireland had already demonstrated his commitment to Catholic American history when he founded the Catholic Historical Society of St. Paul in 1905. At the time, he recruited Father Francis J. Schaefer to be the editor of its new Catholic history publication *Acta et Dicta.* Following Ireland's visit to the Minnesota Historical Society, he assigned Father Schaefer to be one of the five members the Society's museum committee that studied the rune stone in detail. The following year, Schaefer published an article in *Acta et Dicta* declaring to his Catholic audience that the Minnesota stone was a "Catholic artifact."[26]

It is tempting to assume that Catholic claims to the country's origin story had already been firmly established by Christopher Columbus. When the Catholic fraternal order known as the Knights of Columbus was founded in 1882, the Italian explorer, said to be the first European to discover America, was upheld as the "first Catholic in America" and "ancestor of all American Catholics."[27] However, this point was lost among Protestant Americans and even many Catholics until well into the twentieth century. Prior to that, Columbus was widely viewed as a generic, nonethnic symbol of American national identity.[28] Celebrations of the four hundredth anniversary of Columbus's arrival in the New World in 1892 and the World's Columbian Exposition of 1893 were largely devoid of any acknowledgment of Columbus's Italian ethnicity or Catholic religiosity. The Exposition was primarily a tribute "to American national grandeur and [was] fully in the hands of the wealthy elite, inspired . . . by a national rather than 'foreign' sentiment."[29]

Catholic leaders of the early twentieth century were well aware of this historical bias. In a 1916 article in the *Catholic Historical Review*, the editors delivered a strong critique of two then-current textbooks in U.S. history that largely ignored the role of Catholics in American life, stating that one book "deliberately throws the mantle of England around the whole of the Colonization Period" and leads the reader to assume that Catholic explorers such as Columbus, Magellan, and de Soto were simply "workers in the establishment of the English Colonies."[30] The article called on Catholic authors to work toward a new history of the Catholic church in the United States and suggested that the Kensington Rune Stone could play an important role in the narrative. The article noted the Minnesota Historical Society's recently published favorable opinion on the authenticity of the controversial stone and expressed optimism that it would eventually be endorsed by other experts and officially recognized as the earliest written source for the Catholic history of the United States.[31] Although Catholic historians continued to push for broader recognition of Columbus's Catholicity, the endorsement of the Kensington Rune Stone provided another means to establish a foundational presence in U.S. history.

The need to do so only intensified in the coming decades. Writing in the 1930s, one Catholic historian lamented that "an unbroken record of a century and a half of Catholic patriotism" had not cast out the "ghost of political bigotry."[32] Following the First World War, a nativist movement spurred a revival of the Ku Klux Klan, which targeted, among others, immigrant Catholics. Although Midwestern Klan activity was most prevalent in states such as Indiana, an estimated thirty thousand Klan members were in the state of Minnesota by the mid-1920s. An inscription on a piece of the Minnesota Klan's memorabilia illustrates its specifically anti-Catholic doctrine: "I would rather be a Klansman in a robe of snowy white than a Catholic priest in robe black as night. For a Klansmen is an American, and America is his home. But the priest owes his allegiance to a dago pope in Rome."[33] Fears of papal allegiance sparked anti-Catholic rallies throughout the state, including one near the Alexandria area. On the rumor that Pope Pius XI had called Catholics in western Minnesota to stockpile arms for an insurrection, Klan members mobilized 1,500 citizens for a rally during the summer of 1924 near the town of Pelican Rapids. According to local accounts, no Catholics were lynched but an estimated 200 area residents were initiated into Klan membership.[34]

A culture of anti-Catholicism permeated American rhetoric well into the twentieth century. For much of the century, the dominant literature about the role of religion in U.S. history largely ignored the presence and contributions of Catholics. Scholars of religion relied on a narrative of "American religious history" that originated with New England Puritans in the seventeenth century and culminated with liberal Protestantism in the twentieth.[35] During the 1950s, a popular liberal Protestant magazine, *The Christian Century*, provoked fears of a Catholic-led antidemocratic revolution in the United States by publishing a series of articles titled "Can Catholicism Win America?"[36] Also during that time period, the self-proclaimed "anti-Catholic bigot" Paul Blanshard received accolades from prominent American figures such as Albert Einstein and John Dewey for his book warning of the threat of Catholic power.[37]

Viking Blood and the Cult of Catholic American Martyrs

Sacrifice is one of the most pervasive themes in Catholic American historiography during the late nineteenth and twentieth centuries. Catholic historians have frequently written (often in graphic detail) accounts of

American Catholics who heroically gave their lives. As historian Robert Orsi observes, "'America' in the Catholic imagination was initially constituted as a network of places connected by the blood of the saints."[38] One of the more popular martyrdom accounts is that of Fathers Brébeuf and Lalemont, who were dismembered and killed by Indians near a mission in Quebec. In addition to sacrifices made in their encounters with North America's first residents, Catholic historians reminded other Americans of the great sacrifices Catholic citizens had made for the nation during important American events such as the Revolutionary War, the Civil War, and even the world wars. However, as Orsi observes, Catholic martyrdom stories often served a dual purpose. On the one hand, Catholic historians endeavored to shape the American civic narratives by showing how Catholics fit into the national story. These narratives, says Orsi, are fundamentally assimilative and American in their aspirations. On the other hand, martyrdom accounts were also instrumental in shaping what Orsi calls the "American Catholic sacred memory," which is "deeply imbued with Catholic religious sensibility, grounded in the tropes and images of devotional culture, of liturgy, and of Catholic theology, which put it most at odds with the dominant story of the modern American nation." The goal of these memories is "to transform the United States into a Catholic reality."[39]

The two goals of civic and sacred memory production are evident in the writings of Minnesota Catholic leaders who used the Kensington Stone to craft a narrative of sacrifice. In 1952, Catholic historian Father James Michael Reardon published *The Catholic Church in The Diocese of St. Paul: From Earliest Origin to Centennial Achievement.* In his opening chapter, "The First White Men in Minnesota," Reardon began his historical narrative about the "earliest origin" of the Catholic presence in Minnesota:

> Nearly six centuries ago a group of Swedes and Norwegians made a journey west from Vinland and camped beside a lake on what is now Minnesota soil. The written record of that amazing voyage, unique in the annals of travel, tells the story of the heroic and tragic wanderings of this group of Catholic explorers from the distant fjords of Scandinavia who, in their hour of peril, invoked the aid of the Mother of God in the first prayer of which we have any extant account in the Western world.[40]

"This Catholic prayer," said Reardon, served as "the prototype of many others uttered by voyageur and missionary in subsequent years as they ventured into the unexplored region of the upper Mississippi."[41] Reardon asserted that it was Catholic missionaries who were the first to bring "Christ" to the "savage wilderness" in what was one day to become Minnesota. His narrative demonstrated to other white Minnesotans that Catholics too had suffered at the hands of the "savages." It is a Catholic insertion into the larger American narrative of white pioneer sacrifice.[42]

However, Reardon also made a claim that runs counter to the prevailing American civic religious sensibilities of the 1950s. He used the rune stone narrative to claim Minnesota, a state where Protestants were in the majority, as a uniquely Catholic space: "In their hour of danger these Catholic adventurers sought help from heaven by appealing to the Blessed Virgin Mary to save them from evil in an invocation characteristic of Norsemen prior to the Reformation . . . In these far-off days Sweden and Norway were as Catholic as all other Christian nations and cultivated filial devotion to the Mother of God.[43] This claim, he reminded his readers, came at a cost. The runic inscription told a "tragic story" of a "lost colony of Vikings whose visit conferred baptism on the state by a shedding of Catholic blood."[44] However, in contrast to Protestant Americans who viewed pioneer sacrifices as instrumental in establishing a new "Promised Land" on the American frontier, Catholics likely viewed these sacrifices as an end in themselves. In Orsi's view, American Catholic sacred memory was preoccupied with the themes of persecution and pain. Therefore, Catholics saw the purpose of missionary journeys to the New World as being "to suffer and die in cruel northern forests and scorched southern deserts at the hands of 'savages' whom they loved even as they were tortured and mutilated by them."[45] More than thirteen thousand copies of Reardon's texts were printed and distributed to parishes throughout the St. Paul Archdiocese and served to localize the narrative of Catholic American sacrifice.[46]

In 1957, St. Cloud Diocese Bishop Peter W. Bartholome traveled to Alexandria, Minnesota, to dedicate a new Catholic elementary school. In his address, Bartholome evoked the memory of the Catholic Norsemen who "appealed to Our Lady when they were in difficulty and in trial."[47] The bishop went on to affirm the vital role of the Catholic church in educating young people, maintaining that public schools in the United States were deficient because they no longer trained youth in "the think-

ing of Christ." As a result, the country was tragically losing its identity
as a "Christian nation" and was at risk of becoming "a pagan nation."
Bartholome expressed concern that young people were turning away
from the faith in alarming numbers. He said that it was only the Catholic
church and a few others that "realize fully the consequences [of this] to
democracy and freedom." He called on Christians to make "unusual
sacrifices in establishing Christian Catholic schools where true Ameri-
canism, true democracy, and true freedom are taught and trained in the
youth of the land." In other words, Catholic education would be successful by producing students who were willing to sacrifice for the welfare
of the nation. The bishop went on to assert that attending a parochial
Catholic school did not mark a student as less patriotic. To the contrary,
participation in a Catholic school "will make you more of an American."
Bartholome asserted that such schools must utilize diverse methods of
teaching children because "as soon as America becomes standardized,
as soon as education is under the control of a few men as it is in Russia
and countries behind the Iron Curtain, as soon as any activities that
Americans pursue become standardized, we cease to be Americans and
religion will suffer and the rights of man will be trampled upon."[48]

Bartholome's words are typical of American Catholic leadership
during the height of the Cold War. At the time, the standoff between
the United States and the Soviet Union was framed as a religious battle. In the words of one historian, "American leaders understood the
menace of Soviet troops, but they recognized as well that the Cold
War would be won or lost not only at the barrel of a gun but also
within the conflicted souls at home and around the world."[49] Catholics
like Bartholome imagined themselves to be sacrificial defenders of the
nation's religious heritage and they viewed Catholic schools as the means
to cultivate a Christian citizenry. Since the 1930s, Catholics had been
some of the most vehement American critics of Communism, but after
the Second World War, they intensified their critiques as Americans
came to broadly recognize it as "the foremost threat to American
peace and prosperity."[50] During the 1950s, Bishop Fulton J. Sheen was
Catholic America's most articulate spokesperson on the threat that
secularization and Communism posed to American society. Sheen's
anti-Communist rhetoric was a central feature on his weekly prime-
time television show viewed by millions of Americans, including many
Protestants and Jews.[51] Spokespersons like Sheen and Bartholome were

instrumental in integrating Catholics into the prevailing American civic religious discourse of the day.[52]

Devotion to Our Lady of the Runestone

Although Bartholome's speech served assimilationist goals, it must also be noted that he situated his rhetoric in distinctively Catholic sensibilities. The purpose of Bartholome's visit to Alexandria's first Catholic school was to dedicate a shrine to commemorate "Our Lady of the Runestone."[53] The shrine, positioned above the main stairway, consisted of a statue of the Blessed Mother standing next to a replica of the Kensington Rune Stone. A quotation was painted on the wall below it: "Ave Virgo Maria Save us from evil A.D. 1362–1957."[54] In his dedication speech, Bartholome admonished his listeners to pray to Our Lady of the Runestone in times of difficulty and trial.[55]

Local priest and diocesan historian Vincent A. Yzermans first coined the phrase "Our Lady of the Runestone" in a diocesan newspaper in 1954. That same year, a Franciscan nun, Sister Mary Christine, was inspired to sketch a drawing she called "The Saga of the Runestone." In her sketch, the Blessed Mother stands above the forested landscape of North America. A Viking ship, an Indian dwelling, and the celestial Northern Lights are also visible. The rune stone is planted in the ground like a gravestone. The text on the sketch says "Our Lady of the Runestone: Ave Virgo Maria Save Us From Evil." Near the bottom of North America, in what looks to be near Mexico City, is a small star. The star was intended to represent "Our Lady's appearance at Guadalupe."[56] Sister Mary Christine's drawing received widespread attention when it accompanied an article about the Kensington Rune Stone in a St. Cloud Diocese paper a few years later.

Known for his promotion of Marian devotion, Bishop Bartholome saw an opportunity in Sister Mary Christine's artwork. In 1950, Pope Pius XII promulgated the doctrine of the Assumption of Mary; he later declared 1954 to be "a special Marian Year to be observed throughout the church universal."[57] In response, Bishop Bartholome named two parishes after the Assumption of the Blessed Virgin Mary and hosted a special Mary's Day event in a local baseball stadium, which was attended by thirty thousand people. He also brought the Family Rosary Crusade to St. Cloud and Alexandria, where thousands of Catholics signed commit-

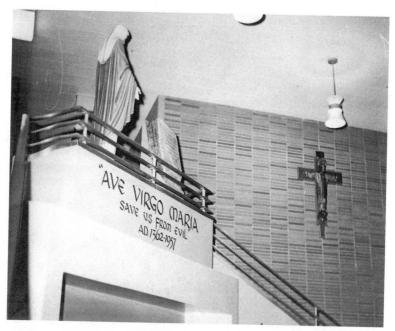

The shrine dedicated to Our Lady of the Runestone at St. Mary's Catholic School in Alexandria, 1957. Courtesy of the Kensington Area Heritage Society.

ment cards to recite the rosary.[58] For Bartholome, promoting devotion to Our Lady of the Runestone would be part of a strategy to foster a localized devotion to Mary. Although Mary had not made an appearance in Minnesota, her presence could be felt in the hearts of lay Catholics through the prayer of the Norsemen.

Although the promotion of Our Lady of the Runestone can be a seen as a Catholic homemaking strategy, it is clear that attempts to Americanize the faith also challenged dominant American religious sensibilities. The use of the Scandinavian stone to promote Marian devotion was not welcomed by Lutherans and led some to disparage the religious practices of the fourteenth-century Norse explorers. J. Edor Larson, historian of the Red River Valley Conference of the Augustana Lutheran Church, criticized the Norse Catholics for chanting "Ave Maria" in their moment of distress. The historian contrasts them with the pioneers who settled western Minnesota in the nineteenth century who were "the spiritual product of the Reformation" and brought with

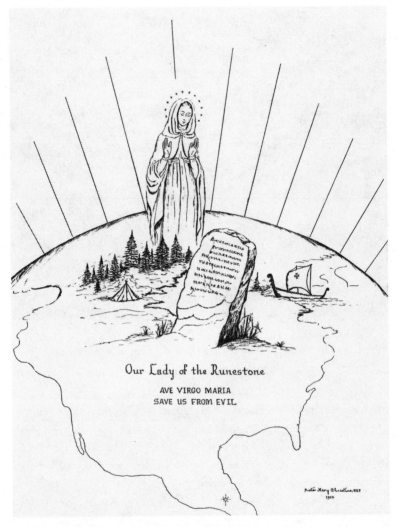

Our Lady of the Runestone

AVE VIRGO MARIA
SAVE US FROM EVIL

"The Saga of the Runestone," by Sister Mary Christine. Courtesy of the Kensington Area Heritage Society.

them Bibles, copies of Luther's Catechism, "sound" books of sermons, and devotional literature. In sum, said Larson, these more recent pioneers "were much more concerned about their spiritual life."[59] The implication is that Catholic religious practices, including devotion to Mary, were inferior to Protestant religion, which emphasized dogma, belief, and ascetic spirituality.

Other Lutherans attempted to wrest control of the Kensington Rune Stone from Catholics by reinterpreting its inscription. To American Catholics such as Ireland and Bartholome, it was self-evident that the letters AVM in the runic inscription reveal a prayer to the Blessed Mother. As already noted, this assertion did not go unchallenged. The Lutheran college professor Johannes Holvik argued that the Latin letters referred not to Ave Virgo Maria but to the Hindu word AUM, which was used in "to call upon the Supreme power."[60] Holvik claimed that after a visit with the Ohman family in 1938, he procured a family scrapbook containing articles about "exotic religions." One such article about the death of the Buddha concluded with the letters, AUM.[61] Holvik said that Ohman, whom he argued was the forger of the inscription, was trying to say, "Supreme power, save us from evil."[62]

It is not known if Holvik was motivated by anti-Catholicism or if he was simply trying to discredit the despised artifact by any means necessary. Nonetheless, Catholic writers lashed out at anyone who questioned the Catholicity of the stone artifact. Father Henry Retzek wrote a scathing review of Erik Wahlgren's *The Kensington Stone: A Mystery Solved*, which had endorsed Holvik's theory. Retzek described rune stone opponents as an "inimical clan of critics" who will not let the stone rest as a tombstone for the Norse Catholic visitors. Retzek said that it should be obvious that Catholics were on this journey and even a child could confirm that the letters AVM refer to Mary, the Mother of God. Retzek evoked the trope of Catholic persecution when he claimed that those who attack Holand's scholarship are guilty of libel.[63]

Viking Altar Rock: Consecrating the Catholic American Landscape

The genesis of Our Lady of Guadalupe began when an apparition of the Mother of God appeared before an Indian peasant named Juan Diego near Mexico City in 1531. Our Lady of the Runestone could claim no such appearance in Minnesota. Nonetheless, Catholic enthusiasts found ways to incorporate her presence into the rural landscape. Although much of Stearns County, Minnesota, had a high concentration of German Catholics in the mid-twentieth century, the town of Sauk Centre had a reputation as a "bastion of Yankeeism" owing to Catholics arriving rather late in the city's development.[64] This Protestant image was reinforced in Sinclair Lewis's popular novel *Main Street*. With the discovery of an unusual rock formation, local Catholic leaders initiated a campaign to promote Catholicism as the region's original religion. In 1943, Holand received a letter from a local priest who claimed he had discovered a Viking mooring stone. Rev. Henry Retzek told Holand that he had been contacted by a parishioner, Frank Gettys, who told the priest about a large rock formation with peculiar-looking holes. As a child, Gettys claimed that he and his brothers used to play at this location and the mysterious holes had "excited our curiosity."[65]

The following spring, Holand visited the site accompanied by Retzek, another priest from the nearby town of Sauk Centre, and Holand's son Harold. Holand found what he described as a large semicircular boulder, twenty-seven feet long by seventeen feet wide with two vertical holes on the top of the boulder and two horizontal holes on the side. Surveying the nearby terrain, he concluded that this boulder had not been used as a mooring stone for Nordic ships because it was too far above water level. Instead, Holand said the stone resembled "the choir of a small church or a miniature amphitheater." In his later writings, Holand argued that this site conformed to Catholic church criteria for constructing temporary chapels to conduct the Eucharist while traveling.[66] The two horizontal holes, he theorized, were used as receptacles for wooden dowels to hold a small portable altar table that would have been earlier consecrated by a bishop. The two vertical holes were used to erect a canopy over the altar in order to shield the candles from the wind. In short, Holand declared the rock to be the site of a Catholic worship service conducted by the same Norse travelers who had carved the inscription on the Kensington Rune Stone.

Holand was not only willing to identify *what* happened at this location; he was also willing to claim exactly *when* it happened: August 15, 1362. If, as he reasoned, the Norse travelers left their larger boats behind at Hudson Bay on June 1, it would be "plausible" that they could have reached this area by the middle of August. The fifteenth of this month, said Holand, was an important day for Catholics: the Feast of the Assumption of the Blessed Virgin:

> [I]t is reasonable to assume that they found a real pleasure in
> giving expression to their gratitude by creating, in this invit-
> ing spot, a semblance of the house of God in their homeland.

And, as their priest stood before the altar arrayed in his full vestments, they must have sung their Te Deum Laudamus with more than customary fervor.[67]

In Holand's account, his son Harold was the first to suggest this idea. Regardless of whose idea it was, it is certain that the priests would have been eager to embrace Holand's imaginative projections. If Holand was correct, this site would be of enormous historical value to local Catholic leaders who sought to spread their religious influence in an area that was still a Protestant holdout. A local newspaper article later affirmed the religious significance of the site, describing it as "the first prepared place of Christian Worship in the New World," and it was widely referred to as the "Viking Altar Rock."[68]

A few years after Bishop Bartholome delivered his address at the dedication of the Our Lady of the Runestone shrine, two Catholic lay-persons from Douglas County approached Bartholome about establishing a new parish near the village of Kensington to serve a small group of Catholics of Czech, German, and Irish descent. Bartholome supported this new parish as a "mission church" because he hoped to attract Catholics to a part of Douglas County heavily populated by Swedish and Norwegian Lutherans.[69] Like Ireland in the early twentieth century, Bartholome saw an opportunity to use the Scandinavian symbol to convert Protestants to the Catholic religion of their Viking forebears. The choice of the name Our Lady of the Runestone originated with the bishop, and it is documented that he expressed interest in purchasing the site where the rune stone was unearthed on Ohman's farm for the construction of the church.[70] However, at the time, this land was not available, and the new church was constructed on a ten-acre parcel of land adjacent to the village of Kensington. The construction of the new church in Kensington was completed in 1964.

The founding of Our Lady of the Runestone parish inspired other Catholic enthusiasts to incorporate Catholic myth into the local landscape. In the summer of 1970 a Chokio, Minnesota, woman unearthed a mysterious-looking stone while tilling her garden. The stone was approximately five inches wide, seven inches long, and a little over an inch thick with markings on the surface. Suspecting it might be an important historical artifact, she contacted local historian and Viking enthusiast Marion Dahm, who recognized its markings to be runic letters.

Dahm consulted a local priest, Father Nicholas Zimmer, and they both quickly concluded that this was an artifact of Catholic significance. Specifically, they believed that the stone was the same kind that a medieval Norse priest would use as a portable table for the Eucharist. They further postulated that this particular stone was used for the Catholic Mass at the Viking Altar Rock and it became known, henceforth, as the "Chokio Altar Stone."[71] Zimmer promoted the stone's discovery in the local media, touting it as "the oldest artifact to substantiate the presence of the Catholic religion on the North American continent."[72] Seeking further validation of his new find, Dahm consulted Professor Ole Landsverk, a retired physicist who traveled to Minnesota from California in the spring of 1971. Landsverk, who had recently authored a book titled *Ancient Norse Messages on American Stones*, concluded that the stone was authentic and that the runic letters were part of a cryptic religious message.[73]

Local Catholic leaders did not seem concerned that Landsverk's credentials were in atomic radiation research and not in runic linguistics or Norse history. As has often been the case with the history of the Kensington Rune Stone, a person with expertise in one field is often perceived by the public to be an expert in any field. With the help of Landsverk's dubious yet influential endorsement of the "altar stone," Catholic enthusiasts accelerated their efforts during the 1970s to portray the Viking Altar Rock as an authentically Catholic site. In 1973, Lloyd Herfindahl, an internationally known artist from southern Minnesota, produced a series of paintings called "Vikings in Minnesota." After reading about the discovery of the Chokio Altar Stone, Herfindahl teamed up with Dahm to produce a visual interpretation of the Viking Altar Rock site. The painting, *Altar in the Wilderness*, is an imagined depiction of the first Catholic Mass in North America. In the painting, the priest stands facing the small altar stone table attached to the side of the curved boulder. Two poles erect a canopy over the wilderness altar and several "Vikings" kneel before it. In producing it, Herfindahl used Dahm as a model for the priest and fragments from the Chokio Altar Stone and the Viking Altar Rock were both mixed into the paint.[74]

In 1975, the local Catholic civic group Knights of Columbus purchased the site to "memorialize the dauntlessness of those long ago Vikings."[75] The Rev. Paul Schmelzer, a parish priest in Sauk Centre, promoted the Viking Altar Rock as a Catholic American site and managed to convince the state legislature to designate a number of area highways as part of a "Viking Trail" with the Viking Altar Rock at its eastern terminus.[76] On Sunday, August 10, 1975, for the Feast of the Assumption of the Blessed Virgin, Rev. Schmelzer conducted a "rededication" ceremony at the site of the Viking Altar Rock and St. Cloud Diocese Bishop George Speltz presided.[77] Smelzer promoted the ceremony as an ecumenical event and invited members of all denominations to attend.[78]

As noted earlier, claims to sacred spaces are often substantiated by acts of symbolic violence. Just as white residents of western Minnesota used the Kensington Rune Stone to claim that they were the rightful heirs to the land, Catholic leaders asserted that Viking blood had been spilled to claim America for the Catholic church. With the help of Viking enthusiasts such as Holand and Dahm, the bishops and priests interpreted rock formations and found artifacts as evidence of this claim. The Catholic leaders used ceremonies as ideological tools to inculcate a disposition in western Minnesotans to recognize (or misrecognize) the Catholic church as the foundational religion in their community. Although the ecumenical invitation to the 1975 service could be seen as a noble attempt to build unity among Christian denominations in Sauk Centre, one cannot ignore the power dynamics at play. The service was a Catholic Mass consecrating a physical space that symbolically represented a Catholic presence near Sauk Centre, preceding the Yankee Protestant settlement of the town by hundreds of years. This was not the first time that Minnesota Catholics had used the rune stone in this strategy. Father Schaefer's 1910 article emphasized that those who carved the Kensington Rune Stone were representatives of a unified Christian church: "It was only after the rise of the Protestant Reformation, that they were led away from the unity of the Catholic Church."[79] The narrative of Catholic missionaries traversing the Minnesota landscape provided a unique form of religious power. Through the promotion of the Knutson expedition, Catholic leaders could argue that representatives of a unified church had touched American soil before the church had splintered into numerous denominations. The "ecumenical" service at Viking Altar Rock was an attempt to strengthen Catholic cultural influence and expand the church's market share of the area's religious adherents.

Viking Origin Myths and Catholic Modernity

By the 1960s and 1970s, Catholic leaders no longer needed the Kensington
Rune Stone to prove to other Minnesotans that Catholics were truly
American. By this period, says Orsi, "Catholics in the United States
seemed to have become indistinguishable from their fellow Americans."[80]
Catholics had made significant gains in political power as evidenced by the
election of John F. Kennedy to the presidency in 1960. In 1968, Congress
dedicated the second Monday of October to commemorate the accomplishments of the Catholic explorer Christopher Columbus. After 1960,
Minnesota Catholics primarily used the rune stone as a means to convert Swedish- and Norwegian-American Lutherans rather than bolster
their credentials as America's founders. However, the Catholic appeal of
the Kensington Rune Stone was always limited. Despite the best efforts
of Bartholome and other Catholics leaders, Our Lady of the Runestone
was never embraced as broadly as other Marian figures among American
Catholics.[81] Neither the Viking Altar Rock nor Ohman's farm site ever
became significant sites of Catholic pilgrimage such as the shrine dedicated to Our Lady of Czestochowa in Pennsylvania or the Holy Hill
National Shrine of Mary, Help of Christians in Wisconsin. Yzermans's
hope for Our Lady of the Runestone to be recognized as Our Lady
of North America never materialized and the number of her devotees
remained small, concentrated in a handful of rural communities.

The limited effectiveness of Holand's rune stone to generate Catholic
religious power can be attributed to at least two factors. First, the
Kensington Rune Stone did not embody a potent nexus of religious
identity and ethnic identity. The utility of a Scandinavian artifact with
a Catholic prayer was limited because so few Norwegian and Swedish
Americans were Catholic.[82] If Ohman had unearthed a stone with a
medieval Catholic prayer written in German, Our Lady of the Runestone
might have achieved worldwide fame among Catholics. The power of
this ethnic overlay is evident in another, more widely known, Catholic
origin myth. Despite the even flimsier evidence that the Catholic priest
St. Brendan had traveled from Ireland to North America in the sixth
century, many Irish Catholics embraced the notion as an assertion of
ethnic pride.[83]

Second, the debate over the Kensington Rune Stone's historical
authenticity affected its value for Catholics. No evidence has been found
indicating that Archbishop Ireland publicly discussed the artifact fol-

lowing the 1909 meeting at the Minnesota Historical Society. One can speculate that Ireland recognized the risks of Catholics extracting social capital from the controversial stone. In a similar way that Holvik and Blegen denounced the Kensington Rune Stone to bolster the social status of Norwegian Americans in the eyes of the academic establishment, Ireland may have sought to protect the social status of Catholics, should the rune stone one day be proven a hoax. He may have been aware that even some highly respected Scandinavian Americans already viewed the rune stone as a hoax.[84] In subsequent decades, prominent national Catholic scholars would also express doubt in the Kensington Rune Stone's authenticity. In a 1925 article, Catholic historian Carl H. Meinberg gives a lengthy account of the medieval Catholic church's American presence in Greenland, but implies that Francis Schaefer's earlier article about the artifact was the work of an "enthusiast." The authenticity of the runic inscription, Meinberg says, was, "to say the least, doubtful." Even John LaFarge's rosy endorsement in 1932 is a qualified one. For LaFarge, the religious value of the Kensington Rune Stone lay not in its authenticity as a historical artifact; its value was in its ability to inspire.[85]

In sum, Catholic leaders used the Kensington Rune Stone narrative in ways that were similar to and different from other devotees of the rune stone. Like other white residents of western Minnesota, Catholics used the stone to situate themselves in the nation's civic memory and demonstrate that their group embodied quintessential American values. At the same time, however, the Viking origin myth also served their own internal purposes that were at odds with dominant American values. The bloody sacrifice of the Catholic Norsemen "baptized" or claimed the nation for the Catholic church and it also provided a model for proper Catholic devotional practices. As of 2014, the *Catholic Encyclopedia* still referred to the Kensington Rune Stone as "the earliest Catholic record of what became afterwards the Diocese of St. Paul."[86]

Toward an Ecumenical Rune Stone Enthusiasm

During the first half of the twentieth century, the Catholic narrative about the Kensington Rune Stone developed in isolation from other Christian groups. Protestants sometimes resented the Catholic claim to the rune stone and they did not readily draw attention to the missionary

impulse of the Norsemen in Holand's narrative.[87] Swedish and Norwegian Lutherans, in particular, were concerned that highlighting the fervent prayer of the Norsemen would amount to endorsing a religion based
on rituals and Mariolatry, rather than on faith and the worship of Jesus
Christ.[88] As a result, non-Catholic Minnesotans in the early twentieth
century used the Kensington Rune Stone primarily to construct ethnic
and civic religious identities rather than denominational ones. Although
the rune stone sometimes caused tensions between Protestants and
Catholics in the first half of the twentieth century, there were moments
where representatives of both sides of the religious divide found common interest in the artifact. In 1910, the membership of the Minnesota
Historical Society committee commissioned to study the stone included
a Swedenborgian minister and a Catholic priest. In addition, the committee's report depended on the research of a Lutheran minister, who
seemed untroubled to declare the runic inscription to be genuine because
of its authentically Catholic prayer.[89] In 1951, Alexandria's Chamber
of Commerce, primarily led by Protestants, enlisted the local Catholic
priest Father William A. Renner to deliver the dedication address for
the installation of a twenty-two-ton rune stone replica along the city's
major traffic artery. In sum, Protestant rune stone enthusiasts (often
motivated by ethnic and civic agendas) collaborated with local Catholic
priests and laity (motivated by a denominational agenda) in producing
spaces that were meaningful for Catholics, Scandinavians, and other
white Americans. In particular, Catholic Americans and Scandinavian-
American Protestants found common ground in their critique of the
Anglo-biased historical narratives of the United States. The Kensington
Rune Stone inspired both constituencies to challenge the cultural hegemony of the academy. In other words, a Catholic Scandinavian artifact
dating from the fourteenth century provided western Minnesotans with
the symbolic power to disrupt the dominant historical-spatial narrative
that the United States began with English Protestants in Massachusetts.

Starting in the 1950s, Protestants and Catholics in western Minnesota increasingly found common ground in using the Kensington
Stone to confront other threats to American religion and identity.[90] During the "fifties revival" of religion in the United States, Catholics and
Protestants began to embrace a common "Christian" identity to help
distinguish American culture from "atheistic Communism." Bishop

Bartholome's jeremiad that the United States was becoming a pagan nation was one that was increasingly shared by a variety of Christian leaders. As we shall see in the next chapter, the rock extracted from Ohman's field would continue to serve as a touchstone for constructing a local civil religious identity.

CHAPTER FIVE

Immortal Rock

Cold War Religion, Centennials, and the Return of the Skrælings

{ We vow Christianity shall not perish there in our day! We shall proclaim . . . a crusade to the West! }

—King Magnus in Margaret Leuthner's *Mystery of the Runestone*

The 1950s was a decade marked by a religious resurgence in the United States. Between 1951 and 1961, membership in religious congregations grew by 31 percent, outpacing population growth, which was only 19 percent during the same period. During the 1930s, a mere 29 percent of Americans believed that religion had an increasingly strong influence on their communities. That number catapulted to 70 percent in 1957.[1] Also in 1957, 96 percent of Americans identified with a religious tradition, even if they did not belong to a congregation.[2] During this time period, American culture was saturated with religious symbols and rhetoric. Americans could watch *The Ten Commandments* at the movie theater and turn on their televisions to see the Catholic bishop Fulton J. Sheen and the Evangelical preacher Billy Graham deliver exhortations to repent from sin and take up the cross of Christ.

This religious revival has been attributed to a variety of factors, including postwar prosperity, the baby boom, and new mass-media forms that created religious celebrities and propagated their messages. Historians of American religion have also noted U.S. policy makers' keen interest in fueling this revival as a way to confront the threat of "atheistic Communism." On Flag Day in 1954, President Dwight D. Eisenhower signed a law that added the words "under God" to the nation's Pledge of Allegiance. In his speech that day, Eisenhower emphasized that "reaffirming the transcendence of religious faith in America's heritage and future" served to "strengthen those spiritual weapons which forever will be our country's most powerful resource, in peace and war." Historian T. Jeremy Gunn observes that following his speech, Eisenhower toured a nuclear bomb shelter used to defend against a possible attack from the Soviet Union.[3] According to Gunn, American political leaders during the 1950s endeavored to distinguish the United States from the Soviet Union by articulating what he calls an "American National Religion."[4] In addition to exalting American military supremacy and the virtues of capitalist free enterprise, this national religion emphasized God as "a first line of defense" against the Soviet Union. In addition to adding the words "under God" to the Pledge of Allegiance, policy makers stamped the phrase "In God We Trust" on the nation's currency in 1955 and adopted it as the national motto in 1956. Also during this period, stone monuments were placed in civic sites throughout the country to honor the Ten Commandments.[5] These public endorsements of religion led many Americans to view national piety as a bulwark against the nation's enemies.

The area around Alexandria, Minnesota, was also swept up in the religious fervor of the early Cold War period. 1958 was a particularly robust year for public expressions of the Christian faith in the region. For local residents, the year was doubly significant as it was both the centennial for the founding of the city of Alexandria and the statehood of Minnesota. Throughout the summer tourist season, the local newspaper printed full-page advertisements sponsored by the Alexandria Ministerial Association. One ad depicts a scene of Christ hanging on the cross and the caption exhorts the viewer to "got to church Sunday and kneel once more before the Cross of Calvary."[6] That same summer, a camp near Alexandria sponsored by the Assemblies of God Church set an all-time attendance record of four thousand.[7] A Family Rosary Crusade sponsored by the Catholic diocese brought an estimated fifteen thousand to the Douglas County fairgrounds. One newspaper article reported that "all roads leading into Alexandria were jammed" prior to the event and additional seating had to be added to accommodate a crowd that far exceeded the seating capacity of the grandstand.[8]

The Kensington Rune Stone, and the religious expedition it symbolized, figured prominently into the local centennial celebrations.[9] The Chamber of Commerce succeeded in raising adequate funds to build a

The building shared by the Alexandria Chamber of Commerce and the Runestone Museum, circa 1962. The Viking ship replica was likely the one used for the Runestone Pageant. Courtesy of the Douglas County Historical Society.

"fitting and permanent home" for the city's sacred civic artifact. The city kicked off its tourist season in June 1958 with a ceremony to dedicate the new Runestone Museum. A detachment of National Guard troops greeted Minnesota Governor Orville L. Freeman at the city airport and escorted him in a military-style parade to the museum, where he delivered a dedication speech before a crowd of war veterans, businessmen, clergy, and other local citizens. Although the governor's speech primarily emphasized the economic benefits of the museum to the local tourist industry, this civic ceremony once again visually juxtaposed military symbolism with the rune stone artifact. At a Kensington Rune Stone monument rally in 1927, National Guard members from the First World War's "Lost Battalion" stood guard over the stone, equating their battle behind enemy lines with the Norsemen who gave their lives in skræling country. In the context of the Cold War religious fervor in 1958, it is likely that locals, once again, saw the artifact as a suitable symbol of bravery in face of the nation's powerful enemies.

A portrait of Hjalmar Holand seated next to a depiction of the Norsemen inscribing the Kensington Rune Stone is on display in the Runestone Museum of Alexandria. Photograph by the author.

In a speech before the local Rotary Club, one rune stone enthusiast expressed pleasure that the artifact had been "resurrected from the dungeon that it had occupied so long."[10] The relic had spent much of the past two decades stored in the old bank vault in the basement of the Chamber of Commerce building, while a replica was displayed in the lobby. Although the actual artifact had been sequestered from public sight in its underground bunker, its religious significance had been promoted for some time. In 1955, the civic organization acquired from Norway a copy of the King Magnus document that Hjalmar Holand claimed was the genesis of the Norse expedition to North America. A local newspaper article reiterated Holand's claim that the purpose of the royal expedition was to restore the missing Greenland colonists back to the faith to prevent Christianity from perishing.[11] Chamber officials displayed this document prominently in the front window of their building. Often the first stop for tourists visiting Alexandria, the Chamber display clearly left the impression that the city of Alexandria had deep Christian roots.

Other civic venues also touted the religious significance of the rune stone. During the centennial festivities, the local newspaper published a series of special editions dedicated to local history, highlighting testimonials of longtime residents and their remembrances of the early settlement of the region. The edition dedicated to the role that churches played in county history also prominently featured the story of the Kensington Stone. Minneapolis attorney Maugridge Robb wrote a lengthy article about "Douglas County's most famous relic," summarizing Holand's standard arguments for the authenticity of the Kensington Stone.[12] Robb's personal religious affiliation is not certain, but he calls on his readers to remember the true motivation of the fourteenth-century Norse explorers, "who came not in search of gold or commercial preferment, but for the glory of God and the salvation of man." Knutson's expedition was commissioned by King Magnus to return to the Christian faith a "lost colony of backsliders" in western Greenland, who had succumbed to "the hostility of the aboriginal Eskimos." As Knutson's men traveled into the heart of North America to find them, the Norse missionaries were confronted with the Indians' "savage practices":

> Between the Viking lines we can hear the whoops and see the onrush of the savages, their copper torsos gleaming in sweat and paint, the feathers of the eagle streaming from their scalplocks . . . We can shudder with him who wrote what he saw. "Red with blood and dead."

In the face of such opposition, Robb praises the Norse Christians' attributes that he thought were noblest, characterizing King Magnus as a "fanatically militant Catholic" who was "alive with zeal to spread the gospel." Robb admires a faith that could "convert unbelievers at sword's point if necessary." The inscribed prayer "Hail Mary save us from evil" testifies to the "deep spiritual character of these men." The story of the rune stone, he proclaims, is an "imperishable account of a real, personal and horrible tragedy—an immortal voice speaking as eloquently as Homer." Their Christian presence on the Minnesota landscape cannot be missed because "their trail is blazed as definitely as the concrete highways which today parallel their route."[13] In the same centennial edition, the motif of white survivors telling of past Indian massacres is also evident in the article "An Army Scout Tells the Story of Gen. Custer's

Vikings in the streets of Glenwood, Minnesota, circa 1962. Courtesy of the
Douglas County Historical Society.

Last Stand." In yet another article, an early pioneer gives an account of
the "Sioux Outbreak of 1862" and describes life inside the walls of the
stockade, where early Alexandrians found refuge from the "savage foe,"
who lurked just outside.[14]

The specter of savage Indians hostile to the Christian faith was juxtaposed with expressions of Cold War anxiety. In the same newspaper
edition is an announcement about a three-night civic history "spectacle"
held during the centennial celebrations. The ninth and final scene of the
performance was titled "The Atomic Age: Is This the Beginning or the
End?" The strength to confront these apocalyptic threats is trumpeted
in a Father's Day advertisement that calls for local men to strengthen
their character through church attendance and daily Bible reading.
Character development was necessary, the ad claimed, to cultivate good,
democratic citizen leaders who could "handle the affairs of the state
in these perilous times." Like other church ads during the summer of
1958, this one was sponsored by local "patriotic individuals and business establishments."

A rune stone enthusiast writing some years later makes even clearer the association between Christian sacrifices of the past with the national threats of the contemporary age. A Wisconsin nun paralleled the Soviet arsenal with the Indian threat, and appealed to the inscription to ask for God's protection from a nuclear holocaust:

> What is the message on the stone for us of the atomic age? It is a prayer of the brave but frightened men, "AVE MARIA, SAVE US FROM EVIL!" the first words of the Hail Mary, the last words of the Our Father. The evil they feared was whatever terrible people had left their companions "red with blood and dead" (probably scalped.) . . . It is also a pointer for us, who live under an atomic cloud as they lived in terror of the unknown Indians, what we should do and say. AVE MARIA, SAVE US FROM EVIL.[15]

Similar to Robb, Sister Dorcy lauds the "militancy" of the fourteenth-century Norse explorers: "The Norsemen in the Viking age were uncommonly handy with a battle ax, and we tend to class them as barbarians, raiders, plunderers, robbers. But this message on the stone also tells us that once converted to Christianity, they became very militant Christians."[16] Sister Dorcy's declaration that the Christian faith and militarism were interdependent resonates well with Cold War claims that religion served as a "spiritual weapon" to fight the global scourge of Communism.[17]

The Birthplace of a Christian Nation

Robb's claim that the trail of the Christian Norsemen in Minnesota is as obvious as modern concrete highways anchors Alexandria as the birthplace of American Christianity. Other rune stone enthusiasts echoed his assertions and the artifact played a role in the public debate over the inclusion of a cross on the seal commemorating the Minnesota state centennial. In 1958, Rev. J. C. K. Preus, director of Christian education for the Evangelical Lutheran Conference, argued that the state's centennial commission "had ample reason for making the cross a part of the centennial emblem" because "the Christian Church had been securely planted on Minnesota soil many years before the state of Minnesota came into being."[18] Preus was weighing in on a debate that took place a year earlier between a coalition of civic and religious groups and the centennial commission. Samuel Scheiner, executive director of the Jewish Community Relations Council of Minnesota, along with representatives of several churches and the American Civil Liberties Union, asked the commission to remove the cross, stating that its inclusion implied the exclusion of non-Christians from being considered Minnesotans.[19]

Other religious Minnesotans vigorously defended the commission's decision to include the cross. Catholic Archbishop William O. Brady wrote in a local Catholic publication that "Jews should not feel the cross was an affront" and he promised that as archbishop he would "defend Jews in times of persecution." He went on to say that "atheists, agnostics and the ACLU had no business protesting the cross . . . because they were not present when Minnesota was founded. 'If today's pressure removes the cross from the emblem that marks the past, tomorrow's pressure will attempt to tear it from our church and our homes.'"[20] Despite the efforts of the protesters, the centennial commission voted to retain the cross.

It is not known if Archbishop Brady called on the Kensington Rune Stone to bolster his claim that Minnesota was originally Christian, but Reverend Preus certainly did. In his article, Preus describes the Viking explorers as "men of religion" whose "earnest prayer" recorded on the stone was the first uttered by "white men" in the state.[21] Preus recognized the utility of the artifact to proclaim the United States to be a Christian nation and Minnesota to be a Christian state. For those claiming Christianity to be America's original religion, the Kensington Rune Stone wielded significant symbolic power.

In addition to substantiating claims that the United States was a Christian nation, rune stone enthusiasts such as Laura Goodman Salverson considered the controversial artifact to be a symbol of the Christian faith. In her novel *Immortal Rock: The Saga of the Kensington Stone*, published in 1954, Salverson's imaginative rendering of the Paul Knutson expedition paralleled the defense of the rune stone with a defense of the Christian faith.[22] Her assertions resonate with Holand's rhetorical flourishes. Holand referred to the artifact as a stone that was once "rejected" but had later been "resurrected" thanks to his research efforts. Chapters 3 and 4 in *A Pre-Columbian Crusade to America* employ these terms to frame his historical narrative about the first decade after the stone's discovery. The rejection–resurrection motif bears a resemblance to New Testament depictions of Jesus Christ. Luke 20:17 refers to Jesus as "the stone

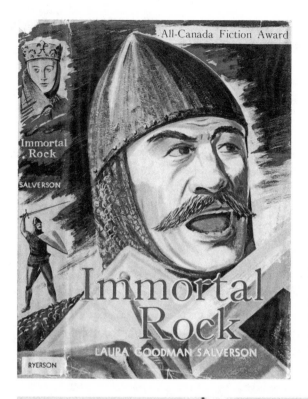

Published in 1954, Laura Goodman Salverson's novel *Immortal Rock* dramatized the Knutson expedition to Minnesota.

LAURA GOODMAN SALVERSON

Immortal Rock
The Saga of The Kensington Stone

BASED ON THE PAUL KNUTSON EXPEDITION TO GREENLAND AND AMERICA IN THE FOURTEENTH CENTURY; COMMISSIONED BY HIS MAJESTY KING MAGNUS ERIKSON OF NORWAY, SWEDEN AND SKAANE; HIS LETTER OF AUTHORITY EXECUTED AT BERGEN, OCTOBER 28TH, 1354, BY ORM OSTENSON, REGENT.

THE RYERSON PRESS ~ TORONTO

which the builders rejected." It cannot be proven that Holand intended this subtle juxtaposition of the Kensington Rune Stone and the Christ figure, but his rhetorical choice would have surely been noted by many Christians, particularly conservative Protestants with a high level of biblical literacy. Holand had spent his younger years among Seventh-day Adventists and he knew intimately the language of Evangelicalism. Although he rejected denominational religion for himself, embracing a form of nature-based spiritualism, he greatly expanded popular support for his artifact by framing it in a narrative of a Christian crusade. However, the cords binding this symbiotic relationship between the Kensington Rune Stone and the Christian faith would begin to fray under the weight of historical and scientific criticisms from the academic establishment.

Runestone Showdown:
Wahlgren's *The Kensington Stone: A Mystery Solved*

Holand and other enthusiasts had been remarkably successful in per-suading the public of the veracity of the Kensington Rune Stone. A 1963 poll conducted by the *Minneapolis Tribune* indicated that 60 percent of Minnesotans believed that Vikings were the first European visitors to Minnesota.[23] Viking mania was so widespread that the state's profes-sional football team became known as the Minnesota Vikings.[24] The publication of Erik Walhgren's book *The Kensington Stone: A Mystery Solved* in 1958 slowly began to chip away at public confidence in the stone, and with it the sacred civic narrative fueling its popularity. Wahlgren, a linguist specializing in Scandinavian and Germanic languages at the University of California, Los Angeles, consolidated the evidence against the stone in his book. He relied heavily on the rune stone criticisms of the researcher Johannes A. Holvik. Holvik had written dozens of newspaper articles and letters on the topic, but had never published an extended academic treatise on the topic. According to Wahlgren, Holvik shared with him his "vast file on the subject" and he commended Holvik for his "generosity" in sharing his research.[25]

Wahlgren's book asserts that it was more than a coincidence that the stone was found in a Scandinavian immigrant community. The decade of the 1890s was especially "propitious . . . to the manufacture of a rune stone among the transplanted Scandinavians" given the pervasive inter-est in pre-Columbian Viking travels in North America (121). Wahlgren criticizes the Minnesota Historical Society investigation for not utilizing formal methods and adequate controls. Because of numerous inconsistencies in the affidavits written and signed by Ohman and his neighbors, Wahlgren is convinced that they had been coached before writing and signing their affidavits (48–58). Wahlgren describes the museum committee's report as a "partisan document" and maintains that its production was driven by "private, promotional interests" (100, 179). Furthermore, the language of the inscription, he says, correlates with the vernacular of the late nineteenth century rather than that of the fourteenth. In conclusion, Wahgren explains the rune stone as follows: "The planting of the Minnesota stone was a clever and understandable hoax with both amusing and tragic consequences, and the Kensington story is an episode in the history of the development of the American frontier" (181).

Rune stone supporters had been confronted with such assertions before via the writings of Holvik, but there are two assertions in Wahlgren's book that particularly provoked the ire of the artifact's defenders. First, he asserts that neither Holand nor any historians had proof that the Paul Knutson expedition to bring apostate Vikings back to the Christian church was ever carried out. Even if a Norse sailing vessel had somehow managed to reach the Hudson Bay, he argues, it would have been almost physically impossible for explorers to travel upstream on the Nelson and Red rivers in the fourteenth century, especially in the fourteen days mentioned in the runic inscription.

Second, Wahlgren takes direct aim at the credibility of Hjalmar Holand: "Holand is not an investigator upon whom one can rely for competent, impartial, and accurate presentation of the rune stone matter" (83). Without Holand's efforts, the stone would have "died a natural death long ago" (81). Wahlgren also criticizes Holand's ignorance of the Norse language and of Latin, which Wahlgren believed was paramount to understanding the medieval sources necessary for the interpretation of the stone's inscription (84). He further attacks Holand's character as "devious," stating that Holand purposefully "distracts and wearies the reader's critical faculties through an accumulation of irrelevant 'examples'" (94). For Wahlgren, Holand's disregard of previous scholarship debunking the stone's authenticity amounted to a rejection of academia, showing a "complete lack of respect for the purposes and function of the scientific inquiry itself" (96). This contempt proves that

Holand was nothing more than a "professional promoter" motivated to seek compensation for his contribution to American history (97).

Supporters of Minnesota's rune stone did not sit idly by and allow their sacred artifact to be maligned and the reputation of their revered prophet to be besmirched in this way. The defense of the rune stone only intensified in response to Wahlgren's book. In 1959, an Alexandria physician and one of the founders of the Runestone Museum was highlighted in a newspaper article titled "Dr. Tanquist's Testimony: Why I Believe in the Runestone." During his speech, Tanquist presented his reasons for why he believed the rune stone to be authentic before a group of local residents and visitors from the Minnesota Historical Society.[26] Also that year, the Runestone Museum Foundation published and distributed a booklet by Holand summarizing the key arguments for the artifact's authenticity. Its title left no doubt as to the motivations of Norse expedition North America: "A Holy Mission to Minnesota 600 Years Ago."

The strident defense of Holand's story of medieval Christian missionaries in Minnesota swelled to a crescendo in 1962, during the civic celebrations of the "600th Anniversary of the Runestone." The Runestone Pageant Play took direct aim at the credibility of academe. "[E]ven though I have a B.A.," said one of the characters, "I [wrongly] thought Columbus discovered America." The driving narrative of the pageant centers on Holand, a marginalized "scholar-historian" outside "the isolated ivory towers" of the academy who mentors a young university student researching Norse exploration history. The script exalts Holand as a populist martyr whose "revelations" challenged the academic orthodoxies of the day.

The Runestone Pageant also attempted to reify the Christian motivations of the Norse explorers in the popular imagination. Widely disseminated during the civic celebration was a comic book titled *Mystery of the Runestone*, which simultaneously defends the authenticity of the Kensington Rune Stone and the veracity of the Christian faith. The comic book targets a youth audience and embeds the saga of the Norsemen into in an adventure narrative with vivid illustrations. Its author, Margaret Barry Leuthner, was an elementary school librarian, an active member of her Catholic parish, and a vehement critic of anyone who questioned the authenticity of the sacred artifact. Years later, the local press described her as a "legend renowned for her unwavering Runestone loyalty . . . While many Alexandrians wearied of the dispute, Leuthner,

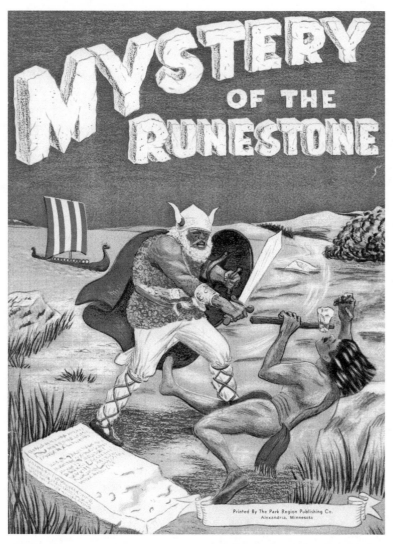

The *Mystery of the Runestone* comic book was written in 1962 by rune stone enthusiast Margaret Leuthner. It was distributed at the Runestone Pageant that same year and at the 1965 World's Fair in New York.

like a mooring stone, kept the faith."²⁷ Like the Runestone Pageant and Robb's centennial article from 1958, Leuthner emphasized the religious militancy of the Norse explorers, describing them as "Christian Crusaders" on a mission to "preserve Christianity."²⁸

Leuthner stays close to Holand's historical narrative but emphasizes and embellishes certain aspects she deems relevant to young people in the early 1960s. Throughout the comic book, she paints a picture of Christianity ever at risk. To keep the faith from perishing, King Magnus sent Knutson and his men on a mission to find the "fallen ones" in Greenland who "gave up all good manner and true virtues" and "turned to the people of America." As the Norse missionaries traveled deeper into the heart of the American wilderness, even they faced the temptation to turn from the Christian faith. One of the explorers asks Knutson whether the Norse fire gods from home also resided in these new lands. He is quickly admonished: "Christian men, don't talk of pagan Gods even in jest, remember our holy mission." They proceed up a narrow and winding river and arrive at a shallow lake littered with dead fish. "The Dead Sea!?" exclaims one of the Norsemen. "God has led us to our deaths!" Whispers of mutiny begin to spread among some: "Let's go back. We find no Greenlanders. They were swallowed by this evil place!" At this point, the priest accompanying the expedition says to Knutson, "Paul, the men are uneasy. We now pray for a sign of God's favor." Knutson responds, "If I am right, God has granted a sign . . . this is the continental divide . . . we have only to find a river running east to Vinland."

The expedition continues eastward and finds a lake good for fishing. Dividing the group into two, Knutson assigns half to stand guard with the boats and half to go fishing. When the fishermen return, they find the "10 men red with blood and dead," killed and scalped by "Sioux" Indians. This is the scene immortalized by the "Runemaster," who carved an inscription to memorialize the "10 Vikings who died for Christ on a crusade in the wilderness." This artifact has survived, said Leuthner, as a monument to the Norsemen's "courage, resourcefulness and an astounding missionary zeal." On the final pages of the comic book, Leuthner praises the vigilant "detective work" of Holand the researcher and exhorts her readers to remember that history is made and truth is discovered by "the man who ventures." The final scene is a pictorial lineup of such heroic American male figures, the first of whom is a Viking, followed by an explorer, a pilgrim, a colonist, a pioneer, a modern man in a business suit, and finally an astronaut.

Leuthner's telling of the rune stone story suggests a high degree of anxiety about the state of the nation and the Christian faith. The inclusion of the astronaut in the comic book must be understood in context of the "space race" between the United States and the Soviet Union at the time. Following the Soviets' launch of the satellite Sputnik in 1957 and the first human into orbit in 1961, many Americans expressed concern that the United States was losing the Cold War. In 1961, President Kennedy escalated the nation's efforts by setting the goal of "landing a man on the moon and returning him safely to earth." In Leuthner's 1962 comic book, both Holand and the Vikings modeled the courage and scientific inquisitiveness needed to compete with the nation's modern foes.[29] These foes, of course, represented an existential threat to Christianity. The Indian in her narrative symbolizes danger of the atheist, or a religious other at least, who could lure vulnerable young people from the one and true faith. Both the savagery of the Indian and the heroic militancy of the Viking explorer are graphically illustrated in a battle scene depicted on the cover of the comic book. In the scene, a muscular Norseman donning a horned helmet, a shield, and a shiny metal sword lunges toward an Indian falling backwards while swinging a primitive stone tomahawk.

Exuberant defenses of the faith and local hostility toward Wahlgren reached a plateau of intensity just as America's religious revival was starting to decline. The percentage of Americans who believed that religion was increasing in influence had declined from a high of 70 percent in 1957 to 45 percent in 1962. By 1965, it plunged even further to 33 percent.[30] The rhetoric of harnessing "spiritual weapons" to confront the Communist threat during the Eisenhower years shifted to an emphasis on American economic and military prowess following John F. Kennedy's election in 1960.[31] Two Supreme Court cases further challenged the civic religious consensus by declaring teacher-led prayer and Bible readings unconstitutional in 1962 and 1963. Hollywood's 1950s love affair with religion also fizzled out during the 1960s. The movie *Elmer Gantry*, released in 1960, painted a dark portrait of Evangelical religion. The film was based on Sinclair Lewis's novel by the same name. Similar to *Main Street*, *Elmer Gantry* did not portray small-town Midwesterners in a positive light. In both the movie and the novel, rural residents appear as dupes, taken in by a wily huckster evangelist offering salvation in exchange for overflowing offering plates.

It is not clear if these shifting national trends had any impact on eroding religious attendance in Minnesota, but Leuthner and other civic leaders seemed concerned that future generations were at risk of abandoning the church and forgetting the Christian origins of their community and nation. The Runestone Pageant Play and the writings of rune stone enthusiasts contain a great deal of religious pedagogy used in an effort to perpetuate the Christian faith. The Norsemen are upheld as moral exemplars of what it means to be a good Christian in the mid-twentieth century. Although they faced the temptation to give up their Christian faith, they remained steadfast in the pursuit of their holy mission. Rune stone supporters portrayed the members of the Knutson expedition as morally superior to other early explorers of the Americas because the former were driven by religion and not by greed. These writings laud the Vikings for the militancy of their faith. The Norsemen were willing to put their lives on the line for spreading the message of Jesus Christ in America. In sum, the story of the Knutson expedition teaches that a good Christian in mid-twentieth-century Alexandria is one who is bold, adventurous, steadfast, militant, self-sacrificial, and motivated by spiritual, not material, concerns.[32]

Although it might seem logical that the Kensington Rune Stone narrative would have inspired advocacy of Christian missionary work, the rune stone enthusiasts clearly emphasized domestic religious concerns. In the various iterations of the story, King Magnus realizes that he had neglected the spiritual welfare of his Norse colonists in Greenland when he was trying to convert the Russians. The implicit moral lesson is that missionary outreach should not distract the church from maintaining the faith of its own. Even in midcentury Alexandria, the "skrælings," in whatever form they take, may still be lurking, posing a threat to the survival of a robust Christian faith. Leuthner, in particular, describes the rune stone discovery site as a place of safety and refuge. In her subsequent writings, she argues that Norsemen had lived in a "Christian colony" in the Alexandria area for some four hundred years, having first settled in the region shortly after Leif Eriksson's expedition to Vinland in the year 1000.[33] What Leuthner has done, whether consciously or not, is mythically reconstruct her small town as a bulwark against the threat of secularization. Through her use of the Kensington

Viking actors on Lake Winona during the 1962 Runestone Pageant. Courtesy of the Douglas County Historical Society.

Rune Stone and her adaptation of Holand's narrative, she inscribed the local landscape with a religious narrative that offered Christians, both Catholic and Protestant, a symbolic tool to resist the perceived decline of religious fervor. Furthermore, she naturalized her community as an originally and exclusively Christian place, pushing to the margins all those in the community who did not conform to her religious vision. Not long after the Runestone Pageant Play in 1962, Alexandrians would find a hospitable national stage on which to tell their exceptional story.

Giant Vikings and Totemic Anxieties at the New York World's Fair

Through the pageant play script, comic book, and other writings of rune stone enthusiasts in the 1950s and early 1960s, locals proclaimed their certainty in the veracity of the artifact and its sacred story. However, as the 1960s wore on, doubts were beginning to take root and western Minnesotans could no longer be certain their region had been visited by

Scandinavian Christian missionaries. Minnesotans were never unanimous in their "belief" in the stone, but now they were becoming more divided than ever. Despite doubts about the rune stone's authenticity, many of the region's business and civic leaders remained undaunted in their endorsement of the artifact. These savvy entrepreneurs came to embrace the controversy surrounding the stone as a means to generate symbolic and, increasingly, economic benefits for their region. Even if the stone were proved a hoax, they could still identify with a more widely embraced American civic religious claim: the belief in economic prosperity and material progress.[34]

In 1965, the Runestone Museum received a request for the sacred artifact to be a part of the Minnesota Pavilion at the New York World's Fair. State exhibits at the World's Fair had the primary purpose of generating publicity for local businesses, which could in turn translate into increased tourism and economic development.[35] The Minnesota exhibit had been part of the fair since it opened in 1964, but owing to mismanagement and a rather uninspiring theme of "Minnesota Brainpower Builds Profits," it had run deeply in debt and attendance was low. The Midwestern artifact was now going to be the new "focal point of interest" by claiming that Minnesota was the "birthplace of America." Organizers hoped that this new attraction would reinvigorate interest and persuade the state government to financially bail the exhibit out.

This change in direction received wide attention in the Minneapolis–St. Paul media, and most of it was negative. A *Minneapolis Star* editorial encouraged Minnesota legislators to "stand firm" in their opposition to approving funding for the exhibit, implying that the inclusion of the dubious artifact would be an embarrassment to the state. On a WCCO television program broadcast statewide, George Rice, the former *Star* journalist who debunked the artifact in a series of articles in 1955, also voiced his opposition to the rune stone being sent to New York. Predictably, rune stone enthusiasts in Alexandria were incensed by these remarks—especially the ones from their old nemesis George Rice. However, the strategy for defending the rune stone shifted from efforts just ten years earlier. An editorial by Alexandria resident John Obert says that he does not criticize Rice for doubting the rune stone story; he chastises him for opposing the inclusion of the artifact at the World's Fair. Obert argues that the authenticity of the rune stone is not what is most important:

We who are pushing the Runestone exhibit at the Fair are
not asking that the controversial artifact be displayed as
indisputably authentic. The slogan for the exhibition will be
"Minnesota—Birthplace of America?" The question mark we
believe is justified. We do not believe the stone has been proved
authentic. But neither do we believe it has been proved a fake. If
the purpose of the various state exhibitions at the World's Fair
is to attract as much attention as possible, we can think of no
other feature which could attract attention to Minnesota.[36]

Throughout most of the artifact's history, Kensington Rune Stone enthusiasts had emphatically argued for its authenticity. However, by 1965,
questions of authenticity were no longer primary, at least not before a
national audience. All that mattered was that the storied stone was getting attention, along with its hometown. Civic leaders had successfully
co-opted the skepticism of academic critics such as Erik Wahlgren to
generate controversy, and hence, interest in their civic totem.

Local residents eagerly supported efforts to send their beloved
rune stone out east. James Stuebner, a representative of the Minnesota
exhibit, worked with Alexandrians to arrange the civic artifact's travel
to the World's Fair. He also solicited their financial help. The Minnesota exhibit was already $225,000 in debt and Stuebner asked the local
officials to try to come up with twenty-five thousand dollars.[37] Chamber
of Commerce officials initiated an intense campaign to raise funds from
private individuals and businesses and sold tickets for a special "Runestone Ball." In several weeks' time, they raised twenty-three thousand
dollars to send their civic totem to New York.[38]

To draw attention to the Minnesota exhibit, a large Viking statue,
later named "Big Ole," was built to stand near its door.[39] The giant
figure stood twenty-eight feet tall and boasted milky white skin, a full,
blond beard, and thick, muscular arms and legs. The Viking was well
armed. A sword hung from his belt. In his right hand, he held a tall
spear, and in his left, a shield with the phrase "Minnesota: Birthplace
of America?" A news article emphasized the strength and resilience of
the Viking giant: "The statue is made of weather-resistant structural
fiberglass . . . weighs four tons and will withstand winds of up to 100
miles an hour."[40] Articles from later years reveal a preoccupation with
the Viking's virility. After an act of vandalism broke off part of his

sword, the local paper celebrated its repair with the headline: "Sword (and Esteem) Now Restored: Big Ole Grins to Welcome Summer."[41] Another article notes that Big Ole "has an estimated shoe size of 50."[42] Plans for the exhibition aroused civic expectations in advance of the artifact's trip to the World's Fair: "What a break this is for Alexandria," declared one article, which wildly predicted that more than 18 million people would be exposed to the rune stone story at the World's Fair.[43] An editorial audaciously claimed: "By the end of next summer, we expect Alexandria and the Kensington Runestone will be household words the length and breadth of the nation."[44]

Alexandria Mayor Marvin E. Hansen declared April 7, 1965, as "Runestone Day," and he hosted a "send-off celebration" for the departure of the rune stone to the World's Fair. The civic event included a high-school band performance and speeches by local politicians and business leaders. Mayor Hansen, who was to accompany the sacred civic symbol to New York, vowed to "sell Alexandria to everyone I talk to from here to New York and back again."[45] For its trip east, the rune stone was mounted in a display case inside the Viking ship used during the 1962 pageant. The ship was loaded on a flatbed truck and traveled the 1,500-mile journey to New York, making several publicity stops along the way. One of the highlights was a visit to Washington, D.C., where the Viking ship was parked in front of the Smithsonian Institution. Over the course of two days, Mayor Hansen reported that more than sixty thousand people had walked by the Runestone.[46] The display made additional stops in Atlantic City and Philadelphia before arriving in New York City on April 19.

Mayor Hansen became a media sensation on his pilgrimage to the World's Fair. He was interviewed by dozens of media outlets along the way and was greeted by high-ranking civic officials. After delivering a speech in Chicago, Hansen claimed that Mayor Richard Daley had asked him to make campaign speeches for him in the next election.[47] Upon arrival in New York, he was interviewed on NBC's *Today* show and was later photographed standing next to Vice President Hubert Humphrey at the Minnesota Pavilion. In the mayor's own assessment, the response to the rune stone display had been "more than terrific." He joked that "if one-tenth of the people who told me they would actually come to Alexandria for a vacation—we will be really crowded!"[48]

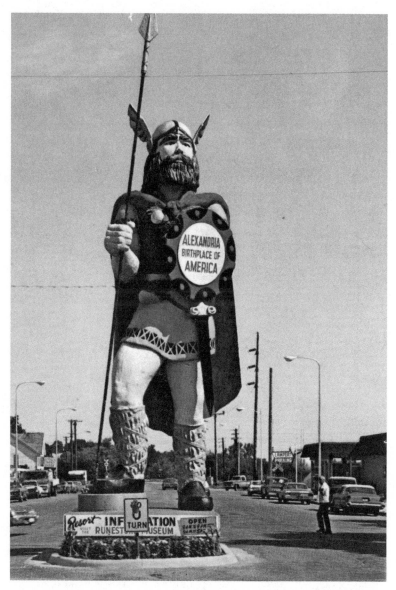

The famous Viking statue "Big Ole" originally stood in the middle of the street near Third and Broadway in downtown Alexandria. It has since been relocated to a small lakeside park across from the Runestone Museum. Courtesy of the Douglas County Historical Society.

Vice President Hubert H. Humphrey after viewing the Kensington Rune Stone in the Minnesota exhibit at the 1965 World's Fair. Courtesy of the Douglas County Historical Society.

In June, the Alexandria newspaper reprinted an article from the *Minneapolis Star* reporting that the presence of the controversial stone had increased attendance at the Minnesota Pavilion from the previous year. The Alexandria editor gleefully highlighted the Minneapolis article's contrition for formerly opposing the rune stone's inclusion in the Minnesota exhibit, but seemed to miss the subtle sarcasm implicit in the Minneapolis article. The article reported that the professional guides hired to tell the story of the rune stone expressed "no doubt that it is the real thing." One guide, whom the article described as "a tall, fresh blonde from St. Petersburg, Florida," said she had never heard of the rune stone until she started her job two weeks earlier. However, now "she spiels about it confidently from the platform where the stone is displayed" four times every hour. She was prepared, in her words, "to fancy the story up" with references to relevant aspects of medieval history if the audience pressed her with questions. The article went on to express skepticism over the interplay between historical pedagogy and civic boosterism in quoting Russell W. Fridley, director of the Minnesota Historical Society. Prior to the rune stone's traveling to the World's Fair,

Russell said that the exhibit would be provocative, but that it should be presented as a controversial object: "Mixing history and commercialization can cause problems . . . if claims are made which exceed evidence supporting them." He warned that the artifact had not been proved and care should be used in interpreting its place in history.[49]

Although the major media outlets based in the Twin Cities insistently declared the rune stone a hoax, non-Minnesota media simply portrayed the artifact as "controversial" but did not take a condemnatory stance.[50] Mayor Hanson's observations corroborate this: "except for Minneapolis, I have only had three who stated that the stone was not authentic. We must convert Minneapolis—Ha!"[51] It is certainly the case that Minnesotans were more familiar with the scientific and historical evidence against the artifact and persons in Chicago and New York were likely enchanted by their first encounter with the storied stone, but urban Minnesota's rejection of the rune stone was likely rooted in sensitivities about Midwestern identity. In a similar way that modern Norwegian Americans and modern Catholics rejected the Kensington Rune Stone in an effort to distance themselves from their filiopietistic and pseudoscientific peers, urban Minnesotans likely emphasized their condemnation of the dubious artifact and kitschy fair exhibit to portray themselves as culturally sophisticated before a New York audience and distinct from their rural and small-town cousins.

While rural, western Minnesotans had grown comfortable with outsiders viewing the rune stone as "controversial" and relished the sensation it caused out east, many expressed anxiety over the safety of their civic totem at the World's Fair. In advance of the trip, the Chamber of Commerce purchased a $1-million insurance policy for the rune stone.[52] However, the worth of the sacred artifact could not be calculated in monetary terms alone. Locals expressed fear that the stone could be subject to vandalism and desecration.[53] Just ten weeks after the stone arrived at the World's Fair, their anxiety intensified greatly. Exhibit officials reported that they would have to shut down the Minnesota Pavilion. Despite the uptick in attendance, funds had been drained to the point that they were not able to ship the rune stone back to Minnesota.[54] The Alexandria Chamber of Commerce was warned that the civic symbol could possibly be subjected to "severe vandalism" if left unattended at the World's Fair. In response, they dispatched Chamber president Harvey Hammergren

Alexandria Chamber of Commerce President Harvey Hammergren rescued the Kensington Rune Stone from possible vandalism at the 1965 World's Fair in New York. Courtesy of the Douglas County Historical Society.

to New York, this time to retrieve the two-hundred-pound stone, which he wrapped carefully in a blanket and carried home in the trunk of his Buick.[55]

Of the nearly 25 million people who attended the fair in 1965, only 187,471 were recorded as having visited the Minnesota Pavilion.[56] This is a fraction of the 18 million predicted a few months earlier, but none-theless Alexandria boosters seemed generally satisfied with the exposure that the rune stone and their town had received. Hammergren acknowl-edged "keen disappointment" that the Minnesota exhibit had closed early, but he attributed the higher number of tourists visiting Alexandria that summer to the appearance of the Kensington Rune Stone at the World's Fair.[57] In December of that year, the giant Viking statue was returned to Alexandria and installed in the middle of the city's most prominent intersection, positioned to greet visitors as they entered the town.[58] Given the popularity of the giant Paul Bunyan statue and his com-panion Babe the Blue Ox in Bemidji, Minnesota, Alexandrians hoped that their giant Viking attraction would draw scores of visitors and boost tour-ist revenue.[59]

The rune stone's visit to the World's Fair was clearly driven by eco-nomic benefit, but it would not be accurate to mark this development strictly as a secular turn for the artifact. As it had in other moments in the history of the region, the collective aspiration for economic prog-ress served as a unifying thread in the sacred civic canopy. The choice to put economic language at the forefront may have been an effort to make rune stone enthusiasm appear to be more rational in the face of an increasingly skeptical audience. Disagreement over the stone's origins need not contradict the fact that it could stimulate a fledgling tourist economy. While the motives of civic boosters were certainly varied, the use of economic language provided cover for those who endeavored to use the exhibition as a platform to promote small-town, Christian values to a national audience.

The 1964–65 World's Fair was a particularly hospitable environ-ment for Minnesota's claim that the nation had been founded by white, Christian missionaries who died at the hands of savage Indians. Under the powerful influence of the fair's president, Robert Moses, the event had an overwhelmingly conservative tone, nostalgic for postwar opti-mism and notions of American innocence. Inspired by Walt Disney's theme park in California, Moses aimed to create a "sanctuary from the cultural storm that was rapidly approaching in the mid-1960s."[60] Early in 1965, Malcolm X had been assassinated, civil-rights activists had been brutally beaten on Selma's Edmund Pettus Bridge, and America's involvement in Vietnam had significantly escalated with a "search-and-destroy" military strategy. As historian Lawrence R. Samuel notes, the fairgrounds were shielded from the emerging "cracks in the nation's foundation" that "were dividing Americans along political, social, and economic lines, a growing sense of cynicism and disillusionment was palatable in the air."[61]

Inside the walls of the World's Fair was a blissful refuge from the raging social turmoil outside. There was no cynicism and disillusionment to be found at the Minnesota exhibit. According to one researcher, it is likely that the only promotional materials at the exhibit were Holand's booklet *A Holy Mission to Minnesota 600 Years Ago* and Leuthner's comic book *Mystery of the Runestone*.[62] These two documents would affirm nostalgic depictions about the virtue of rural Americans and the sacredness of the nation's origins. Christians from Scandinavia on a divine mission to save the church were likely embraced by East Coast fairgoers as suitable substitutes for New England Puritans who traveled to North America to build a "city on a hill." The savage Indians in the rune stone narrative would have been easily recognized by exhibit attendees as symbolic of the various threats to God's chosen and innocent nation—both past and present. The Viking statue towering over the exhibit boldly proclaimed the superiority of the Nordic male body and likely served to invoke in the fairgoers a sense of nostalgia for an imagined past that was whiter than the present. Although the facticity of the rune stone story was open to debate, the narrative contained enduring truths that resonated with a popular version of American history and culture under threat.

The True Believers

In the aftermath of the media spectacle at the World's Fair, academics continued to be dismayed that scientific and historical arguments were not enough to extinguish public interest in the dubious artifact. In 1968, Theodore Blegen, a distinguished history professor at the University of Minnesota and unrivaled expert on the history of the state, wrote an extended treatise titled *The Kensington Rune Stone: New Light on an Old Riddle* to further strengthen the evidence against the stone's authenticity.[63] As noted in chapter I, Blegen was instrumental in founding the Norwegian-American Historical Association in the 1920s and was an early critic of Holand's pseudohistorical writings. In this latest volume, Blegen argued that Ohman and two of his neighbors, Andrew Anderson and Sven Fogelbad, were responsible for creating the hoax. Although

Holand had portrayed Fogelblad as a lazy drunk incapable of perpetrating a hoax, Blegen showed that Fogelblad was an iconoclastic intellectual with knowledge of runic writing and an interest in Swedish history.[64] In contrast to Holand's depictions of Ohman as a simple, uneducated farmer, Blegen observed that he was described much differently by a Minnesota Historical Society researcher, who referred to him as an "intellectual man." Blegen also mentioned the testimony of a local dentist who described Ohman as "one of the keenest and best informed men he had ever met."[65] Less is known about Andrew Anderson, but Blegen writes that Newton Winchell's 1910 report had described him as "a political agitator" and that if a hoax had been perpetrated, it would have been by Ohman, Fogelblad, and Anderson working together.[66]

The true believers were undeterred by Blegen's historical evidence and they turned to new and increasingly bizarre techniques to validate the rune stone. An entire subgenre of belief sought to identify secret messages embedded in the inscription. Ole G. Landsverk, a physicist from the University of Chicago, teamed up with a retired U.S. Army cryptographer, Alf Monge, to research a theory that runic inscriptions are actually cryptograms that "record secret calendrical data pertaining to the perpetual calendar of the Catholic Church."[67] Through his decoding method, Monge claimed he could pinpoint the exact date of the origin of runic inscriptions. He dates the rune stone inscription to April 24, 1362. Landsverk's and Monge's findings were published in a 1969 volume *Ancient Norse Messages on American Stones.*[68] Monge's method has been widely discredited: "his work was based on so many arbitrary assumptions and allowed so many exceptions to the rules that he could read messages into anything."[69] Even other rune stone enthusiasts agree that his cryptography theory was "unsupportable" and one laments that it has "created a credibility problem for advocates of the Stone."[70]

Lay Catholic Margaret Barry Leuthner built on many of Landsverk's arguments about the presence of codes in the runic inscription. She argued that she had a special ability to read codes embedded in the runes, unlike Holand, who she said could only offer a translation.[71] This mystical gift enabled her to recognize that the inscription had multiple, layered meanings that revealed the names of all the members of the Norse expedition and even the author of the inscription, whom she referred to as "Ivar." Leuthner asserts that Ivar has incorporated several maps into the inscription.[72] One map is supposed to be of the site of discovery in which one of the letters points in the direction of "mooring stones" that were found nearby. Regarding the so-called grammatical mistakes on the inscription, Leuthner says:

> [The Vikings] were not ignorant; their broken grammar was deliberate to clue us to codes and ciphers and acrostics that reveal the whole story of their stay. They were clever; they chose runes that were crosses so that the memorial they carved became a shrine for the lost colony they came to restore to the Christian faith.[73]

Perhaps the most bizarre claim she makes is that the name of the Minnesota state mascot, "GOPHER," is hidden in an anagram of English letters found on the inscription.[74] Despite her sometimes outlandish yet imaginative claims, she maintains that "the one thing she can't stand is . . . an illogical argument."[75]

Retaking Runestone Hill

By the 1970s, many local residents had grown weary of the increasingly desperate attempts to defend the authenticity of the stone. Wahlgren and other rune stone critics had largely succeeded in dismantling the notion of Christian crusader Vikings. The effect was to remove a core reason many Minnesotans used to suspend disbelief. Locals continued to embrace the significance of the artifact in bringing visitors to the area in addition to the area's recreational attractions, but the rune stone never became a primary draw. Some residents seemed increasingly embarrassed by the discredited artifact, and especially by the garishly painted fiberglass Viking standing in the center of town. Over time, Big Ole the Viking migrated further and further from the city's premier intersection at Third and Broadway. Its final resting place is a quiet lakeside park, where he is easily missed if a visitor is not looking for him.

Although most efforts to defend the rune stone had become unmoored from anything resembling scientific credibility, the die-hard enthusiasts struggled to keep the dream of pre-Columbian Vikings alive in the public imagination. At times, they were successful. During the 1970s, there was one moment in particular when rune stone enthusiasts successfully

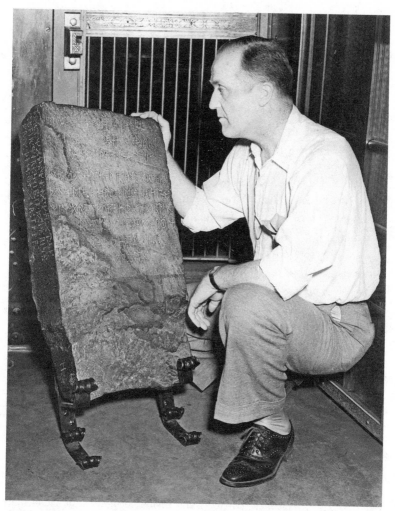

An unidentified researcher in a reflective moment with the Kensington Rune Stone. Courtesy of the Douglas County Historical Society.

evoked the narrative of martyred Norsemen to address a civic need in the final days of America's involvement in Vietnam.[76]

Marion Dahm, a farmer from Chokio, Minnesota, spent half his life collecting what he called Norse artifacts from throughout the upper Midwest. Sometimes referred to as the "outlaw archaeologist," Dahm claimed that he had identified and "validated" more than three hundred mooring stones in the region, far more than the thirteen that had anchored Holand's mythic map. Dahm employed a number of unconventional methods to prove that Vikings had not only visited Minnesota but had lived there in large numbers since the year 1000. Dahm used dowsing rods to locate what he hoped would be Viking graves, and local newspaper articles depicted him donning scuba gear while diving for Viking artifacts in Minnesota lakes. Although his research methods have been criticized, he was revered by many rural Minnesotans as a folk hero.[77]

In 1971, Dahm used an infrared camera to photograph the landscape on Ohman's farm. After viewing the results, he concluded that there were at least five Viking habitations dating to the fourteenth century buried just beneath the soil.[78] The Ohman farm had recently been purchased by the county and was in the midst of being transformed into a park dedicated to the Kensington Rune Stone. Dahm said of the location, "We have a national heritage right here . . . It's perhaps the most important site in the country . . . let's dig it up and prove it."[79]

Dahm finally got his wish three years after he made his "discovery." On a rainy October Saturday, a group of Viking enthusiasts watched as an army helicopter descended on the Ohman farm piloted by local politician and National Guard Captain Dave Fjoslien. Dressed in full battle uniform, Fjoslien and nine other guardsmen leaped out of the chopper armed with metal detectors.[80] The soldiers were greeted by Dahm and an archaeologist from the University of Minnesota. The rune stone supporters were not only eager to find Viking habitations; some, like Margaret Leuthner, were hopeful that Viking graves would be found. Leuthner was convinced that this was the location of the final resting place of the Knutson expedition's victims. Although Holand claimed that they were buried near Lake Cormorant, the site where they were massacred, Leuthner maintained that the bodies had been brought back to their "home" in the "Christian colony" near Kensington, where they were given a proper "Christian burial."[81]

Throughout the day, the guardsmen scanned the terrain near where Ohman had unearthed the stone. Every time the detectors began to squeal, it would "arouse curious onlookers to huddle around in anticipation of a big discovery." The guardsmen and the archaeologist managed to unearth a few scraps of metal, but the archaeologist identified them as rusty nails and broken pieces of farm machinery.

Although the archaeological dig did not yield physical evidence of fourteenth-century Norsemen, the account of the day's activities suggests the occurrence of a sacred civic event. Photographs in the local newspaper are pregnant with symbolism. One depicts a Vietnam War–era transport helicopter positioned at the top of Runestone Hill next to the four flagpoles representing Norway, Sweden, the state of Minnesota, and the United States of America.[82] In another photo, a scowling guardsman crouches near the ground while an archaeologist carefully probes the soil in search of evidence of slain Vikings.

Such evocative imagery requires that the day's events be placed in historical context. America's unpopular and failed involvement in the Vietnam conflict was nearing an end. The last U.S. troops would withdraw from Saigon when the city fell to the Communists the following April. As Richard Slotkin has observed, U.S. military leadership had often compared the fight against the Viet Cong to the "Indian Wars" of the nineteenth century. The parts of Vietnam controlled by the Viet Cong were frequently referred to as the "frontier" and the South Vietnamese who lived there were characterized as "settlers." One military strategy required the "settlers" to live within "stockades" in order be protected from the savages outside.[83]

Although Fjoslien likely orchestrated the theatrical approach to the excavation in hopes of fortifying his prospects in an upcoming election, the event unintentionally served as a civic religious ritual. As some scholars have observed, American civil religion during this era was fragmenting. Widely embraced notions of American innocence were called into question by the masses protesting the Vietnam War and the integrity of the nation's leaders was heavily damaged in the aftermath of the Watergate scandal.[84] The guardsmen, the archaeologist, and the remnant of rune stone enthusiasts at the Ohman farm effectively consecrated the site as significant in the larger American narrative of mourning in the mid-1970s.[85] Despite the unraveling of Holand's sacred narrative undergirding the Kensington Rune Stone, the ritual seemed to convey the notion that neither the imagined Christian Vikings of the past nor the U.S. troops of the present age had given their lives in vain. Just as the descendants of Vikings would one day help anchor a new nation's westward expansion, so too would the United States reassert itself in global affairs. The excavation is best understood as a symbolic "retaking" of Runestone Hill serving to reassert American military prowess and honor while memorializing the sacrifices of fallen American warriors, both past and present.

Throughout the history of the Kensington Rune Stone in the twentieth century, memories of an ancient battle were repeatedly evoked to address the concerns about more recent battles.[86] The skræling endured as a convenient symbol of the threats posed by secularization, urbanization, and diversification. As sociologist Richard K. Fenn observes, "Any society is a reservoir of old longings and ancient hatreds. These need to be understood, addressed, resolved and transcended if a society is to have a future that is different from its past." Furthermore, when a society does not adequately confront its past, it perpetually finds "a new target that resembles but also differs from the source of original conflict."[87] If Fenn is correct, old enemies will continue to emerge in the face of new enemies unless Minnesotans can understand, address, resolve, and transcend the state's original sin: the unjust treatment of the region's first inhabitants.

CONCLUSION

The Enduring Legacy of American Viking Myths

Not long after the episode at Runestone Hill, the Runestone Museum of Alexandria built a replica of the stockade first constructed in the aftermath of the "Sioux Outbreak" of 1862. The museum expansion was dedicated during the week of July 4, 1976—the nation's bicentennial. Ten-foot-high log walls were erected to enclose a recently purchased lot adjacent to the museum. Within the perimeter of "Fort Alexandria," the museum exhibited a collection of agricultural implements and other tools used by early pioneers to transform the wilderness into a productive landscape. In the ensuing years, replicas of a country school, a pioneer church, and a general store were also included. Today, inside the walls of the museum building rests the storied Kensington Rune Stone, encased in a Plexiglas case, with spotlights trained on its inscribed surface. Along one wall of the museum's inner sanctum is a collection of purported Norse artifacts—rusty spears, swords, battle-axes, and the so-called Chokio altar stone—long since discredited as proof of pre-Columbian visitors to the area. Although the museum takes no official stance on the authenticity of the rune stone, it endeavors to make the rune stone "available to any serious researcher."[1]

The controversy continues to attract visitors to Alexandria from around the world.[2] Across the street from the museum and fort stands the statue of Big Ole the Viking holding a spear in his right hand and a shield in his left. The twenty-eight-foot-tall giant looms over a quiet street as a civic sentinel. On almost any warm summer day, one can see parents encouraging their children to stand in front of the blond, bearded Viking while they snap photos. Within minutes, they are on their way to the lake for a swim or to take a bike ride down the adjacent recreational trail. If the tourists are paying attention, they may also notice, just across Lake Agnes, a replica of the Statue of Liberty standing next to an American flag. On the base of the statue is another prominent inscription with the words "One Nation, Under God." Although the visitors and residents alike experience their visit to the museum and photo-op with the giant Viking as innocent fun, the symbols of triumphant militarism, divine national blessing, American national origins, and the glorified Nordic male body continue to evoke the enduring themes of the Kensington Rune Stone story.

By now, it should be evident to the reader that the history of Kensington Rune Stone does not end with the academic critiques of Erik Wahlgren, Theodore Blegen, Tom Trow, Birgitta Wallace, and others. For many, the mystery of the rune stone has yet to be solved. A new crop of rune stone defenders has brought the artifact back to life. Many of these enthusiasts have continued the tradition of defending the honor of Olof Ohman against those who accuse him of being a forger.[3] Others, such as anthropologist Alice Beck Kehoe, postulate that the Norsemen came to Minnesota to establish new fur-trading networks after the Black Death had weakened Sweden's trade in Russian furs.[4] Another enthusiast claimed that the Norsemen died not at the hands of violent Indians, but of the bubonic plague.[5] One of the more influential rune stone defenders is Richard Nielson, an American-born engineer of Danish descent. Nielson is a self-taught researcher who has spent more than twenty years studying the runic inscription and once claimed that its language bears a similarity to dialects spoken on the Swedish island of Gotland during the fourteenth century.[6]

Cultural expressions regarding pre-Columbian explorations to the heart of North America have also continued to flourish. Don Coldsmith authored a novel called *Runestone: A Novel of Adventure,* which tells the story of a Viking expedition that traveled to the heart of modern-day Oklahoma to carve an inscription on a rock formation near the town of Heavener. Jack Selmela's novel *Of Vikings and Voyageurs* tells the story of seventeenth-century French fur traders who found, and later lost, Viking treasure in the Minnesota wilderness. The Kensington Rune Stone was also the feature of a 2011 U-Haul promotional campaign called "Venture across America," in which 2,300 moving vans were painted with a "SuperGraphic" depicting the Minnesota artifact towering over a Viking ship.[7] At the 2014 Minnesota Fringe Festival, the artifact's story was dramatized in a musical titled *The Ohman Stone* directed and written by rune stone enthusiast Sheridan O'Keefe.[8]

No one has brought more attention to the rune stone in recent times than Scott Wolter, a forensic geologist who was featured in a 2009 History Channel documentary titled *Holy Grail in America*. In 2000, the Runestone Museum of Alexandria hired Wolter to study the physical features of the rune stone—particularly the engraved characters of the inscription.[9] Although he found evidence of fresh scratches deep in the runic grooves, he also discovered what he claims to be evidence of weathering along the sides of grooves.[10] Based on research, he concludes that the physical evidence indicates that the inscription is at least two hundred years old and, most likely, dates to 1362.[11] Along with former collaborator Richard Nielson, Wolter coauthored *The Kensington Rune Stone: Compelling New Evidence* in 2006. Not long after the book was published, Nielson substantially revised his conclusions about the runic inscription and eventually challenged the integrity of Wolter's research methods.[12] Given the "rough handling" of the rune stone over the years, scholars have remarked on how difficult it is to accurately assess the physical condition of the stone.[13] Nielson began to collaborate with a Swedish runic scholar, Henrik Williams, from the University of Uppsala. Williams concluded that the Kensington inscription bears no resemblance to known runic writings from the fourteenth century but instead shares similarities with recently discovered documents in Sweden dating to the 1880s.[14] He claims that Swedish-American immigrants in the late nineteenth century could have been familiar with the particular runic characters used to create the Kensington Rune Stone inscription.

Wolter is undaunted by the betrayal of his former research partner and holds firm to his own conclusions. However, he is not content to let his geological evidence stand alone.[15] Like other rune stone enthusiasts, he embeds his research in a fantastic historical narrative. Although his expertise is in the physical science of stones, he now speaks as an authority for fields in which he has no formal training. He claims that the Goths and Norsemen who carved the inscription were members of the order of the Knights Templar, who had used the stone as a land claim to prove that they had been the first to discover the land.[16] In Wolter's view, the chiseled boulders that Holand had understood to be mooring stones for Viking ships were actually markers to guide future explorers to this Nordic land claim. Furthermore, Wolter claims that the Knights

Templar had come to North America to establish their order and hide treasure (including the Holy Grail) acquired during the Crusades. Wolter is following the same strategy as Holand and many other rune stone enthusiasts who have long believed that sensationalism is the key to proving the artifact to be true. Not long after his first appearance on the History Channel in 2009, Wolter got his own television show, *America Unearthed*, in which he frequently speaks of his efforts to expose the conspiracies that have hidden the true history of North America. He takes advantage of the popular distrust of the academic establishment, as did Holand. Popular media outlets such as the History Channel often blur the lines between fact and myth and the public is often unable to discern the difference.[17] Fantasies about Cistercian monks traveling to North America to find the Holy Grail are entertaining, but they ought to be relegated to the genre of mythic literature rather than history.

Despite their dubious conclusions, there is perhaps one thing to be celebrated in the arguments of contemporary rune stone enthusiasts. They have by and large refrained from resurrecting Holand's debunked thesis that the United States was birthed by the sacrifices of Nordic Christian missionaries who died at the hands of bloodthirsty savages. Yet, they expend a great deal of energy speculating on who *might* have been in North America prior to Columbus rather than on the people who were known to be here. In Wolter's television series *America Unearthed*, the majority of episodes deal with found artifacts and rock formations that he claims indicate the presence of non-Indian people in North America prior to the exploration of Columbus. In the spirit of Carl Christian Rafn, Caleb Atwater, and Hjalmar Holand, Wolter has found an audience tantalized by the notion of an imagined ancient America populated by more than just Indians.[18]

The American fascination with a pre-Columbian presence of Europeans has often functioned to render invisible, or at least marginal, the region's first inhabitants. Indian history is evoked in Alexandria's Runestone Museum by a collection of Indian artifacts situated next to a wildlife exhibit filled with stuffed deer, bears, and raccoons. Following a visit by members of Minnesota's White Earth Ojibwe tribe, the museum announced plans for changes to make the Indian exhibit "more accurate and sensitive to Native American cultures," including the construction of an "authentic" diorama of an Ojibwe village.[19] One wonders if this same cultural sensitivity will extend to other areas of the museum where Indian history is mentioned. In a space dedicated to the early history of Alexandria is a small television that plays a looping video about Clara Kinkaid, one of the first pioneer settlers of Alexandria. In 1862, Kinkaid recorded a detailed account in a diary of her experiences during the Dakota War. She conveyed her fears and frustrations about having to abandon the home she and her husband had recently built to seek refuge at the fort in St. Cloud. The film's narrator interprets the events by stating that in 1862, the Indians were trespassers on land that no longer belonged to them. They had ceded their land and were paid fairly for it.[20] Rather than acknowledge the moral complexities of the events of 1862, this simplistic rendition serves to reify the notion that the white settlement of Minnesota was a purely innocent endeavor.[21] A small placard located near the television heightens the rhetoric of white victimhood by proclaiming that the word *Sioux* was a synonym for *terror* in the days of the pioneers.[22]

As the rune stone story exemplifies, the controversial artifact has been used to generate group pride, but also to demarcate who does and who does not belong. Rune stone enthusiasts have been creative and entrepreneurial in their efforts to portray their region of Minnesota as significant in the larger American story. Yet, these proclamations of exceptionalism have been wedded to assertions of victimhood. Norwegian immigrants, small-town Midwesterners, Catholic leaders, and others have used the Kensington Rune Stone story to advance persecution narratives. In doing so, these groups have often ignored (whether consciously or unconsciously) their own privileged status as white, Christian Americans.

Minnesota has become an increasingly diverse place in recent decades. New immigrants from Somalia, Laos, and Latin America have changed the racial and ethnic makeup of the state. Even rural communities now have sizable populations of Mexican Americans and other immigrant groups. The religious landscape of Minnesota is also more diverse than ever. Protestant and Catholic Christians still dominate the culture of the state, but there are now Muslims, Buddhists, Hindus, and a growing segment of the population that identifies as nonreligious. In light of the history of the Kensington Rune Stone in the twentieth century, it is appropriate to inquire whether the specter of the savage skræling will be revived to confront the anxieties aroused by the presence of a new "other."

ACKNOWLEDGMENTS

This project could not have been completed without the support, love, and encouragement of many people. First, my wife has been an anchor for me throughout my years at graduate school and writing this book. I am grateful to our children's grandparents, aunts, and uncles who have stepped up to watch the kids whenever I needed to "make just one more revision to my manuscript." Writing a book is a lot like farming. They both require the ability to be self-motivated and work independently. I am grateful to my dad, a lifelong farmer, for modeling these strengths for me. My mother likes to think that I chose to write about my home-town so that I could visit her more often; I have enjoyed numerous trips to Minnesota over the past several years that combined research and treasured family time. I am indebted to my sister and brother-in-law, who have been consistently present with my parents while I have lived far away.

I trace the genesis of this book to the classroom of Richard K. Fenn's Religion and Society course at Princeton Theological Seminary in 2003. Dr. Fenn is an inspiring teacher and was a big encouragement to me as I wrote my first paper about the civic myths of my home-town. This book first took shape as I researched and wrote my disserta-tion during my graduate studies at Temple University's Department of Religion. I am enormously grateful to the members of my dissertation committee. Terry Rey is the most generous and kind graduate studies chair a student could ask for: he read every word of my dissertation in at least three different iterations and nurtured creativity in my writ-ing. Jon Pahl's research on religion and violence has made an important impact on this project; I have relished my conversations with Jon over the years and I appreciate the opportunities he provided me to deliver lectures in his classes at Lutheran Theological Seminary and Princeton University. Rebecca Alpert has been very encouraging to me throughout my graduate-school experience and beyond; she is a reliable source of pragmatic advice and helped me to establish a discipline of writing. I am grateful to Andrew Isenberg of Temple University's Department of History, who read my dissertation and served as a valuable resource on the history of the American West. David Watt played a critical role in introducing me to many of the scholars to whom I refer in this book. His practical advice and bibliographic brilliance were invaluable to my graduate studies experience. Finally, I am indebted to John Raines, who chaired my graduate exam committee. As a fellow Minnesota native who spent his childhood summers on Alexandria's Lake L'Homme Dieu, he brought a unique perspective to this project. Dr. Raines has been an inspiration to my scholarship and church-based activism. His prophetic challenge still echoes in my mind and heart: to reveal the arbitrary nature of exploitative systems that appear natural or ordained by God.

Several other people were helpful in transforming my dissertation into a book manuscript. Laura S. Levitt has been a terrific cheerleader and guide in writing a book proposal. Audra J. Wolfe was invaluable in helping me to navigate the process of securing a publishing contract. Karen Schnitker patiently and carefully edited countless versions of this manuscript. I am grateful to my Minnesota friends David W. Bauer, Travis Larson, Jon Larson, Edward Godfrey, Darwin Johnson, Pastor Craig Dahl, and others who provided helpful feedback at various points in my research and writing. I have been privileged to have had insightful conversations about my topic with other scholars who write about religion, history, and culture, including Nathan Wright, Kipp Gilmore-Clough, Christy Croxall, Brian McAdams, Beth Lawson, Kime Lawson, Omer Awass, Sean Sanford, Katie Oxx, Jennifer Graber, and, most recently, Arthur Remillard, Eric Ecklund, Mathew Sayers, Grant Julin, and Joseph Williams.

This book has been shaped by my recent teaching experience as an adjunct professor and church-based educator. My honors undergraduate students at Rutgers University–Camden and my graduate students at the Rutgers branch at the Joint Base McGuire–Dix–Lakehurst read an earlier draft of this book for my Religion and American Culture seminars. Thanks to Nema Buruschkin, John Dunbar, Adam Jadick, Jasmine King, Sarah Morris, Kimberly Nguyen, Jamila Pascal, Yekaterina Rasstrigina, Argenis Reyes, John Yosko, Tinisha Bass, Shuan Brock, Julie Hafeez, Brian Harriet, William Lanehart, Samuel Lewis, Douglas Paley,

Margarita Urgiles, and Thomas Weaver. I am particularly grateful to students Alissa Valeriano, Julia Lehman, Madison Rogers, Ashley Lewis, and Michael Weldon, who wrote insightful book reviews posing helpful questions to clarify and enhance my arguments. Church study groups at Arch Street United Methodist and Germantown Mennonite in Philadelphia; Rochester Mennonite Church in Rochester, Minnesota; and Christ United Methodist's Inquiring Spirits class have all been stimulating environments for my thinking about the ethical themes raised in this book.

A number of people and institutions have been of great assistance in my research. Thanks to Mel and Mary Conrad of the Kensington Area Heritage Society for their hospitality. They meticulously compiled hundreds, if not thousands, of articles related to the history of the Kensington Rune Stone. Their archives and museum center located in the town of Kensington should be a first stop for research. Thanks to Carol Keller, who escorted me on a visit to Our Lady of the Runestone Catholic Church, also located in Kensington. Thanks to the staff of the Douglas County Historical Society in Alexandria, Minnesota; executive director Rachel Bardson and research director Kim Dillon helpfully answered my questions and pointed me in the right direction for research. I appreciated my conversations with Julie Blank and Jim Bergquist of the Runestone Museum in Alexandria and with the staff at the Newport Historical Society in Rhode Island. Finally, I am particularly grateful for the superb research library and archives at the Minnesota Historical Society in St. Paul.

NOTES

Introduction

1. The pageant depends a great deal on music from Wagner, whose music was banned in Israel during this time because of its association with the Nazis and notions of Aryan racial supremacy. The song "Ride of the Valkyries" was famously used in the climactic scene of D. W. Griffith's 1915 film *Birth of a Nation* to dramatize the charge of the Klu Klux Klan and the rescue of white captives from black soldiers. See Smith, "American Valkyries," 221–42.

2. All quotations from Merling, *The Runestone Pageant Play* (1962).

3. Larry J. Zimmerman, an archaeologist from the Minnesota Historical Society, asks why many cultural groups do not believe what the scientific community tells them about their past: "Many will not accept the pasts that archaeologists construct for them are correct, no matter how well-reasoned the archaeological arguments or how solid the evidence." Zimmerman argues that scientists need to make a distinction between "truth" and "validity." Scientists are concerned with validity, which demands evidence and proof. Truth, however, may not. Zimmerman suggests that the truth has more to do with the centrality that cultural myths may have for a particular community. In this sense, the rune stone is experienced as true for its enthusiasts even if the evidence for it is not valid. See Zimmerman, "Unusual or 'Extreme' Beliefs about the Past, Community Identity, and Dealing with the Fringe," 55.

4. The 1963 poll is cited in Hughey and Michlovic, "'Making' History," 338.

5. Other names that were considered include Chippewas, Miners, and Voyageurs. The name "Vikings" was chosen in part to "to recognize the venturesome people who first populated the state" (Dick Cullum, "Minnesota Is Designation of Pro Grid Team," *Minneapolis Tribune*, August 6, 1960, 21).

6. The term "collective memory" is best associated with French sociologist Maurice Halbwachs. In translator Lewis Coser's words, "For Halbwachs, the past is a social construction mainly, if not wholly, shaped by the concerns of the present" (in Halbwachs, *On Collective Memory*, 25).

7. The book will interchangeably use the terms "Native American," "Indian," and "Native peoples" to refer to the first residents of North America. For a discussion of the usage of such terms, see King, *The Inconvenient Indian*, xii–xiii.

8. The term *skræling* in the Norse language has pejorative connotations meaning "wretches" or "people who screech." See Kolodony, *In Search of First Contact,* 3.

9. Sawyer, *The Viking-Age Rune-Stones,* 16–18, and Gräslund, "Religion, Art, and
Runes," 69.

10. Blegen, *The Kensington Rune Stone,* 36–39.

11. Wahlgren, *The Kensington Stone,* 181.

12. McCloud, *Divine Hierarchies,* 14.

13. Mancini, "Discovering Viking America," 877.

14. Hjalmar Holand wrote dozens of books and articles, most notably *Westward
from Vinland* and *Explorations in Minnesota before Columbus.* The two most famous scholars to argue against the stone in book-length treatments are Wahlgren, *The Kensington Stone,* and Blegen, *The Kensington Rune Stone.* A recent defense of the rune stone
is Nielson and Wolter, *The Kensington Rune Stone.* The Minnesota Historical Society
has published articles that have summarized the history of the debates, including
Gilman and Smith, "Vikings in Minnesota," 1–34, and Gilman, "Kensington
Runestone Revisited," 61–65.

15. Dregni, *Minnesota Marvels,* 10.

16. See Michlovic and Hughey, "Norse Blood and Indian Character," 79–94;
Hughey and Michlovic, "'Making' History," 338–60; Michlovic, "Folk Archaeology in Anthropological Perspective," 103–7. David A. Sprunger wrote an article
illuminating the divisions between Norwegian Americans in their endorsement
and opposition to the rune stone: "Mystery and Obsession," 140–54. Chris Susag
and Peter Susag illustrate the close relationship between the commercialization
of the rune stone and its ability to generate ethnic identity in the late twentieth century in "Scandinavian Group Identity," 30–51. A graduate student from
the University of Minnesota wrote an insightful thesis illustrating how the pau-
city of words in the rune stone inscription provided space for Minnesotans to
project their own interpretations upon it. See Mealey, "Qualitative Research in
Anthropology."

17. The role of religion in the Kensington Rune Stone phenomenon has been
briefly explored by Hughey and Michlovic, "'Making' History," 338–60, and
Mancini, "Discovering Viking America," 868–907. However, theorizing rune
stone enthusiasm as a cultural religion has been not been explored in depth.

18. Holand, "An Explorer's Stone Record Which Antedates Columbus."

19. Holand, "A Fourteenth Century Columbus."

20. Holand did not identify himself as an adherent Christianity and was, in
fact, quite critical of it. As a young, traveling book salesman for Seventh-Day
Adventists in rural Wisconsin, he mocked religious people for what he described
as their "indifference to the printed page." As he observed, the only book in most
homes was the family Bible, which was used primarily for decoration. Holand
goes on to describe church members as legalistic, intolerant, militant, and overly
argumentative (Holand, *My First Eighty Years,* 48, 65–66).

21. Catherine L. Albanese illustrates how "cultural" and "civic" religions in

the United States combine elements of traditional religion to form new religious hybrids that often exist alongside denominational religion (*America*, 275–301).

22. Historians in the United States have often assumed that religion is practiced in private and the public is secular. As Kathryn Lofton observes, the lack of an established faith in the United States does not preclude the emergence of religious discourse in realms assumed to be secular: "These forms are unfamiliar to students of history and religion, as they are without bounds, without permanent structure, and without imprinted creed." The task of the present analysis is to render visible what Lofton calls this "ceaseless commingling" of religion and culture. See Lofton, *Oprah*, 10–12. As Danièle Hervieu-Léger argues, religion in the modern world often functions independently of traditional institutions. Religion continuously "re-emerges, revives, shifts ground, [and] becomes diffuse." When religious beliefs are liberated from institutions of believing, "all symbols are interchangeable and capable of being combined and transposed. All syncretisms are possible, all retreads imaginable" (Hervieu-Léger, *Religion as a Chain of Memory*, 24, 75).

23. "Dr. Tanquist's Testimony: Why I Believe in the Runestone," *Park Region Echo* (Alexandria, Minnesota), July 21, 1959.

24. "Holand to Autograph Books at Herbergers," *Park Region Echo*, May 17, 1956.

25. "Hoax of the Century? Runestone Forgery Claimed," *Lake Region Press* (Alexandria, Minnesota), August 9, 1974.

26. Brian Branston, "An Open Letter to Cliff Roiland, the Runestone Rambler," *Lake Region Press*, November 22, 1974. Branston's choice of inflammatory language likely helped him to generate publicity for his recently released film documentary *Riddles of the Runestone*.

27. Peter Berger writes that religion had suffered a "crisis of plausibility" (*Sacred Canopy*, 127). In later writings, Berger acknowledged that religious adherence had not declined as he had predicted (Berger, *The Desecularization of the World*).

28. Danièle Hervieu-Léger writes: "If science and technology have removed most of the mystery from the world, they clearly have not obliterated the human need for assurance, which is at the source of the search to make life intelligible and which constantly evokes the question of why" (*Religion as a Chain of Memory*, 73).

29. Hervieu-Léger observes that cultural religions or religious hybrids often emerge in response to rapid social change, dislocation, or experiences of group trauma. These conditions can evoke appeals to collective memory and the construction of new "sacred canopies" and collective identities (ibid., 141).

30. Bellah, "Civil Religion in America," 3, 18.

31. In a 1985 essay, N.J. Demerath and Rhys Williams called on scholars to address "the contexts and uses of civil religious language and symbols, noting how specific groups and subcultures use versions of civil religion to frame, articulate, and legitimate their own particular political or moral visions" ("Civil Religions in an Uncivil Society," 166). Although the scholarly conversation about civil religion dissipated in the 1980s, recent scholars have responded to Demerath and

Williams's challenge. See Remillard, *Southern Civil Religions*; Walker "Liberators for Colonial Anáhuac," 183–203.

32. Rather than think of American civil religion as a static, well-defined national religion, this analysis sees it as a fluid cultural repertoire from which civic and cultural leaders can select, adapt, and apply in order to advance their own particular agendas. As a local sect, it both affirms and challenges many of the popular assertions of American civil religion. It should be noted that civil religion is not necessarily a substitute for traditional Christian expressions, but often exists alongside of them. Kensington Rune Stone enthusiasts have frequently been practicing Lutherans, Catholics, and Evangelicals. This analysis demonstrates how civil religions and traditional religions often coexist in a symbiotic relationship.

33. For an excellent overview of American myths and the historical contexts from which they emerged, see Hughes, *Myths Americans Live By*. As Bruce Lincoln observes, myths are really "ideology in narrative form" (*Theorizing Myth*, 147).

34. Pahl, *Empire of Sacrifice*, 2.

35. Conservative Christian activist and pseudohistorian David Barton has been a tireless advocate for the notion the United States was founded as a Christian nation (http://www.npr.org/2012/08/08/157754542/the-most-influential-evangeslist-youve-never-heard-of).

36. Gunn, *Spiritual Weapons*, 9.

37. The U.S. Supreme Court declared teacher-led prayer and Bible readings in public schools to be unconstitutional in *Engel v. Vitale* (1962) and *Abington School District v. Schempp* (1963). Additionally, the popular 1960 film *Elmer Gantry* portrayed Christian leaders as hucksters.

38. As some scholars have observed, sacrifices are necessary for enduring groups to cohere. See Marvin and Ingle, *Blood Sacrifice and the Nation*, 1. The present analysis shows that even imagined sacrifices can forge collective identity.

39. Øverland, *Immigrant Minds, American Identities*, 150.

40. Protestant Christians are often depicted as concerning themselves with the spiritual rather than the material dimension of religion. This analysis shows that the typically austere and iconoclastic Swedish and Norwegian Lutherans found in Kensington Rune Stone enthusiasm an outlet to express their religious impulses in material and spatial forms. Colleen McDannell observes that Protestants have often freely incorporated material culture into their religious expressions (*Material Christianity*, 6).

41. Writing in the early twentieth century, Durkheim researched the religious beliefs and rituals of several indigenous ethnic groups in Australia and noted that various clans within the tribe identified themselves with an image of a particular plant or animal. Durkheim referred to this image as a totem, which was used as a marking on all persons and things belonging to the clan. In modern societies, the totem can be understood to be a flag or coat of arms that represents a particular group or nation. See Marvin and Ingle, *Blood Sacrifice and the Nation*, 29–40.

42. Durkheim, *Elementary Forms of the Religious Life*, 208. Durkheim's totemic theory

and observation of the importance of public rituals in the maintenance of social/religious cohesion are utilized in this analysis with an important revision: Durkheim does not ask the question of who controls the collective rituals and whose interests are served by them. See Cristi, *From Civil to Political Religion*, 40. Durkheim portrays totemic symbols as given; he plays little attention to the process by which totems come to be accepted. The present analysis illustrates the process by which civic boosters appropriated the rune stone as a sacred totem to represent the identity and aspirations of western Minnesotans.

43. Eliade, *Patterns in Comparative Religion*, 216.

44. For some, the stone discovered in Ohman's field functioned as a land claim to prove that white Minnesotans were destined to be there. Their presence on the landscape was a "justified" and a "natural" progression of the Norse expedition in the fourteenth century.

45. Jonathan Z. Smith reminds us that sacred spaces are not ordained as such by divine decree; they are actively constructed by human agents who have the power to do so ("The Wobbling Pivot," 141). Thomas Tweed's theory of religion is helpful in gaining perspective on the ways that rune stone enthusiasts fashioned the fields, forests, and waterways of Minnesota into a sacred landscape or "sacroscape." Tweed understands homemaking, or "dwelling," to signify the ways that religious people map, build, and inhabit physical and imagined spaces (*Crossing and Dwelling*, 74). However, it is clear that claims to landscapes are not benign. The production of sacred space is an operation of naturalization. What is in reality a completely arbitrary claim to a landscape is made to appear as natural or determined by God. Sociologist Pierre Bourdieu would refer to this process of naturalization as an act of symbolic violence. See Rey, *Bourdieu on Religion*, 53–55.

46. Karen Fields, "Translator's Introduction," in Durkheim, *Elementary Forms of the Religious Life*, xli.

47. Historian David Glassberg sees historical pageantry of the early twentieth century as being based on "the belief that history could be made into a dramatic public ritual through which the residents of a town, by acting out the right version of their past, could bring about some kind of future social and political transformation" (*American Historical Pageantry*, 1).

1. Westward from Vinland

1. The Kensington Rune Stone is thirty-six inches long, fifteen inches wide, about six inches thick, and weighs 201 lbs., 7 oz. See Kehoe, *The Kensington Runestone*, 3.

2. Holand, *Westward from Vinland*, 110–12.

3. Ibid., 97.

4. Holand claimed that "thousands" of residents viewed the stone (*Westward from Vinland*, 97). Theodore C. Blegen questioned Holand's claim that the artifact was even put on public display and points to the curious lack of local media coverage as evidence (*The Kensington Rune Stone*, 42).

5. "A Stone Bearing Runic Inscriptions," *Alexandria Post News*, February 23, 1899, I. This article was also published the previous day in the *Minneapolis Journal*.

6. Wahlgren, *The Kensington Stone*, 9.

7. Holand, *Westward from Vinland*, 99.

8. Lovoll, *The Promise of America*, 7.

9. It should be noted that in the mid-nineteenth century, Columbus was not perceived to have an ethnic identity. Rather, he was an American symbol. Columbus did not begin to emerge as an icon of Italian-American identity until the early twentieth century. See Øverland, *Immigrant Minds, American Identities*, 63–76.

10. There is a long tradition of marginalized groups in U.S. history making the claim that their ancestors had traveled to North America prior to Columbus. Another example is Ivan Van Sertima's 1976 text *They Came before Columbus*. Van Sertima claims that there is evidence that Africans who traveled to North America had a strong influence on pre-Columbian American cultures. See Feder, *Frauds, Myths, and Mysteries*, 105–10.

11. Øverland, *Immigrant Minds, American Identities*, 146.

12. New England historians in the middle of the nineteenth century had embraced the notion of pre-Columbian Norse visits to North America decades before Anderson's book was published. The seminal texts were Henry Wheaton's *History of the Norsemen*, published in 1831, and Dane Carl Christian Rafn's *Antiquitates Americanae*, published in 1837. These texts mark a significant departure from most scholars of the day, who considered the Norse sagas to be simply legend and devoid of historical value. Rafn claimed that the Vikings had traveled as far south as New Jersey. J. M. Mancini demonstrates that many New England historians and literary producers used Viking history as a means to bolster notions of Anglo-Saxon racial identity over and against newer immigrant groups arriving in the United States (Mancini "Discovering Viking America," 868–907).

13. Rafn was the first scholar to claim a Norse origin for these artifacts in his 1837 work. Most contemporary scholars attribute the carvings on the Dighton Rock to the work of Native Americans. Excavations of the Newport Tower site in the 1940s yielded evidence that the edifice was constructed during the colonial period. See Williams, *Fantastic Archeology*, 213–19.

14. See Mancini's analysis of Anderson's work, "Discovering Viking America," 883–84.

15. Anderson, *America Not Discovered by Columbus*, 51.

16. Øverland, *Immigrant Minds, American Identities*, 158.

17. Anderson, *America Not Discovered by Columbus*, 63.

18. Øverland, *Immigrant Minds, American Identities*, 149.

19. Ibid., 157.

20. Mancini, "Discovering Viking America," 883.

21. Anderson's cultural production was also adopted by some Swedish-American writers. The journalist Johan A. Enander used Viking history prominently in his popular historical writings of the late nineteenth century in his Chicago-based

newspaper *Hemlandet* (Homeland) (Øverland, *Immigrant Minds, American Identities*, 155). In addition to the cultural capital found in Viking discovery narratives, Swedish Americans could claim deep roots in the United States by reminding Anglo-Americans that the Swedes had founded a colony along the Delaware River in the seventeenth century. This may help to explain why Swedish Americans were less prolific in their production of filiopietistic historiography about Viking discovery narratives. See Barton, "Swedish Americans and the Viking Discovery of America," 61–78.

22. Wahlgren, *The Kensington Stone*, 123.

23. Berger, *Sacred Canopy*, 51.

24. In Sweden, it was illegal to be anything but Lutheran until 1860. This is not to say that there were not religious options for persons in Norway and Sweden in the mid-nineteenth century. Mormons, Baptists, and Pietist missionaries were active in Scandinavian countries starting in the 1850s.

25. Lovoll, *The Promise of America*, 143. Lovoll's chapter "The Spirit and the Mind" describes in more detail the reasons for the fragmentations among Norwegian Lutherans.

26. See Lovoll, *Norwegians on the Prairie*, 65–71. This is a central reason why Norwegian immigrants have been more enthusiastic about Viking discovery narratives than Swedish immigrants. Swedish Americans also benefited from their association with the early colonial efforts in North America. Immigrants from Sweden colonized the Delaware Valley in the 1640s.

27. Danièle Hervieu-Léger observes that periods of accelerated social change are often accompanied with appeals to collective memory (*Religion as a Chain of Memory*, 141.

28. Tweed, *Crossing and Dwelling*, 54.

29. Tweed understands the process of homemaking as the ways that religious people map, build, and inhabit physical and imagined spaces (ibid., 74).

30. Lago, *On the Viking Trail*, 59.

31. Around 850,000 Norwegians settled in the United States between 1825 and 1928 and an overwhelming majority of them settled in Minnesota. The peak years of arrival were 1866–73, 1880–93, and 1900–1910. See Carlton C. Qualey and Jon A. Gjerde, "The Norwegians," in Holmquist, *They Chose Minnesota*, 220. From 1845 to 1930, 1,250,000 Swedes immigrated to the United States and the majority of them arrived in Minnesota as well (John G. Rice, "The Swedes," in Holmquist, *They Chose Minnesota*, 248).

32. Wahlgren, *The Kensington Stone*, 121.

33. This was a typical path of Scandinavian immigration to the Midwest from the mid- to late nineteenth century.

34. Kjaer, "Runes and Immigrants in America," 26.

35. Williams, *Fantastic Archeology*, 205.

36. In 1869, a farmer in Cardiff, New York, Stub Newell, unearthed a ten-foot-long stone object in the shape of a large man. Local observers concluded that this

was a petrified giant, dating from the antediluvian era mentioned in the biblical book of Genesis. Within days of the discovery, Newell erected a tent over the giant and began to charge money for admission. Hundreds of people flocked to Newell's farm each day. After a few short weeks, Newell had collected more than seven thousand dollars in admission fees—a staggering sum for 1869. However, the hoax was exposed and the business enterprise soon came to an end. Newell's cousin admitted that the "giant" was a simply a carved statue made of gypsum.

37. Mulder, "Mormons from Scandinavia, 1850–1900."

38. Holand, *History of Norwegian Settlements*, 34–35.

39. Sawyer, *The Viking-Age Rune-Stones*, 16–18.

40. Gräslund, "Religion, Art, and Runes," 69.

41. Blegen, *The Kensington Rune Stone*, 36–39.

42. "The Stone Is Resurrected" is the title of one Holand's chapters in *A Pre-Columbian Crusade to America*.

43. See Blegen, *The Kensington Rune Stone*, 49. Marion John Nelson argues that Holand saw the rune stone in terms of a historical monument that would commemorate Norwegian Americans. Nelson also compares Holand with the Norwegian folk character Askeladden, who is known for picking up mundane and discarded objects. Although his brothers make fun of him, Askeladden uses these objects to win the heart of a princess and half of the kingdom. Nelson parallels this story of Holand picking up the Kensington Rune Stone: an artifact that had been rejected and relegated for use as a step for Ohman's granary. See "Material Culture and Ethnicity: Collecting and Preserving Norwegian Americana before World War II," in Nelson, *Material Culture and People's Art among the Norwegians in America*, 3–10.

44. Holand, *My First Eighty Years*, 185–88.

45. Ibid. The depiction of Ohman as an uneducated but honest farmer would come to be a frequently used trope to glorify Scandinavian farmers.

46. Ibid., *My First Eighty Years*, 186. That the stone was used as a stepping stone is likely a literary device used in Holand's storytelling. Ohman's sons later testified that the stone was stored in the shed and was never used in such a way. See Wahlgren, *The Kensington Stone*, 191–92n.

47. Just after he acquired the stone, Holand carved his initial "H" on the side. The newly inscribed letter is still visible on the stone today. See Nielson and Wolter, *The Kensington Rune Stone*, 25.

48. Ibid., 238.

49. Ibid., 239.

50. For many years, Ohman appealed unsuccessfully to Holand to return the stone. Finally, in 1923, Holand sent Ohman a letter explaining that he was trying to get some compensation for all of the money he had spent researching the stone. Holand offered Ohman a rather empty promise to share some compensation with Ohman if he were ever in need. Ohman eventually pursued legal help in making a claim against Holand. However, on his attorney's advice, Ohman chose not to sue

Holand because of the high legal fees associated with suing a resident of another state. Holand remained a resident of Ephraim, Wisconsin. For a more detailed documentation of the debate over the ownership of the Kensington Rune Stone, see ibid., 237–48.

51. Holand, *Norwegians in America*, 157.

52. Ibid., 3. Holand's blindness to the complicity of his immigrant brethren with the systemic violence perpetrated by U.S. policy toward Native Americans will be addressed in chapter 2.

53. Holand, *Westward from Vinland*, 262.

54. Copies of these documents exist but the originals were supposedly destroyed during a fire at Holand's house in 1934 (Blegen, *The Kensington Rune Stone*, 58.

55. "University and Educational News," *Science* 31, no. 791 (February 25, 1910): 297.

56. Blegen, *The Kensington Rune Stone*, 72. Wahlgren points to a number of inconsistencies in Winchell's claims (Wahlgren, *The Kensington Stone*, 63–64).

57. Blegen, *The Kensington Rune Stone*, 89.

58. Kehoe, *The Kensington Runestone*, 8.

59. Nielson and Wolter, *The Kensington Rune Stone*, 430.

60. Holand had clear aspirations to pursue a literary career. While attending graduate school at the University of Wisconsin–Madison, he pondered his future plans: "It was a somewhat vague expectation of going to New York and there taking up a literary occupation. It seemed to me that literary people got more out of life than others." As an aspiring writer, he had disdain for those who wrote about the "commonplace." He saw the novelist as a true "knight of the pen" who could pursue creative endeavors through fostering an inner life. "When he retires to his den and rubs the Aladdin's lamp of his imagination, he enters a different world of lovely ladies and heroic men whose conversation sparkles with wit and humor. Or there is the historian who in the profundity of his research meditates only on the high and the mighty of mankind" (Holand, *My First Eighty Years*, 98–99).

61. The Swedish-born archaeologist Birgitta Wallace researched the numerous artifacts that Holand and other Norse enthusiasts claimed were from the fourteenth century. As of 1982, Wallace claimed that sixty-nine artifacts, allegedly of Norse origin, have been found throughout the Midwest. She concluded that some of the artifacts are legitimate in that they date from the medieval period, but it cannot be verified that they were actually unearthed in Minnesota. However, others are clearly fakes dating from the nineteenth century (Wallace, "Viking Hoaxes," 64–65).

62. Farmers used dynamite to break boulders into smaller pieces in order to clear land and collect building materials for foundations. As archaeologist Tom Trow has observed, there are hundreds of chiseled boulders scattered throughout the landscape. Holand identified only thirteen to support his theory of a fourteen-day journey. Archaeologists such as Trow have concluded that in the fourteenth

century it would not have been possible to travel by a large boat from Hudson Bay to Douglas County as Holand had claimed. The group would have had to use small boats such as canoes that could be portaged over long distances. These boats, says Trow, would not have required mooring stones (Trow, "Small Holes in Large Rocks," 125–26). In his 1986 book, Wahlgren argues that some of the stones were surveyor markings and others were used to anchor fish traps (Wahlgren, *The Vikings and America*, 110–11).

63. Holand, *Westward from Vinland*, 262.

64. Ibid., 266.

65. Ibid., 272. Catlin is known for his theory that the Mandan were descendants of Prince Madoc, a Welsh prince who is said by some to have sailed to North America in 1170. Holand is quick to denounce that theory (275–76).

66. Ibid., 263–64.

67. Ibid., 278.

68. Ibid., 264.

69. Michlovic and Hughey, "Norse Blood and Indian Character," 83.

70. Evidence from as early as 1893 suggests that some Scandinavian Americans were growing weary of immigrant homemaking arguments. This might be an indication that in some sectors of the immigrant community, homemaking arguments were thought to be increasingly unnecessary. Anderson is portrayed almost as a rambling old coot by the publication *Skandinaven*. See Øverland, *Immigrant Minds, American Identities*, 225n33.

71. Wahlgren observed that Holand first said the tree was twenty-five years old in his 1908 book. In a 1910 article, Holand maintained the tree was forty years old and, in his later writings, claimed it was seventy. Wahlgren concluded that Holand had a growing need to increase the age of the tree as his linguistic evidence was challenged (Wahlgren, *The Vikings and America*, 32). Scandinavian Americans who questioned the Kensington Rune Stone were often portrayed as ethnic traitors. Regarding attacks on Holvik, see Sprunger, "Mystery and Obsession," 149. Erik Wahlgren also experienced attacks, which he describes in "Reflections around a Rune Stone," 37–49.

72. Sprunger, "Mystery and Obsession," 144.

73. Holvik found a copy of the letter that a Kensington resident had sent to the *Swedish American Post* in 1899. This letter contained a copy that J. P. Hedberg claimed he had made of the inscription. Holvik observed numerous discrepancies between it and the actual rune stone inscription. He concluded that the Hedberg copy was a draft used by the stone carvers. Furthermore, following a visit with Ohman's daughter, Manda, Holvik discovered that Ohman had owned a copy of the Swedish text by Carl Rosander, *The Well-Informed Schoolmaster*. According to Holvik, the text would have been a sufficient help in producing a runic inscription and even included the phrase "save us from evil" (ibid., 148).

74. Holvik's strident attacks on Holand's scholarship were also fueled by a personal quarrel with Holand when they met in Norway in 1911. See ibid., 142.

75. Ibid., 151.

76. It was the first professional historical society founded by an immigrant group in the United States (Lovoll, *The Promise of America*, 330).

77. Christianson, "Myth, History, and the Norwegian-American Historical Association," 64–65.

78. Blegen, "The Kensington Rune Stone Discussion and Early Settlement in Western Minnesota," 370–71.

79. Holand, *Explorations in America before Columbus*, 344. Holand includes a reproduction of Anderson's article in the *Minneapolis Journal* from June 2, 1910.

80. Ibid., 342. Notably, Holand was a student of Ramus B. Anderson at the University of Wisconsin and even rented a room from him until they had "a falling out" (Nielson and Wolter, *The Kensington Rune Stone*, 484).

81. Anderson, "Another View of the Kensington Rune Stone," 414. It is well established that Goths did indeed participate in Viking expeditions.

82. Lovoll, *The Promise of America*, 118.

83. Matthew Frye Jacobson illustrates how the Johnson-Reed Act of 1924 favored immigration from Northern and Western Europe and restricted arrivals from Southern and Eastern Europe (*Whiteness of a Different Color*, 83).

84. Schultz, "'The Pride of the Race Had Been Touched,'" 1265.

85. Lovoll, *Norwegians on the Prairie*, 229. Coolidge, in earlier writings, praised persons from the Nordic race for their superior ability to become assimilated Americans. He contrasted them with other races that showed evidence of "deterioration" (Jacobson, *Whiteness of a Different Color*, 90).

86. Lovoll, *The Promise of America*, 303.

87. *Bygdelags* were Norwegian-American cultural organizations that were popular in the first decades of the twentieth century. Members of a particular *bygdelag* could trace their ancestry to a particular village or region in Norway. See Lovoll, *A Folk Epic*, 174–96; Lovoll, *The Promise of America*, 224.

88. This is an estimated percentage based on the census date recorded in Sletto's *Douglas County's Immigrants*, 22.

89. Øverland, *Immigrant Minds, American Identities*, 147.

90. This is not to suggest that ethnicity no longer played a factor in enthusiasm for the rune stone. Odd Lovoll coined the term "chamber of commerce ethnicity" to describe the ways that small towns capitalize on the so-called ethnic revival of the 1960s and 1970s by promoting ethnic-themed civic celebrations. These celebrations serve to generate financial gain from appeals to ethnic nostalgia (Lovoll, *Norwegians on the Prairie*, 262–70). As the following chapters reveal, appeals to ethnic pride persisted throughout the twentieth century.

2. Knutson's Last Stand

1. Holand, "An Explorer's Stone Record Which Antedates Columbus," 15.

2. Mancini, "Discovering Viking America," 872.

3. One example of this is Elliott, *New England History from the Discovery of the*

Continent by the Northmen, A.D. 986, to the Period When the Colonies Declared Their Independence, A.D. 1776, vol. I.

4. Mancini, "Discovering Viking America," 874.

5. The armor on the skeleton was actually made from copper and years later was determined to be made by precontact Algonquian Indians—not Norse travelers. See Kolodny, *In Search of First Contact,* 151–52.

6. Williams, *Fantastic Archaeology,* 191–92.

7. Ibid., 193.

8. Mancini, "Discovering Viking America," 877.

9. Ibid., 886.

10. Kolodny, *In Search of First Contact,* 29.

11. Ibid., 27–28.

12. Ibid., 23–25.

13. Ibid., 33–34.

14. See Anderson, *Kinsmen of Another Kind.*

15. Wingerd, *North Country,* 24.

16. Andrew Isenberg tells the story of Presbyterian missionaries in the 1830s who lived in a mutually beneficial relationship with Indians at the Lac qui Parle mission. These missionaries viewed their life on the Minnesota River as a utopian retreat from what they saw as a degenerate white civilization (Isenberg, "'To See inside of an Indian,'" 218–40).

17. Wingerd, *North Country,* 191.

18. Ibid., 185–96.

19. Brown, *Bury My Heart at Wounded Knee,* 39.

20. Wingerd, *North Country,* 307, 347.

21. Ibid., 320.

22. Ibid., 297. Clergy members were often the only white Minnesotans willing to stand in defense of the Dakota. However, most offered "no more than a timid protest" (316). Whipple was a notable exception known for his staunch advocacy of the Dakota.

23. Ibid., 319.

24. Ibid., 327.

25. One such physician, Dr. William Mayo, of Mayo Clinic fame, acquired the body of a man he referred to as "Cut Nose" and used it to teach his sons about medicine. The remains of "Cut Nose," or Marpiya Okinajin, were kept at the Mayo Clinic until 1998 when they were finally returned to his descendants and buried at Lower Sioux Agency. See Bessler, *Legacy of Violence,* 61, 66.

26. Wingerd, *North Country,* 315.

27. Ibid., 338. For accounts of the Dakota War from the perspective of the Dakota, see Anderson and Woolworth, eds., *Through Dakota Eyes.* Some six thousand Anishinaabe (Ojibwe) tribal members continued to live throughout northern Minnesota. By 1870, they were relegated to a handful of reservations.

28. Folwell, *A History of Minnesota,* 3:58.

29. Wingerd, *North Country,* Plate Caption 119.
30. Ibid., Plate Caption 126.
31. Ibid., Plate Caption 132.
32. Having served as Minnesota's second lieutenant governor and as a U.S. congressman, Donnelly was well known in Minnesota. His novel *Atlantis,* published in 1882, sold more than 1 million copies and has a number of references to Goths and to Odin as the god of the runes. Erick Wahlgren suggests that Donnelly's novel was a direct inspiration for the creators of the Kensington Rune Stone (*The Kensington Stone,* 126).
33. Turner, "The Significance of the Frontier in American History," 227.
34. Theodore Roosevelt argued that "overcivilized" men in the East should be encouraged to spend time in vigorous physical activity, such as hunting and camping in the western wilderness, in order to renew their connection to life in the pioneer era. The push to send U.S. troops to Cuba and the Philippines during the Spanish-American War was largely driven by the desire to "provide an outlet for men's robust energies." See Rosemary Radford Reuther, *America, Amerikka,* 113, and Hoganson, *Fighting for American Manhood,* 8.
35. "The Old Settlers' Reunion," *Alexandria Citizen,* July 12, 1900.
36. "Old Settlers Get Together," *Alexandria Post,* July 5, 1900.
37. In 1914, Lucy Leavenworth Wilder Morris published her collection of pioneer accounts, which was widely read and well received by the public: *Old Rail Fence Corners.*
38. In 1912, a monument was put up to commemorate the fifty-year anniversary of the execution of the thirty-eight Dakota men in Mankato. It was located at a prominent intersection at Front and Main Streets and was marked by a two-by-five-foot plaque. Local white residents complained bitterly and it was eventually removed. It was not until 1997 that a monument was dedicated at the site. It is now called Reconciliation Park and is marked by a large statue of a buffalo. In recent years, Dakota tribal members have made an annual pilgrimage via horseback from the Lower Brulé Indian Reservation in South Dakota to Mankato. The 2012 documentary *Dakota 38* tells the story: http://smoothfeather.com/dakota38/. Another group has participated in a biennial walk retracing the steps of 1,700 Dakota persons who were forcibly marched from Mankato to Fort Snelling after the Dakota War of 1862 (http://www.twincities.com/ci_21984103/dakota-commemorative-walk-remembers-1862-forced-march-fort).
39. Dahlin, *Dakota Uprising Victims,* xvi.
40. Faust, *This Republic of Suffering,* 83.
41. It should be noted that sacred spaces are often contested spaces. The meaning of the site where General Custer met his demise on the Montana prairie in 1876 has long been contested. It is a place where two different groups have competed over a national story. During the 1970s, Native American groups protested the name of the site: Custer Battlefield National Monument. The park had originally been dedicated as a memorial to General Custer, who was seen as sacrificing his

life to open the frontier for white settlement. Native Americans had long contested this claim and aimed to see it transformed into a site that commemorated the Indians who had died there. By 1991, the activists were successful in persuading the National Park Service to change the name to Little Big Horn National Monument. See Chidester and Linenthal, "Introduction," in Chidester and Linenthal, *American Sacred Space*, 17–20.

42. Holand, *Westward from Vinland*, 262.

43. Holand, "Further Discoveries concerning the Kensington Rune Stone," 332–33.

44. Ibid., 337.

45. Holand, *Westward from Vinland*, 198.

46. Holand, *My First Eighty Years*, 230. The number of those who accompanied him is modified again in 1962 when he writes that twenty-five to thirty men visited the site during the fall of 1919. This latest account also tells a more dramatic story of Holand arriving in a sleepy town "early one Sunday morning after an all-night [train] ride in a day coach." The only person Holand could find was a local minister preparing to leave for church. After feeding him breakfast, the minister drove Holand in his buggy near to Lake Cormorant, where Holand began his research (Holand, *A Pre-Columbian Crusade to America*, 121–23).

47. Johannes A. Holik found evidence that at least one of the mooring stones was chiseled by a farmer at Lake Cormorant (Sprunger, "Mystery and Obsession," 146).

48. In response, Holand collected the testimonies of other area farmers who claimed that they had seen the so-called mooring stone holes prior to 1908. See "More Criticism Directed at Runestone by Holvik," *Park Region Echo*, December 28, 1948.

49. See "Historical Discoveries," *Ashby Post*, December 3, 1909.

50. Wahlgren, *The Kensington Stone*, 77. In Holand's 1940 account, he says that a day's journey is seventy-five miles and the fourteen-day journey would be 1,050 miles. This is but one example of Holand's willingness to revise numbers in order to fit his theory.

51. "Iowan to Search for Viking Explorer Clues in Area" (date of article and newspaper name are unknown), Archives of the Kensington Area Heritage Association.

52. "Seeking Runestone Evidence—Divers Search Bottom of Big Cormorant Lake," *County Record* (Detroit Lakes, Minnesota), July 8, 1965.

53. Mircea Eliade speaks of sacred spaces as an *axis mundi* or "fixed point" that provides orientation (*The Sacred and the Profane*, 20–21).

54. Larson, *History of Douglas and Grant Counties*, 83.

55. Mircea Eliade illustrates the sacred significance that rocks and stones have held for many human cultures: "The hardness, the ruggedness, and permanence of matter was in itself a hierophany in the religious consciousness of the primitive. And nothing was more direct and autonomous in the completeness of its strength,

nothing more noble or more awe-inspiring, than a majestic rock, or a boldly-standing block of granite . . . Rock shows the [human] something that transcends the precariousness of his humanity." Of particular relevance to understanding the cultural role of the Kensington Rune Stone is to understand how stones function in commemorating violent deaths. Eliade notes that some groups in central India believe that the soul of a person who died violently would remain at the location, resentful that he had been cut off from the community. Stone markers placed at the site were believed to contain the dead, requiring them to help rather than harm the living. These burial stones are symbolic of protecting life against death. See Eliade, *Patterns in Comparative Religion*, 216, 218–19. For Christians, gravestones also function as symbols of immortality and resurrection (McDannell, *Material Christianity*, 17).

56. Cichy. *A History of Millersville, Minnesota, Douglas County*, 75.

57. Many of the army commanders who fought in the Philippines were veterans of the America's Indian Wars. Filipinos were often described by American soldiers as "Natives," "Injuns," or "savages" who were incapable self-rule and "only understood force" (Ruether, *America, Amerikka*, 125). This was also evident among Minnesota soldiers. See Penick, "A Test of Duty," 300. Subsequent chapters of this book demonstrate that Indians would serve as a recurring proxy for a wide variety of external and internal enemies. For another account of the battle, see McKeig and Geving, *The 1898 Battle of Sugar Point.*

58. Matsen, "The Battle for Sugar Point," 270.

59. Ibid., 269.

60. Bagone-giizhig continued to evade arrest, but most of his associates received light prison sentences and fines. The following January, President McKinley issued full pardons to all members of the Pillager band on the recommendation of the local commissioner of Indian affairs.

61. "No Indian Uprising," *Alexandria Citizen*, July 5, 1900. In 1890, the Ghost Dance had become a popular ritual for Indian tribes across the American West. It was widely known by white Americans and many feared that it could lead to a mass uprising. Practice of this ritual led to the massacre of more than 150 Lakota men, women, and children at Wounded Knee, South Dakota. For a scholarly treatment of both Indian and white perspectives on the Ghost Dance, see Andersson, *The Lakota Ghost Dance of 1890.*

62. Sheldon Solomon, "Introduction to Ernest Becker," http://www.ernestbecker.org/images/stories/pdf/transcript.pdf (accessed August 14, 2014).

63. Solomon, Greenberg, and Pyszczynski, "The Cultural Animal," 24.

64. Larson's depiction is a contrast to most white American depictions of Indians in the early twentieth century, which tended to be romantic. This was particularly true of writing originating in eastern states, where violent encounters with Indians had occurred generations earlier. See Marsh, "Penn's Peaceable Kingdom," 654.

65. Larson notes that another white settlement was founded near Holmes City

during the same summer of 1858 (Larson, *History of Douglas and Grant Counties*, 125). This location was just six miles from where the rune stone was later unearthed.

66. "Census of Douglas County for 1860," Douglas County Historical Society Archives.

67. Larson, *History of Douglas and Grant Counties*, 131.

68. After a few days, a group of twenty armed settlers ventured back to the Alexandria area to check on their farms. Two of the settlers out in front of the group, Andrew Austin and Ben Lewis, were ambushed by a band of forty Indians and shot at close range. Lewis managed to escape on his horse, but Austin was killed. The others settlers decided not to engage in battle with the larger group of Indians and retreated to the military stockade in Sauk Centre. A dispatch of troops was later sent out to give a "proper burial" to Austin. When the troops found the body, Larson writes that "the savages had cut off Austin's head and one of his hands and then had cut out his heart" (ibid., 150). In the 1890s, local newspapers ran articles about the sacrifices of early white settlers. One such article referred to Andrew Austin as "Douglas County's first white martyr" ("Alexandria in Early Days," *Alexandria Post News*, July 15, 1897).

69. The fort became the center of commercial and social activity for the next few years. Troops were stationed there until the spring of 1866.

70. Larson, *History of Douglas and Grant Counties*, 131–32.

71. Ibid., 143. His figure of eight hundred is at the highest end of the range estimated by historians of his day. The conflict actually took place over several weeks.

72. Ibid., 148.

73. Ibid., 72.

74. Ibid., 83.

75. For a brief summation of Girard's theory, see Pahl, *Empire of Sacrifice*, 28–29. Girard's classic text on the topic is *Violence and the Sacred*.

76. Pahl, *Empire of Sacrifice*, 28.

77. See, for example, Marvin and Ingle, *Blood Sacrifices and the Nation*.

78. Holand's historical narrative of the Viking massacre was ritually dramatized in several local historical pageants throughout the twentieth century. These pageants played an important role in forging civic identity and community spirit. As Marvin and Ingle assert, "violent, blood sacrifices make enduring groups cohere" (ibid., 1).

79. Weber, *The Sociology of Religion*, 107.

80. Eliade notes the ways stones function in biblical literature to demarcate sacred spaces. In the book of Genesis, God speaks to Jacob while he was resting his head on a stone. God tells Jacob that the land on which he was sleeping would be the land that would belong to him and his descendants. When Jacob arose the next morning, he took the stone, poured oil on it, and named the place "Bethel" or "house of God." See Eliade, *Patterns in Comparative Religion*, 228–29. In this sense,

the stone yields physical proof that God had given the land to one group and not to another.

81. As Frieda Knobloch observes, the expansion of agriculture is inherently an act of colonization (*The Culture of Wilderness,* 49).

82. Joseph Smith's discovery of the golden plates also functioned as a land claim for his followers. It situated the Mormon American story inside a larger biblical narrative.

83. Wingerd, *North Country,* Plate Caption 135.

84. See Southwick, *Building on a Borrowed Past.* Although flesh-and-blood Indians were not often visible to whites in west-central Minnesota at the turn of the century, they were present. Boarding schools for Indian children were located in Pipestone and in Morris, which is less than thirty miles from where the rune stone was unearthed. This Morris school was operated by the Catholic Sisters of Mercy from 1887 to 1909 and educated more than two thousand children who were brought there from Ojibwe, Dakota, and Lakota reservations. Indian boarding schools separated children from their families for long periods of time and forbade them to speak their tribal languages or practice tribal customs.

85. The state seal was modified slightly in 1983 so that the Indian appears to be riding south instead of west in order to "better represent the Indian heritage of Minnesota." However, appreciation of this Indian heritage still is mediated by the presence of a gun. See "State Seal," https://web.archive.org/web/20050905003524/http://www.leg.state.mn.us/webcontent/leg/symbols/sealarticle.pdf.

86. Anderson, "The Great Seal of Minnesota." The phrase "L'Etoile du Nord" or "North Star" is the Minnesota state motto.

87. Wingerd, *North Country,* Plate Caption 134.

88. "Runestone Days Has Small Attendance," *Park Region Echo,* June 30, 1938.

89. "Indian Baritone," *Park Region Echo,* June 30, 1938. Indians have long played starring roles in dramatic productions that portray Indians as violent. Perhaps the most notable example is the participation of Sitting Bull in William "Buffalo Bill" Cody's Wild West Show. See Warren, *Buffalo Bill's America,* and Deloria, *Indians in Unexpected Places.*

90. The comic book *Mystery of the Runestone,* written a few decades later, makes a distinction between violent Sioux Indians and peace-loving Chippewa Indians (Leuthner, *Mystery of the Runestone*). The comic book perpetuated a good Indian/bad Indian dichotomy that expresses the white desire for peaceful, compliant Indians who accept white domination. See Deloria, *Playing Indian,* 20.

91. Holand, *Norwegians in America,* 167.

92. Rølvaag, *Giants in the Earth,* 41.

93. Pahl, *Empire of Sacrifice,* 4.

94. Holand, *History of Norwegian Settlements,* 1.

95. Ibid., 282.

96. Perhaps one of the most potent symbols of innocent domination is Francis

Davis Millet's painting *The Signing of the Treaty of Traverse des Sioux*. In the words of Mary Lethert Wingerd, the painting is a representation of white Minnesotans' understanding of the history of Indian land cessions: "His vista of a peaceful and majestic ceremony, conducted under a waving American flag, provides no hint of coercion or desperation" (Wingerd, *North Country*, Plate Caption 128).

97. Holand, *Norwegians in America*, 3.

98. Ibid., 95. Holand fashioned for himself his own pioneer experience. After graduate school, he purchased a piece of land in sparsely populated Door County, Wisconsin. He planted a fruit orchard, which eventually financed much of his research.

99. Graber, "Mighty Upheaval on the Minnesota Frontier," 76–108.

100. As indicated earlier, contemporary historical accounts demonstrate that white–Indian relations in Minnesota prior to the Dakota War of 1862 were far more nuanced than these Manichaean accounts portray.

101. Holand, *History of Norwegian Settlements*, 255.

102. Holand, *Norwegians in America*, 34.

103. In 1904, the building was later moved to the Luther Seminary campus in St. Paul, where it still stands today.

104. This ideology has a lineage that traces back to John Locke's ideological defense of private property. Writing in the late seventeenth century, Locke asserts that Europeans were entitled to claim land in North America because they mixed their labor with the fruit of the landscape: "As much land as a man tills, plants, improves, cultivates, and can use the product of, so much is his property." Although God had given land to humans in common, he did not intend for it to remain unclaimed and uncultivated. Locke claims that God desires land to be in the hands of the "industrious and rational" (Locke, *Second Treatise of Government*, 21).

105. In Mark Juergensmeyer's theory, cosmic wars often "evoke great battles of a legendary past, and they relate to metaphysical conflicts between good and evil (*Terror in the Mind of God*, 146).

3. In Defense of Main Street

1. The U.S. Census recorded a loss of 226 residents in Douglas County from 1920 to 1930 (Sletto, *Douglas County's Immigrants*, 22).

2. Campion and Fine, "'Main Street' on Main Street," 80.

3. See Orvell, *The Death and Life of Main Street*.

4. Morris Dickstein, "Introduction," in Lewis, *Main Street*, xiv.

5. Lingeman, *Sinclair Lewis*, 159.

6. Orvell, *The Death and Life of Main Street*, 73.

7. "Sauk Centre Man Has Arrived as an Author," *Sauk Centre Herald* (Sauk Centre, Minnesota), March 13, 1921.

8. Lingeman, *Sinclair Lewis*, 201.

9. Campion and Fine, "'Main Street' on Main Street," 83.

10. Ibid., 88.

11. Ibid., 89, 84.

12. Writing in the early twentieth century, French sociologist Émile Durkheim researched the religious beliefs and rituals of indigenous groups in Australia. He observed that various clans within the tribe identified themselves with an image of a particular plant or animal. Durkheim referred to this image as a totem, which was used as a marking on all persons and things belonging to the clan. In modern societies, the totem can be understood to be a flag or coat of arms that represents a particular group or nation. Durkheim maintains that totemic identification is at its heart a religious process. Members of social groups worship themselves through identifying with collective totems. In Durkheim's view, society is God (Durkheim, *Elementary Forms of Religious Life*, 208).

13. "They Banished 'Main Street': Library Censors at Alexandria, Minn, Put Ban on Lewis's Book," *Kansas City Star*, August 31, 1921, 7.

14. This point was also stated in an article in the *St. Cloud Times* and in the *Milwaukee Journal*.

15. "Alexandria Denies Banning of Book," *Sauk Centre Herald* (Sauk Centre, Minnesota), September 15, 1921.

16. Price, *Indianapolis Then and Now*, 102.

17. Glass, "Alexanders All."

18. "Bjorklund's Opinion and Dream on the Runestone Memorial," *Glenwood Herald* (Glenwood, Minnesota), May 5, 1927. At some point, Bjorklund changed the name of his pharmacy to "Runestone Pharmacy."

19. "Kensington Plans Monument to Norsemen," *Park Region Echo*, April 14, 1927.

20. Fahlin was Swedish-American and his family members were among the very first white settlers of Douglas County.

21. "Thousands View Famous Stone and Hear Its History," *Park Region Echo*, June 2, 1927.

22. "Everybody Bound for Oscar Lake on June 1st," *Park Region Echo*, May 19, 1927.

23. Elna Thompson, "The Kensington Runestone," circa 1928; from the archives of the Kensington Area Heritage Society.

24. Local residents were not unanimous in recognizing the value of building a monument to the Kensington Rune Stone. One editorial stated that it would be more appropriate to build a monument to the pioneers who settled and founded the community: "The adventure of the Norsemen resulted in no benefit to themselves or anybody else. They came to their deaths in a swamp near Kensington and the world was bettered not one iota for their having lived and died, if the story about them is true." The editor quipped that it would be more beneficial to build a monument to "the dairy cow—the real discoverer of Douglas County" ("If We Put Up a Monument," *Park Region Echo*, April 14, 1927).

25. "Committee Chosen to Head Runestone Monument Project," *Park Region Echo*, June 23, 1927.

26. There was some debate among monument promoters about keeping the

actual artifact at the monument site for fear that it could be damaged or defaced unless it was guarded continually ("Everybody Bound for Oscar Lake on June 1st," *Park Region Echo*, May 19, 1927).

27. "Kensington Plans Monument to Runestone Norsemen," *Park Region Echo*, April 14, 1927.

28. "Committee Chosen to Head Runestone Monument Project," *Park Region Echo*, June 23, 1927.

29. Robert Belmont Freeman Jr., "Design Proposals for the Washington National Monument," *Records of the Columbia Historical Society, Washington, D.C.* 49 (1973/1974): 163; http://www.jstor.org/stable/40067740 (accessed April 14, 2010).

30. At least one genealogist in the late nineteenth century argued that the lineage of George Washington can be traced to the Norse God Odin. See Welles, *The Pedigree and History of the Washington Family Derived from Odin, the Founder of Scandinavia. B.C. 70, Involving a Period of Eighteen Centuries, and Including Fifty-Five Generations, Down to General George Washington, First President of the United States.* It is not known if local monument boosters would have been aware of this claim.

31. Completed in 1929 and standing at 447 feet, Minneapolis's Foshay Tower became the tallest building west of the Mississippi River. Wilbur Foshay based his design of the tower on the Washington Monument in Washington, D.C. It is possible that Bjorklund and other monument supporters found some inspiration in Foshay's project, especially because local residents were involved in its construction ("Tower Built by Men Dedicated," *Park Region Echo*, August 1, 1929).

32. "Mystery of the Kensington Rune," *Ogden Standard*, January 7, 1910. Latin inscriptions frequently utilize the character "V" for a "U."

33. Wahlgren, *The Kensington Stone*, 164–65.

34. Jolicoeur and Knowles, "Fraternal Associations and Civil Religion," 6, 17.

35. "Large Crowd Attends Runestone Rally at the Armory," *Park Region Echo*, December 1, 1927.

36. Skog, *The Kensington Runestone*, 5.

37. Ibid.

38. Odd Lovoll coined the term "Chamber of Commerce ethnicity" to describe the ways that small towns capitalized on the so-called ethnic revival of the 1960s and 1970s by promoting ethnic-themed civic celebrations. He points to the example of Madison, Minnesota, which declared itself "Lutefisk Capital USA" in 1983. The celebration of this traditionally Scandinavian dish was a way to generate financial gain from an appeal to ethnic nostalgia. The civic boosterism with the rune stone at its center is an example of commercial interests capitalizing on ethnic nostalgia much earlier in the twentieth century. See Lovoll, *Norwegians on the Prairie*, 262–70.

39. "Memorial for Norsemen Approaches Reality as Result of Festival Here," *Park Region Echo*, December 1, 1927.

40. "Commerce Club Bid Accepted," *Park Region Echo*, February 16, 1928.

41. "Runestone Attracts Much Attention," *Park Region Echo*, September 12, 1929.

42. "Runestone Park Foundation Discusses Future of Kensington Runestone Park," *Hoffman Tribune*, January 13, 2005.

43. "Famous Runestone is Mounted in a New Case," *Park Region Echo*, August 1, 1929.

44. "Kensington Plans Monument to Norsemen," *Park Region Echo*, April 14, 1927.

45. To this day, many residents in Kensington resent the fact that the stone resides in Alexandria. They feel that their artifact was taken from them.

46. The persons who put up money were listed as follows: Phil Noonan, Carl V. Anderson, C. O. Franzen, Judge C. J. Gunderson, Dr. A. D. Haskell, Gustav A. Kortsch, Constant Larson, J. O. Shulind, T. A. Syvrud, and J. A. Wedum.

47. The Alexandria businessmen were not as concerned as the Minnesota Historical Society over the question of legitimate ownership. They took Holand's word that he was indeed the owner. Throughout the twentieth century, some residents of the village of Kensington have felt that their rune stone had been stolen by the bigger city of Alexandria. In the gift shop of the Kensington Area Heritage Society, there are T-shirts with the phrase "Kensington, Minnesota: the Real Home of the Kensington Rune Stone."

48. "Hometown Opportunities," *Park Region Echo*, February 9, 1928.

49. Ibid.

50. An editorial from the preceding year expresses the futility of banning "sensational" books by authors like Lewis because it only boosts sales. See "Boosting Sinclair Lewis" (*Park Region Echo*, March 31, 1927).

51. Karen Fields, "Translator's Introduction," in Durkheim, *Elementary Forms of Religious Life*, xli.

52. "Everybody Bound for Oscar Lake on June 1st," *Park Region Echo*, May 19, 1927.

53. "Famous Stone Is to Stay Here," *Park Region Echo*, February 9, 1928.

54. "Runestone Story to Reach Many," *Park Region Echo*, January 26, 1933.

55. "Runestone Days Is On in Full Blast," *Park Region Echo*, June 23, 1938.

56. "Finance Plan for Runestone Days," *Park Region Echo*, April 21, 1938.

57. Southwick, *Building on a Borrowed Past*, 129.

58. Glassberg, *American Historical Pageantry*, 1.

59. "Runestone Days Program Ready," *Park Region Echo*, May 19, 1938.

60. "Runestone Days Celebration Is On in Full Blast," *Park Region Echo*, June 23, 1938.

61. "150 Actors on Big Open Air Stage," *Park Region Echo*, June 16, 1938.

62. "Runestone Tokens Prove Popular," *Park Region Echo*, August 18, 1938. These rune stone replicas or tokens bear a resemblance to "churingas," which Durkheim studied among the Arunta people of Australia. Churingas were often polished pieces of stone with an engraved design representing the totem of the

group. They often played a role in group ritual but were also used by individuals to provide "strength, courage, and perseverance, while depressing and weakening their enemies." Likewise, rune stone replicas provided individuals with a ritual object that evoked an image of Nordic heroism and a pioneer spirit. Placed on a display shelf or an office desk, the rune stone replica had the power to inspire greatness in the modern age. See Durkheim, *Elementary Forms,* 118–22.

63. "150 Actors on Big Open Air Stage," *Park Region Echo,* June 16, 1938.

64. "Did You Know," *Park Region Echo,* August 11, 1938.

65. In the latter, Holand discussed at length a controversial stone tower in Newport, Rhode Island. Although most historians had concluded that it was likely a windmill dating to the early colonial period, there were some who argued that it was built by Vikings in the twelfth century. Anthropologist Philip Ainsworth Means makes this claim in *Newport Tower.* Holand argued that the tower was a Norse fortress and a stopping point for the Knutson expedition on its way to Minnesota.

66. "Runestone May Be Displayed in U.S. National Museum," *Park Region Echo* (Alexandria, Minnesota), December 16, 1947.

67. Wahlgren cites page 343 of the *National Geographic Magazine* (vol. 94, September 1948), which includes a photo of Neil M. Judd, Curator of Archaeology at the Smithsonian, inspecting the stone with a magnifying glass. The quote listed below the photo states: "Later studies indicate that it was carved by white men who had traveled far into North America long before Columbus's first voyage" (Wahlgren, *The Kensington Stone,* 5).

68. "Danish Scientist Surveys Runestone Site Saturday," *Park Region Echo,* October 5, 1948.

69. "Runestone Verified by Noted Scientist," *Park Region Echo,* November 23, 1948.

70. "Runestone Pictured in Sunday Tribune," *Park Region Echo,* March 30, 1948.

71. "Runestone Given Spotlight at Museum, Baker Reports," *Park Region Echo,* February 15, 1949.

72. "Runestone Attracts 60,000 Visitors at State Fair," *Park Region Echo,* September 8, 1949.

73. Gilman and Smith, "Vikings in Minnesota," 16.

74. See Wahlgren, *The Kensington Stone,* 5.

75. Ibid., 182n3.

76. "Danish Scholar Expresses Doubt over Runestone," *Park Region Echo,* January 27, 1955.

77. Sprunger, "Mystery and Obsession," 148.

78. Holvik acquired the books from Amanda with the understanding that they would be returned. Holvik refused to do so and sent her a check for five dollars as compensation. Amanda refused the check and sent it back. Holvik's mistreatment of Amanda is frequently mentioned by defenders of the rune stone. See Nielson and Wolter, *The Kensington Stone,* 158–63.

79. "Professor at Concordia Claims Runestone Is Fake," *Park Region Echo*, December 21, 1948.

80. "More Criticism Directed at Runestone by Holvik," *Park Region Echo*, December 28, 1948.

81. "Holvik Continues Runestone Query," *Park Region Echo*, October 18, 1949.

82. Susag and Susag, "Scandinavian Group Identity," 34.

83. Inspired by Holand's theory about the Kensington Rune Stone, two teenage boys, Eric Sevareid and Walter Port, embarked on a 2,250 mile canoe trip from Minneapolis to the Hudson Bay in Canada in 1930 to trace the journey of the Norsmen. Sevareid's account of the journey, *Canoeing with the Cree*, details the hardships and dangers the boys experienced on their journey. The account is revealing of the twentieth-century nostalgia for the physical hardships of the frontier period. Immediately following his trip, Sevareid notes that he had the physical strength to overpower his older and larger brother—until life back in the city led to "sedentary habits that softened my flesh." Sevareid also notes that he was part of the first generation to grow up "without the American West shining before the eye of the mind as the vision of the future" (Sevareid, *Not So Wild a Dream*, 16, 23.

84. This motif resonates with Thomas Tweed's theory of religion, which describes how religious adherents draw upon "human and suprahuman forces" to cross boundaries. In this instance, the boundary to be crossed is the challenge for the rural, Midwestern community to be recognized as significant in American culture. See Tweed, *Crossing and Dwelling*, 73.

85. Holand's defense of Ohman is ironic given Holand's mistreatment of him. Holand was more eager to defend Ohman the symbol than Ohman the person.

86. Holand, *Explorations in America before Columbus*.

87. Holand, *A Holy Mission to Minnesota 600 Years Ago*.

88. Holand, *Explorations in America before Columbus*, 175.

89. Ibid., 162; Holand, *A Holy Mission to Minnesota 600 Years Ago*. In addition to the Kensington Rune Stone, Ohman himself emerged as a totem for rural, western Minnesotans.

90. Editor's note, "Curious Slab Still Center of Controversy," *Minneapolis Star*, April 11, 1955. This series of articles titled "Kensington Rune Stone: Hoax or History?" appeared in the *Minneapolis Star* from April 11 to April 16 in 1955.

91. Ibid.

92. George Rice, "Stone's Finder No Stranger to Books, Runes," *Minneapolis Star*, April 12, 1955.

93. Ibid.

94. George Rice, "Where Could Ohman Learn English?" *Minneapolis Star*, April 13, 1955.

95. Ralph S. Thornton, "Claims of Hoax Attacked: Backers Defend Authenticity of Runestone," *Minneapolis Star*, May 18, 1955.

96. Ralph S. Thornton, "Was Ohman a Genius? Rune Forgery Held Impossible and Illogical," *Minneapolis Star*, May 19, 1955.

97. "Runestone Tale Still Attracting News Headlines," *Park Region Echo*, April 7, 1955.

98. Ibid.

99. "Kiwanis Talks Flays Critics of Runestone," *Park Region Echo*, April 21, 1955.

100. Ibid.

101. "Los Angeles Times Publicizes Kensington Runestone Story," *Park Region Echo*, February 12, 1957.

102. Sean McCloud discusses how class is both externally ascribed to groups and freely chosen as a part of identity formation in *Divine Hierarchies*, 16–21. Arthur J. Vidich and Joseph Bensman show that small-town boosters often paint their residents as morally superior to big-city dwellers (*Small Town in Mass Society*, 36–38).

4. Our Lady of the Runestone and America's Baptism with Catholic Blood

1. "Keep Runestone in Washington," *St. Cloud Register*, May 21, 1954, 4.

2. Holand cites the work of nineteenth-century Norwegian historian Gustav Storm, *Studier over Vinlandsreiserne* (Holand, *Westward from Vinland*, 91).

3. Ibid., v.

4. Anderson, *America Not Discovered by Columbus*, 84.

5. See Blanck, *The Creation of an Ethnic Identity*, 167.

6. Mancini, "Discovering Viking America," 884.

7. Ibid., 885n45.

8. "Search Started for Old Runic Treasure," *St. Paul Dispatch*, December 14, 1909.

9. Reardon, *The Catholic Church in the Diocese of St. Paul*, 9. Ireland's argument for the authenticity of the Kensington Rune Stone was later cited in the Minnesota Historical Society's investigative committee's preliminary report in 1910. See *The Kensington Rune Stone: Preliminary Report to the Minnesota Historical Society by Its Museum Committee* (St. Paul: Minnesota Historical Society Press, December, 1910), 33.

10. John Ireland, "Letter of the Most Reverend Bishop," December 20, 1909, St. Paul, Minnesota, Roll 11, Letter 50, John Ireland Papers, M454, Minnesota Historical Society, St. Paul.

11. Wingerd, *North Country*, 61, 115–20.

12. Regan, "The Irish," 130.

13. Johnson, "The Germans," 167–68. The Catholic church was instrumental in facilitating this growth. When the Benedictine monastery was founded in 1856, the region's "German and Catholic future was assured" (Conzen, "Peasant Pioneers," 262).

14. Johnson, "The Germans," 153.

15. Reardon, *The Catholic Church in the Diocese of St. Paul*, 288.

16. O'Connell, *John Ireland and the American Catholic Church*, 267.

17. Ireland demanded that German-speaking parishes (and other "national" parishes) use some English. He also imposed a style of Catholicism that empha-

sized respect for clergy. This distinctly Irish style of Catholicism was not well received by other immigrant Catholics (Regan, "The Irish," 144–45).

18. Dolan, *The American Catholic Experience*, 202.

19. Zeidel, "Knute Nelson and the Immigrant Question," 335; Dolan, *The American Catholic Experience*, 202. As Robert Orsi notes, "Public support for war against Spain in Cuba was whipped up by anti-Catholic hysteria." U.S. soldiers were guilty of numerous acts of desecrating Catholic sites in the Philippines (Dolan, "U.S. Catholics between Memory and Modernity," 20).

20. During the period from 1920 until 1966, ten of twelve governors were Lutheran. See Eric Ostermeir, "Will Minnesotans Elect a Catholic Governor in 2010?" (April 5, 2010); http://blog.lib.umn.edu/cspg/smartpolitics/2010/04/will_minnesotans_elect_a_catho.php (accessed August 9, 2014).

21. This is not to say that Catholics did not exert significant political power in certain localities. This can be seen particularly among the Irish Catholics of St. Paul and the German Catholics of central Minnesota. See Regan, "The Irish," 140–44, and Johnson, "The Germans," 173–75.

22. Reardon, *The Catholic Church in the Diocese of St. Paul*, 281, 283.

23. Orsi, "U.S. Catholics between Memory and Modernity," 22.

24. Reardon, *The Catholic Church in the Diocese of St. Paul*, 289.

25. In the terms of Pierre Bourdieu's sociology, both Catholics and Scandinavian immigrants knew that they had to play by the rules of the game. Their collective habitus had already been inculcated with the notion that origin myths generated cultural capital in American society. Protestants had their foundational religious discourse rooted in the myths of Puritan origins; now Minnesota Catholics could create their own origin myth. For a description of Bourdieu's concept, see Rey, *Bourdieu on Religion*, 10–11, 154.

26. Schaefer, "The Kensington Rune Stone," 209.

27. Øverland, *Immigrant Minds, American Identities*, 68.

28. Ibid., 70–72.

29. Ibid., 69–70.

30. "Notes and Comments," *Catholic Historical Review* I, no. 4 (January 1916): 485.

31. Ibid., 484. In 1932, the Kensington Rune Stone was also mentioned in an article from the influential Jesuit publication *America: A Catholic Review of the Week*. Rev. John LaFarge summarized a number of Holand's recently published arguments about the authenticity of the artifact. LaFarge specifically endorsed Holand's theory that the stone inscription was carved by a Catholic priest from the Paul Knutson expedition. He said that the priest's "shuddering remembrance of the spectacle would naturally have expressed itself in those prayers which are most familiar to Catholics of all times and lands, the Hail Mary and the Our Father" (LaFarge, "The Medieval Church in Minnesota," 323).

32. Orsi, "U.S. Catholics between Memory and Modernity," 24.

33. Hatle and Vaillancourt, "One Flag, One School, One Language," 370.

34. Ibid., 364. See also *Fergus Falls Daily News*, June 6, 1924. The article estimates that there were two hundred registered KKK members in the area. See Roger Pinckney, "Klu Klux Klan Organizes Pelikan [sic] Rapids but Nobody Is Kluxed"; http://www.pelicanrapidschamber.com/historyhappenedhere (accessed October 1, 2010).

35. This is evident in writing as late as the 1970s. An example of this can be seen in Ahlstrom, *A Religious History of the American People*.

36. Dolan, *In Search of an American Catholicism*, 166.

37. Ibid., 167. Paul Blanshard's book, *American Freedom and Catholic Power*, was published in 1949.

38. Orsi, "U.S. Catholics between Memory and Modernity," 30.

39. Ibid., 23.

40. Reardon, *The Catholic Church in the Diocese of St. Paul*, 3.

41. Ibid., 9.

42. Kelly J. Baker illustrates the interplay between white racial identity and Protestant religion: "Nationalism and faith in American character combined whiteness, Protestantism, and patriotism to signify who American citizens really were" (*Gospel according to the Klan*, 190).

43. Reardon, *The Catholic Church in the Diocese of St. Paul*, 8.

44. Ibid., 10.

45. Orsi, "U.S. Catholics between Memory and Modernity," 27.

46. "Priest Historian Calls Kensington Runestone Genuine," *Park Region Echo*, November 11, 1952.

47. "At School Dedication, Bishop Bartholme States Church Has a Right to Teach, Praise People and Priests," *Saint Cloud Visitor*, December 8, 1957.

48. Ibid.

49. Herzog, *The Spiritual-Industrial Complex*, 6.

50. Ibid., 61.

51. Winsboro and Epple, "Religion, Culture, and the Cold War," 217.

52. Historian T. Jeremy Gunn observes that Cold War civic religion in the United States placed a priority on three values: governmental theism, military supremacy, and capitalism as freedom (*Spiritual Weapons*, 8–11).

53. According to Roman Catholic Code of Canon law, diocesan bishops are authorized to designate sacred spaces as shrines. An apparition of Mary is not required: *Code of Canon Law*, "Shrines," http://www.vatican.va/archive/ENG1104/__P4J. HTM (accessed September 30, 2010).

54. "Many Attend Catholic School Open House," *Park Region Echo*, November 19, 1957.

55. The placement of the shrine in the new Catholic school drew national attention and was even noted in the "World of Religion section of the *Philadelphia Inquirer*, December 30, 1957.

56. A picture and caption can be found in the *St. Cloud Visitor* from December 8, 1957.

57. Yzermans, *The Spirit in Central Minnesota*, 1:378.

58. Ibid., 379.

59. Larson, *History of the Red River Valley of the Augustan Lutheran Church*, 15–16.

60. Sprunger, "Mystery and Obsession," 145.

61. Ibid.

62. Wahlgren's appropriation of Holvik's claim is found in *The Kensington Stone*, 162–73.

63. Henry Retzek, "No Mystery Solved, but Scholar Attacked, Says Critic of Runestone Book," *St. Cloud Visitor*, July 26, 1959.

64. Yzermans, *The Spirit in Central Minnesota*, 2:792.

65. Holand, *A Pre-Columbian Crusade to America*, 151. The site is located approximately five miles northeast of Sauk Center in Section 26 of Birchdale Township, Todd County. Most residents in this area are Catholic and of German descent. Holand first published his research of his "Altar in the Wilderness" in his 1946 book *America, 1355–1364*.

66. Holand quotes from the *Catholic Encyclopaedia* for guidelines on portable altars (Holand, *A Pre-Columbian Crusade to America*, 154).

67. Ibid., 157.

68. Gary M. Suow, "Sauk Lake Altar Stone: Giant Rock on Sauk Lake May Be a Symbol of Worship," *St. Cloud Daily Times*, November 29, 1956.

69. Yzermans, *The Spirit in Central Minnesota*, 2:657.

70. Leonard and Bemetta Green to Dr. Piroch, May 22, 1995, Kensington Area Heritage Society Archives.

71. "Is the Chokio Stone of Viking Origin?" *Morris Tribune* (Morris, Minnesota), September 24, 1970.

72. "Catholic Historian Studies Local Altar Stone," *Chokio Review* (Chokio, Minnesota), September 24, 1970, 10.

73. Landsverk, *Ancient Norse Messages on American Stones*; "Landsverk Is Impressed by Altar Stone," *Chokio Review*, May 13, 1971, 2.

74. "Dahm Featured in Herfindahl Paintings," *Chokio Review*, March 21, 1974. It is not known if Dahm was affiliated with a religious tradition.

75. Gilman and Smith, "Vikings in Minnesota," 4.

76. Ibid.

77. Bishop Speltz also presided over a Mass at the Ohman farm on August 15, 1981.

78. "Altar Rock to be Re-dedicated in Celebration of Mass this Sunday," *Sauk Centre Herald*, August 7, 1975.

79. Schaefer, "The Kensington Rune Stone," 333.

80. Orsi, "U.S. Catholics between Memory and Modernity," 11.

81. Popular Marian figures such as the "Madonna of 115th Street" and "Our Lady of Charity" were successful because they embodied both ethnic and religious identity (Orsi, *The Madonna of 115th Street*; Tweed, *Our Lady of the Exile*).

82. This likely explains why Catholic Americans have not widely embraced

Leif Eriksson as a Catholic "founder of America" despite the efforts of some Catholic historians. Appeals to Leif Eriksson have been primarily advanced by Scandinavian Protestants, who ironically overlooked the Catholic identity of the Viking explorer.

83. Øverland, *Immigrant Minds, American Identities,* 185.

84. Rasmus B. Anderson, "Thinks Rune Stone Fake," *Minneapolis Journal,* June 2, 1910, 7.

85. See Meinberg, "The Norse Church in Medieval America," 179–216; LaFarge, "The Medieval Church in Minnesota," 323.

86. The article acknowledges that "not all the Scandinavian scholars are agreed on the authenticity of this text," but nevertheless, "the internal evidence seems to be all in its favour; and nothing has been found so far to contradict its contents" See "Saint Paul (Minnesota)," *Catholic Encyclopedia* 13 (New York: Robert Appleton Company, 1912); http://www.newadvent.org/cathen/13366b .htm (accessed August 11, 2014).

87. Protestants were sometimes irritated by the Catholic claim about the rune stone. When Kensington Runestone Park was opened to the public in 1975, Minnesota's secretary of state gave a dedication talk that specifically noted the Catholic faith of the Viking explorers. According to an interview with the priest of Our Lady of the Runestone Church, "a few local Lutherans were so scandalized that they rejected both the stone and the whole idea of a local Viking presence" (Hughey and Michlovic, "'Making' History," 350).

88. One Lutheran historian disparaged the character of Holand's Catholic Vikings (Larson, *History of the Red River Valley of the Augustana Lutheran Church,* 15–16).

89. *The Kensington Rune Stone: Preliminary Report to the Minnesota Historical Society by Its Museum Committee* (St. Paul: Minnesota Historical Society, 1910), 61.

90. Protestant views of Catholics in the 1950s began to shift and the faith of the latter was increasingly imagined by the former to be a legitimate path to becoming "American." Writing in 1955, sociologist Will Herberg writes of the United States' "triple melting pot," in which Catholicism, Protestantism, and Judaism came to be recognized as legitimate means to be recognized as "American" (*Protestant, Catholic, Jew,* 6).

5. Immortal Rock

1. Herzog, *The Spiritual-Industrial Complex,* 170–71.

2. Gaustad and Schmidt, *The Religious History of America.*

3. Gunn. *Spiritual Weapons,* 2.

4. Gunn takes care to distinguish his concept of American national religion from Robert Bellah's understanding of American civil religion. According to Gunn, the latter evokes "God" in a way that is a "less spiritually evocative and more politically insistent 'spiritual weapon' to attack atheistic communism" (ibid., 9).

5. Ibid., 8–9.

6. *Park Region Echo,* August 28, 1958.

7. "4,000 Attend Lake Geneva Bible Camp," *Park Region Echo*, July 8, 1958.

8. "Huge Crowd Jams Alex Fairgrounds for Prayer Crusade," *Park Region Echo*, September 25, 1958.

9. Minnesota statehood and the founding of the city of Alexandria by the Kinkaid brothers both occurred in 1858.

10. "Henry Moen Tells Runestone Story," *Park Region Echo*, September 9, 1958.

11. "More Evidence on Runestone Now on Display at Alex Chamber," *Park Region Echo*, July 12, 1955.

12. Maugridge S. Robb, "The Runestone . . . Douglas County's Most Famous Relic," *Park Region Echo*, June 12, 1958. The following quotations, unless otherwise indicated, are from this article.

13. This rhetorical strategy is reminiscent of Pierre Bourdieu's notion that the powerful try to naturalize the arbitrary. See Rey, *Bourdieu on Religion*, 53–55. In this instance, the rune stone defender makes "concrete" what is ultimately an imagined history.

14. The centennial edition also reprinted an *Alexandria Post* article from July 21, 1876, that describes the "dreadful slaughter" that culminated in the death of General George Custer. See also "An Army Scout Tells the Story of Gen. Custer's Last Stand," *Park Region Echo*, June 12, 1958.

15. Dorcy, "Ave Maria, Save Us from Evil," 42.

16. Ibid.

17. Gunn, *Spiritual Weapons*, 1.

18. Preus wrote this article as part of a series on the history of religion in the state for the *Minnesota Farmer* magazine ("Runestone Story Gets a New Play," *Park Region Echo*, March 11, 1958).

19. Faster, "A Cross to Bear," 103.

20. Ibid., 106.

21. "Runestone Story Gets a New Play," *Park Region Echo*, March 11, 1958.

22. Salverson was born in Winnipeg, Manitoba, to Icelandic-born parents. Starting in the 1920s, she wrote novels about immigrant pioneer life on the Canadian prairie. One of the major themes of her writings is the long-term cultural and spiritual consequences of immigration. See Bookrags Staff, "Laura Goodman Salverson," http://www.bookrags.com/biography/laura-goodman-salverson-dlb/ (accessed October 1, 2010). Four years before Salverson's book was published, Elizabeth Coatsworth published her novel *Door to the North: A Saga of Fourteenth-Century America*. Her novel was published as part of the "Land of the Free Series," which told stories of heroism from various groups that settled in the United States.

23. Hughey and Michlovic, "'Making' History," 338.

24. Other names that were considered include Chippewas, Miners, and Voyageurs. The name "Vikings" was chosen in part to "to recognize the venturesome people who first populated the state" (Dick Cullum, "Minnesota Is Designation of Pro Grid Team," *Minneapolis Tribune*, August 6, 1960, 21).

25. Wahlgren, *The Kensington Stone*, viii. Subsequent references are given in the text.

26. "Dr. Tanquist's Testimony: Why I Believe in the Runestone," *Park Region Echo*, July 21, 1959.

27. Dennis Dahlman, "Leuthner: Runestone 'a Hoax,'" *Echo Press*, November 4, 1988.

28. Leuthner, *Crusade to Vinland*, 3.

29. Wolfe, *Competing with the Soviets*, 93. In 1975, NASA used the name "Viking" for two space probes that were sent to Mars.

30. Herzog, *The Spiritual-Industrial Complex*, 172.

31. Ibid., 183–86.

32. There is evidence of other local Christian leaders using the rune stone narrative in Christian education. Pastor Maynard Anderson of the Bethlehem Evangelical Covenant Church of Wheaton, Minnesota, invited Viking enthusiast Marion Dahm to speak at his church. In a letter to Dahm, Pastor Anderson encouraged him to include something "of a spiritual nature" in his presentation (letter from Maynard Anderson to Marion Dahm, November 5, 1970, Kensington Area Heritage Society).

33. Leuthner, *Crusade to Vinland*, 14.

34. Gunn describes capitalist free enterprise as a central component of "American National Religion." The word *capitalist* was eschewed by many politicians during the 1920s and 1930s. Up until the 1940s, socialism was embraced in a more mainstream way—including endorsement of Keynes's theory of economics. Milton Friedman and other economists in 1947 began to characterize capitalism as a "moral doctrine." During the early 1950s, the word *socialist* became associated with *communist* and was vilified. Billy Graham taught that Jesus valued private property. "By the 1950s, capitalism and free enterprise were understood by many as a religiously sanctioned economic doctrine that also could be mustered as a weapon of freedom to fight the evils of socialism and communism" (Gunn, *Spiritual Weapons*, 11).

35. Lawrence R. Samuel notes the strong commercial orientation of this fair in contrast to previous ones (*The End of Innocence*, xx).

36. John C. Obert, "And Which *Minneapolis Star* Do You Read?" *Park Region Echo*, March 4, 1965.

37. "Alex Delegation to Meet Thursday with Gov. Rolvaag, Jim Stuebner," *Park Region Echo*, March 16, 1965.

38. "Runestone Ball Big Success: Another Planned for 1965," *Park Region Echo*, May 6, 1965.

39. The name Ole is pronounced "Oh-lee" and is a stereotypical name commonly used in Scandinavian-American humor.

40. "Ship Arriving, Runestone Set for World's Fair Trip," *Park Region Echo*, April 6, 1965.

41. Article by Dennis Dahlman in the *Echo Press,* June 7, 1996.

42. "'Big Ole' Looks 10 Years Younger," *Echo Press,* August 2, 1996.

43. "Kensington Runestone to go to 1965 World's Fair," *Park Region Echo,* January 12, 1965.

44. "Editorial," *Park Region Echo,* February 18, 1965.

45. "Runestone Leaves Alex for World's Fair Trip," *Park Region Echo,* April 8, 1965.

46. "60,000 Inspect Stone in Washington Visit; World's Fair Opens," *Park Region Echo,* April 26, 1965.

47. Ibid.

48. Ibid.

49. "Runestone Attracting Big Attention at Fair," *Park Region Echo,* June 3, 1965.

50. "The Days of the Roaring Mud Baths," *Chicago Daily Defender,* April 20, 1965, 14; "What to Look For: A Guide to Exhibits," *New York Times,* April 18, 1965, SM55.

51. "60,000 Inspect Stone in Washington Visit; World's Fair Opens," *Park Region Echo,* April 26, 1965.

52. "Runestone Leaves Alex for World's Fair Trip," *Park Region Echo,* April 8, 1965.

53. "Hammergren Off to World's Fair to Check on Runestone Display," *Park Region Echo,* May 6, 1965.

54. "State Pavilion Closes at Fair; Runestone to Be Brought Home," *Park Region Echo,* July 8, 1965.

55. "Hammergren Returns Kensington Runestone to Alexandria Home," *Park Region Echo,* July 22, 1965.

56. "State Pavilion Closes at Fair; Runestone to Be Brought Home," *Park Region Echo,* July 8, 1965.

57. "Hammergren Returns Kensington Runestone to Alexandria Home," *Park Region Echo,* July 22, 1965.

58. At the World's Fair, the shield held by the Viking had the phrase "Minnesota: Birthplace of America?" When installed in Alexandria, the question mark was removed and the shield read "Alexandria: Birthplace of America" in the form of a declarative statement.

59. After the installation of Paul Bunyan and Babe the Blue Ox in 1937, tourism to Bemidji's annual parade increased from fifteen thousand to one hundred thousand the next year (Dregni, *Weird Minnesota,* 12).

60. Samuel, *The End of Innocence,* xv–xvi.

61. Ibid., xv.

62. Hjorthen, "A Viking in New York," 10.

63. Blegen, *The Kensington Rune Stone,* 4–5.

64. Ibid., 111–12.

65. Ibid., 113.

66. Ibid., 118. Blegen gathered this information from Newton Winchell's field research notes from 1910.

67. Wahlgren, *The Vikings and America*, 132.

68. Landsverk, *Ancient Norse Messages on American Stones*.

69. Gilman and Smith, "The Vikings in Minnesota," 20.

70. Nielson and Wolter, *The Kensington Rune Stone*, 156.

71. "Viking Homes Buried at Runestone Site? Infra-Red Photos Say Yes," *Lake Region Echo*, October 23, 1974, 1.

72. Leuthner, *Crusade to Vinland*, 87.

73. Ibid.

74. Ibid., 63.

75. Nancy Piga, "Leuthner: Tapioca Pudding Got Me My First Job," *Lake Region Press*, May 20, 1989.

76. The image of Viking prowess was also adopted by the Minnesota National Guard. The 47th Infantry Division was known as the "Viking Division" and had the motto "Furor Vikingorum." Specially trained for Arctic warfare, the division served for the duration of the Cold War period from 1946 to 1991. See http://en.wikipedia.org/wiki/47th_Infantry_Division_(United_States) (accessed August 1, 2014).

77. Dahm also inspired countless other amateur archaeologists, such as Orval Friedrich, who claimed to have found evidence for forty-two Viking settlements and numerous buried Viking ships throughout Iowa and Minnesota (Friedrich, *The Great Ice Sheet and Early Vikings*, 3).

78. There had already been at least two excavations at the site. One was an informal excavation carried out by Kensington-area residents in the spring of 1899. The second was led by the Minnesota Historical Society, which carried out a partial excavation of the area in 1964. See Blegen, *The Kensington Rune Stone*, 135–36n1.

79. "Viking Homes Buried at Runestone Site? Infra-Red Photos Say Yes," *Lake Region Echo*, October 23, 1974.

80. Ibid.

81. Leuthner, *Crusade to Vinland*, 14.

82. This was likely a "Huey" helicopter that became an iconic symbol of the Vietnam War.

83. Slotkin, *Gunfighter Nation*, 494–96.

84. Raymond Haberski Jr. argues that the American civil religion during the mid-1970s became "contrite" as Americans wondered whether war, political corruption, and social unrest would lead to moral collapse of the nation (*God and War*, 99).

85. As Jonathan Z. Smith observes, sacred spaces are frequently "built ritual environments." Rituals enable religious adherents to focus their attention on objects or places, a process by which a place becomes sacred (*To Take Place*, 104).

86. The linking of present battles to past battles is indicative of what Mark Juergensmeyer would call a "cosmic war." In Juergensmeyer's theory, cosmic wars often "evoke great battles of a legendary past, and they relate to metaphysical conflicts between good and evil" (*Terror in the Mind of God,* 146).

87. Fenn, *The Return of the Primitive,* 33.

Conclusion

1. Interview with Julie Blank, former director of the Runestone Museum, "Runestone Museum; Alexandria, Minnesota," https://www.youtube.com/watch?v=4PJZp9NI-zo&feature=youtu.be (Prairie Public Broadcasting, uploaded February 22, 2011).

2. The local newspaper reported that five hundred Norwegians and Icelanders traveled to the Runestone Museum in the fall of 2013 alone (Blaze Fugina, "Renovations at the Runestone Museum," *Echo Press,* January 8, 2014).

3. One example is Barry J. Hanson's extended treatise *Kensington Runestone.*

4. Kehoe, *The Kensington Runestone,* 15–16. Robert G. Johnson and Janey Westin's *The Last Kings of Norse America* also develops a fur-trade-expansion thesis and links the Kensington Rune Stone to the Spirit Pond Rune Stone discovered in coastal Maine in 1971.

5. Thomas E. Reiersgord notes that the rune stone phrase "red with blood and dead" could refer to the way a person typically died of the plague—expelling blood from the mouth shortly before death (*The Kensington Runestone and Its Place in History,* 8).

6. Nielson's interest in the rune stone was first piqued by Robert A. Hall Jr.'s *The Kensington Rune-Stone Is Genuine.* Hall was a linguistics professor from Cornell University who asserted that the language in the runic inscription contained vernacular expressions that conformed to known Norse writings of the fourteenth century. Hall's work received mixed reviews from other academics, but it inspired a new generation of rune stone defenders. For a summary of Nielson's earlier conclusions about the runic inscription, see Nielson and Wolter, *The Kensington Rune Stone,* 215–17.

7. http://www.uhaul.com/SuperGraphics/262/1/Enhanced/Venture-Across-America-and-Canada-Modern/Minnesota/Minnesota-Runestone (accessed August 6, 2014).

8. O'Keefe was inspired to take on this project after seeing a presentation on the Kensington Rune Stone given by Scott Wolter. A pervasive theme of the musical is that Ohman and his family have been treated unfairly and that scholars are often wrong.

9. Wolter is the founder of the American Petrographic Services, which had previously performed research on the structural concrete of the Pentagon following the attacks of 9/11.

10. Ohman admitted that he had scraped out the grooves of the letters with a

nail shortly after unearthing it in 1898 (Nielson and Wolter, *The Kensington Rune Stone*, 23–25). For an exchange between Wolter and Miklovic about the rune stone, see https://www.youtube.com/watch?v=4PJZp9NI-zo.

11. Ibid., 221–25.

12. Richard Nielson, "Review of Wolter (2011), 'Report of Digital Microscopic Examination,'" November 26, 2011. Revision 1, February 26, 2012; http://www.richardnielsen.org//PDFs/Review%20of%20Wolter%20(2011)%20Report%20of%20Digital%20Microscopic%20Examination%20Final%20v3.pdf (accessed August 6, 2014). In 2008, Nielson conducted a 3-D imaging study of the rune stone and has since been banned from the Runestone Museum for not making the results public.

13. Runo Löfvendahl notes that the stone throughout the years has been "cleaned with different liquids, scratched with nails or similar, molded a number of times, polluted with gypsum; all these and other unknown interferences changing the appearance of the stone." See Henrik Williams, "Dotted Runes: What Are They and What Significance Do They Have for the Dating of the Kensington Runestone?" July 25 (revised August 20), 2011; http://www.nordiska.uu.se/digitalAssets/79/79636_dotted-runes.pdf (accessed August 6, 2014).

14. Williams, "The Kensington Runestone," 3–22.

15. Larry J. Zimmerman, former chair of the Department of Archaeology at the Minnesota Historical Society, says that Wolter's data has some merit, but it has not been submitted for adequate peer review. Wolter's eagerness to prove his theory has aroused ongoing suspicion from scientists (Zimmerman, "Unusual or 'Extreme' Beliefs about the Past, Community Identity, and Dealing with the Fringe," 72). Wolter has been an outspoken critic of the biases he sees as inherent in the academic peer review process. See Scott Wolter, "Reviewing Peer Review" (April 12, 2014); http://scottwolteranswers.blogspot.com/2014/04/reviewing-peer-review.html#comment-form (accessed August 6, 2014).

16. Nielson and Wolter, *The Kensington Rune Stone*, 234. See Wolter's more enhanced arguments in *The Hooked X*.

17. Brad Lockwood, "High Ratings Aside, Where's the History on History?" *Forbes Online* (October 17, 2011); http://www.forbes.com/sites/bradlockwood/2011/10/17/high-ratings-aside-wheres-the-history-on-history/.

18. In order to have a just and accurate understanding of American history, scholars must continue to research and tell the stories of the continent's first inhabitants. Numerous books give an account of the history of the place that would one day become Minnesota, including Westerman and White, *Mni Sota Makoce*; Treuer, *Ojibwe in Minnesota*; and Wingerd, *North Country*.

19. Jessica Sly, "Runestone Museum's Native American Exhibit Re-Opens," *Echo Press*, April 25, 2014.

20. Paraphrase of the video *The Diary of Clara Kinkaid* from the author's visit to the Runestone Museum on July 21, 2014.

21. Wingerd, *North Country*, 185–224.

22. It is not known when this placard was produced, but in a post-9/11 world, the use of the word *terror* to refer to Dakota people evokes President George W. Bush's "War on Terror." This association is further solidified by observing that this placard is located within a few feet of a display about the participation of local residents in the U.S. military and in several wars. This spatial juxtaposition implies that the viewer should recognize the contemporary military interventions by the United States as the latest efforts to eradicate the savages, reify national security, and carry out an exceptional American calling in the world.

BIBLIOGRAPHY

Archives

Douglas County Historical Society, Alexandria, Minnesota
Kensington Area Heritage Society, Kensington, Minnesota
John Ireland Papers, Minnesota Historical Society, St. Paul, Minnesota

Ahlstrom, Sydney. *A Religious History of the American People.* New Haven, Conn.: Yale University Press, 1972.

Albanese, Catherine L. *America: Religions and Religion.* 5th ed. Boston: Wadsworth Cengage Learning, 2013.

Anderson, Gary Clayton. *Kinsmen of Another Kind: Dakota–White Relations in the Upper Mississippi Valley, 1650–1862.* St. Paul: Minnesota Historical Society Press, 1997.

Anderson, Gary Clayton, and Alan R. Woolworth, eds. *Through Dakota Eyes: Narrative Accounts of the Minnesota Indian War of 1862.* St. Paul: Minnesota Historical Society Press, 1988.

Anderson, Gertrude E. "The Great Seal of Minnesota." In *Minnesota Skyline: Anthology of Poems about Minnesota,* ed. Carmen Nelson Richards, 7. St. Paul: League of Minnesota Poets, 1944.

Anderson, Rani-Henrik. *The Lakota Ghost Dance of 1890.* Lincoln: University of Nebraksa Press, 2009.

Anderson, Rasmus B. *American Not Discovered by Columbus: An Historical Sketch of the Discovery of America by the Norsemen in the Tenth Century.* Chicago: S. C. Griggs and Company, 1891.

Anderson, Rasmus B. "Another View of the Kensington Rune Stone." *Wisconsin Magazine of History* 3, no. 4 (June 1920): 413–19.

Andersson, Rani-Henrik. *The Lakota Ghost Dance of 1890.* Lincoln: University of Nebraska Press, 2008.

Appleby, R. Scott, and Kathleen Sprows Cummings, eds. *Catholics in the American Century: Recasting Narratives of U.S. History.* Ithaca, N.Y.: Cornell University Press, 2012.

Baker, Kelly J. *Gospel according to the Klan: The KKK's Appeal to Protestant America, 1915–1930.* Lawrence: University Press of Kansas, 2011.

Barton, H. Arnold. "Swedish Americans and the Viking Discovery of America." In *Interpreting the Promise of America: Essays in Honor of Odd Sverre Lovoll*, ed. Todd W. Nichol, 61–78. Northfield, Minn.: Norwegian-American Historical Association, 2002.

Bellah, Robert. "Civil Religion in America." *Dædalus: Journal of the American Academy of Arts and Sciences* 96, no. 1 (winter 1967): 1–21.

Berger, Peter L. *Sacred Canopy: Elements of a Sociological Theory of Religion*. New York: Anchor Books, 1969.

————, ed. *The Desecularization of the World: Resurgent Religion and World Politics*. Grand Rapids, Mich.: William B. Eerdmans Publishing Company, 1999.

Bessler, John D. *Legacy of Violence: Lynch Mobs and Execution in Minnesota*. Minneapolis: University of Minnesota Press, 2003.

Blanck, Dag. *The Creation of an Ethnic Identity: Being Swedish American in the Augustana Synod, 1860–1917*. Carbondale: Southern Illinois University Press, 2006.

Blegen, Theodore C. "Frederick J. Turner and the Kensington Puzzle." *Minnesota History* 39, no. 4 (winter 1964): 133–40.

————. "The Kensington Rune Stone Discussion and Early Settlement in Western Minnesota." *Minnesota History* 6, no. 4 (December 1925): 370–74.

————. *The Kensington Rune Stone: New Light on an Old Riddle*. St. Paul: Minnesota Historical Society Press, 1968.

————. *Norwegian Migration to America, 1825–1860*. Northfield, Minn.: Norwegian-American Historical Association, 1931.

Brown, Dee. *Bury My Heart at Wounded Knee: An Indian History of the West*. New York: Holt, Rinehart and Winston, 1970.

Campion, Amy, and Gary Alan Fine. "'Main Street' on Main Street: Community Identity and the Reputation of Sinclair Lewis." *Sociological Quarterly* 39, no. 1 (winter 1998): 79–99.

Cherry, Conrad, ed. *God's New Israel: Religious Interpretations of American Destiny*. Chapel Hill: University of North Carolina Press, 1998.

Chidester, David, and Edward T. Linenthal, eds. *American Sacred Space*. Bloomington: Indiana University Press, 1995.

Christianson, J. R. "Myth, History, and the Norwegian-American Historical Association." In *Nordics in America: The Future of Their Past*, ed. Odd S. Lovoll, 63–72. Northfield, Minn.: Norwegian-American Historical Association, 1993.

Cichy, Helen Joos. *A History of Millersville, Minnesota, Douglas County: Our Founders' Legacy*. Alexandria, Minn.: North Star Books, 1981.

Coatsworth, Elizabeth. *Door to the North: A Saga of Fourteenth-Century America*. Philadelphia: John C. Winston Company, 1950.

Coldsmith, Don. *Runestone: A Novel of Adventure*. New York: Bantam Books, 1995.

Conzen, Kathleen Neils. "Peasant Pioneers: Generational Succession among German Farmers in Frontier Minnesota." In *The Countryside in the Age of Capitalist*

Transformation, ed. Steven Hahn and Jonathan Prude, 259–92. Chapel Hill: University of North Carolina Press, 1985.

Cristi, Marcela. *From Civil to Political Religion: The Intersection of Culture, Religion and Politics.* Waterloo, Ontario: Wilfrid Laurier University Press, 2001.

Dahlin, Curtis A. *Dakota Uprising Victims: Gravestones and Stories.* Edina, Minn.: Beaver's Pond Press, 2007.

Deloria, Philip J. *Indians in Unexpected Places.* Lawrence: University Press of Kansas, 2004.

——. *Playing Indian.* New Haven: Yale University Press, 1999.

Demerath, N. J., III, and Rhys H. Williams. "Civil Religions in an Uncivil Society." *Annals of the American Academy of Political and Social Science* 480 (July 1985): 154–66.

Dolan, Jay P. *The American Catholic Experience: A History from Colonial Times to the Present.* Notre Dame: Notre Dame University Press, 1985.

——. *In Search of An American Catholicism: A History of Religion and Culture in Tension.* New York: Oxford University Press, 2002.

Dorcy, Mary Jean. "Ave Maria, Save Us from Evil: A Viking Message on the Kensington Stone for Us in the Atomic Age." *Our Lady's Digest* 37, no. 2 (fall 1983): 37–42.

Dregni, Eric. *Minnesota Marvels: Roadside Attractions in the Land of Lakes.* Minneapolis: University of Minnesota Press, 2001.

——. *Weird Minnesota: Your Travel Guide to Minnesota's Local Legends and Best Kept Secrets.* New York: Sterling Publishing Company, 2006.

Durkheim, Émile. *Elementary Forms of the Religious Life.* Trans. Karen Fields. 1912. Reprint edition with introduction by Karen Fields. New York: Free Press, 1995.

Eliade, Mircea. *Patterns in Comparative Religion.* New York: Sheed and Ward, 1958.

——. *The Sacred and the Profane.* Trans. Willard R. Trask. New York: Harcourt, Brace and World, 1958.

Elliott, Charles W. *New England History from the Discovery of the Continent by the Northmen, A .D. 986, to the Period When the Colonies Declared Their Independence, A.D. 1776.* Vol. I. New York: Charles Scribner Press, 1857.

Faster, Karen. "A Cross to Bear: The Minnesota Centennial Emblem Debate." *Minnesota History* 61, no. 8 (winter 2010): 102–13.

Faust, Drew Gilpin. *This Republic of Suffering: Death and the American Civil War.* New York: Vintage Books, 2008.

Feder, Kenneth L. *Frauds, Myths, and Mysteries: Science and Pseudoscience in Archaeology.* Boston: McGraw-Hill, 2006.

Fenn, Richard K. *The Return of the Primitive: A New Sociological Theory of Religion.* Burlington, Vt.: Ashgate Publishing Company, 2001.

Fitzhugh, William W., and Elisabeth I. Ward, eds. *Vikings: The North Atlantic Saga.* Washington, D.C.: Smithsonian Institution Press, 2000.

Folwell, William Watts. *A History of Minnesota*. Rev. ed. Vol. 3. St. Paul: Minnesota Historical Society Press, 1922.

Friedrich, Orval. *The Great Ice Sheet and Early Vikings*. Elma, Iowa: Self-published, 1993.

Gaustad, Edwin, and Leigh Schmidt. *The Religious History of America: The Heart of the American Story from Colonial Times to Today*. San Francisco: Harper San Francisco, 2002.

Gilman, Rhoda R. "Kensington Runestone Revisited: Recent Developments, Recent Publications." *Minnesota History* 60, no. 2 (summer 2006): 61–65.

Gilman, Rhoda, and James P. Smith. "Vikings in Minnesota: A Controversial Legacy." *Roots* 21, no. 2 (spring 1993): 1–34.

Girard, Rene. *Violence and the Sacred*. Trans. Patrick Gregory. Baltimore: Johns Hopkins University Press, 1977.

Glass, Matthew. "Alexanders All: Symbols of Conquest and Resistance at Mount Rushmore." In *American Sacred Space*, ed. David Chidester and Edward T. Lilenthal, 152–86. Bloomington: Indiana University Press, 1995.

Glassberg, David. *American Historical Pageantry: The Uses of Tradition in the Early Twentieth Century*. Chapel Hill: University of North Carolina Press, 1990.

Graber, Jennifer. "Mighty Upheaval on the Minnesota Frontier: Violence, War, and Death in Dakota and Missionary Christianity." *Church History* 80, no. 1 (March 2011): 76–108.

Gräslund, Anne-Sophie. "Religion, Art, and Runes." In *Vikings: The North Atlantic Saga*, ed. William W. Fitzhugh and Elisabeth I. Ward, 55–69. Washington, D.C.: Smithsonian Institution Press, 2000.

Greenberg, Jeff, Sander L. Koole, and Tom Pyszczynski, eds. *Handbook of Experimental and Existential Psychology*. New York: Guilford Press, 2004.

Gunn, T. Jeremy. *Spiritual Weapons: The Cold War and the Forging of American National Religion*. Westport, Conn.: Praeger Press, 2009.

Haberski Jr., Raymond. *God and War: American Civil Religion since 1945*. New Brunswick, N.J.: Rutgers University Press, 2012.

Hall Jr., Robert. *The Kensington Rune-Stone Is Genuine: Linguistic, Practical, Methodological Considerations*. London: Hornbeam Press, 1982.

Hanson, Barry J. *Kensington Runestone: A Defense of Olaf Ohman, the Accused Forger*. Kearney, Neb.: Morris Publishing, 2002.

Hatle, Elizabeth Dorsey, and Nancy M. Vaillancourt. "One Flag, One School, One Language: Minnesota's Klu Klux Klan in the 1920s." *Minnesota History* 61, no. 8 (2009): 360–71.

Herberg, Will. *Protestant, Catholic, Jew: An Essay in Religious Sociology*. Garden City, N.Y.: Doubleday, 1955.

Hervieu-Léger, Danièle. *Religion as a Chain of Memory*. New Brunswick, N.J.: Rutgers University Press, 2000 [1993].

Herzog, Jonathan P. *The Spiritual-Industrial Complex: America's Religious Battle against Communism in the Early Cold War*. New York: Oxford University Press, 2011.

Hjorthen, Adam. "A Viking in New York: The Kensington Runestone at the 1964–1965 World's Fair." *Minnesota History* 64, no. 1 (spring 2012): 4–14.

Hoganson, Kristin L. *Fighting for American Manhood: How Gender Politics Provoked the Spanish American and Philippine-American Wars.* New Haven, Conn.: Yale University Press, 1998.

Holand, Hjalmar Rued. *America, 1355–1364: A New Chapter in Pre-Columbian History.* Ephraim, Wis.: Self-published, 1946.

———. "Are There English Words on the Kensington Runestone?" *Records of the Past* 9 (September–October 1910): 240–45.

———. *Explorations in America before Columbus.* New York: Twayne Publishers, 1956.

———. "An Explorer's Stone Record Which Antedates Columbus." *Harper's Weekly* 53, no. 2755 (October 9, 1909): 15.

———. "First Authoritative Investigation of 'Oldest Native Document in America.'" *Journal of American History* 4 (second quarter, 1910): 165–84.

———. "A Fourteenth Century Columbus." *Harper's Weekly* 54, no. 2779 (March 26, 1910): 25.

———. "Further Discoveries concerning the Kensington Rune Stone." *Wisconsin Magazine of History* 3, no. 6 (May 1920): 332–38.

———. *History of Norwegian Settlements: A Translated and Expanded Version of the 1908 De Norske Settlementers Historie and the 1930 Den Siste Folkevandring Sagastubber fra Nybyggerliviet i Amerika.* Trans. Malcolm Rosholt and Helmer M. Blegen. Waukon, Iowa: Astri My Astri Publishing, 2006.

———. *A Holy Mission to Minnesota 600 Years Ago.* Alexandria, Minn.: Park Region Publishing Company, 1959.

———. *My First Eighty Years.* New York: Twayne Publishers, 1957.

———. *Norwegians in America: The Last Migration: Bits of Saga from Pioneer Life.* 1930. Trans. Helmer Blegen. Original Title: *Den Siste Folkevandring Sagastubber fra Nybyggerlivet i America.* Sioux Falls, S.D.: Center for Western Studies at Augustana College, 1978.

———. *A Pre-Columbian Crusade to America.* New York: Twayne Publishers, 1962.

———. *Westward from Vinland: An Account of Norse Discoveries and Explorations in America, 982–1362.* New York: Duell, Sloan & Pearce, 1940.

Holmquist, June Drenning, ed. *They Chose Minnesota: A Survey of the State's Ethnic Groups.* St. Paul: Minnesota Historical Society Press, 1981.

Hughes, Richard T. *Myths Americans Live By.* Urbana: University of Illinois Press, 2003.

Hughey, Michael W., and Michael Michlovic. "'Making' History: The Vikings in the American Heartland." *International Journal of Politics, Culture, and Society* 2, no. 3 (spring 1989): 338–60.

Isenberg, Andrew, "'To See inside of an Indian': Missionaries and Dakotas in the Minnesota Borderlands." In *Conversion: Old Worlds and New,* ed. Kenneth Mills and Anthony Grafton, 218–40. Rochester, N.Y.: University of Rochester Press, 2003.

Jacobson, Matthew Frye. *Roots Too: White Ethnic Revival in Post-Civil Rights America.* Cambridge, Mass.: Harvard University Press, 2006.

———. *Whiteness of a Different Color: European Immigrants and the Alchemy of Race.* Cambridge, Mass.: Harvard University Press, 1998.

Johnson, Hildegard Binder. "The Germans." In *They Chose Minnesota: A Survey of the State's Ethnic Groups,* 153–84. St. Paul: Minnesota Historical Society Press, 1981.

Johnson, Paul Christopher. "Savage Civil Religion." *Numen: International Review for the History of Religions* 52, no. 3 (2005): 289–324.

Johnson, Robert G., and Janey Westin. *The Last Kings of North America: Runestone Keys to a Lost Empire.* Edina, Minn.: Beaver's Pond Press, 2012.

Jolicoeur, Pamela M., and Louis L. Knowles. "Fraternal Associations and Civil Religion: Scottish Rite Freemasonry." *Review of Religious Research* 20, no. 1 (autumn 1978): 3–22.

Juergensmeyer, Mark. *Terror in the Mind of God: The Global Rise of Religious Violence.* Berkeley: University of California Press, 2000.

Kehoe, Alice Beck. *The Kensington Runestone: Approaching a Research Question Holistically.* Long Grove, Ill.: Waveland Press, 2005.

The Kensington Rune Stone: Preliminary Report to the Minnesota Historical Society by Its Museum Committee. St. Paul: Minnesota Historical Society, 1910.

King, Thomas. *The Inconvenient Indian: A Curious Account of Native Peoples in North America.* Minneapolis: University of Minnesota Press, 2012.

Kjaer, Iver. "Runes and Immigrants in America: The Kensington Stone, the World's Columbian Exposition in Chicago and Nordic Identity." *Nordic Roundtable Papers* 17 (July 1994): 19–24.

Knobloch, Frieda. *The Culture of Wilderness: Agriculture as Colonization in the American West.* Chapel Hill: University of North Carolina Press, 1996.

Kolodny, Annette. *In Search of First Contact: The Vikings of Vinland, the Peoples of Dawnland, and the Anglo-American Anxiety of Discovery.* Durham, N.C.: Duke University Press, 2012.

Kunz, Virginia Brainerd. *Muskets to Missiles: A Military History of Minnesota.* St. Paul: Minnesota Statehood Centennial Commission, 1958.

LaFarge, John. "The Medieval Church in Minnesota." *America: A Catholic Review of the Week* 47, no. 14 (July 9, 1932): 322–23.

Lago, Don. *On the Viking Trail: Travels in Scandinavian America.* Iowa City: University of Iowa Press, 2004.

Landsverk, Ole G. *Ancient Norse Messages on American Stones.* Glendale, Calif.: Norseman Press, 1969.

———. *The Kensington Runestone: A Reappraisal of the Circumstances under Which the Stone Was Discovered.* Glendale, Calif.: Church Press, 1961.

Larson, Constant. *History of Douglas and Grant Counties: Their People, Industries, and Institutions.* Indianapolis: B. F. Bowen & Company, 1916.

Larson, J. Edor. *History of the Red River Valley of the Augustana Lutheran Church.* Blair, Neb.: Red River Valley Conference, 1953.

Leuthner, Margaret Barry. *Crusade to Vinland: The Kensington Runestone.* Alexandria, Minn.: Explorer, 1988.

————. *Mystery of the Runestone.* Alexandria, Minn.: Park Region Publishing Company, 1962.

Lewis, Sinclair. *Main Street.* 1920. Reprinted with introduction by Morris Dickstein. New York: Bantam Books, 1996.

Lincoln, Bruce. *Theorizing Myth: Narrative, Ideology, and Scholarship.* Chicago: University of Chicago Press, 1999.

Linenthal, Edward T. *Sacred Ground: Americans and Their Battlefields.* Urbana: University of Illinois Press, 1993.

Lingeman, Richard. *Sinclair Lewis: Rebel from Main Street.* New York: Random House, 2002.

Locke, John. *Second Treatise of Government.* Indianapolis: Hackett Publishing Company, 1980.

Lofton, Kathryn. *Oprah: The Gospel of an Icon.* Berkeley: University of California Press, 2011.

Lovoll, Odd S. *A Folk Epic: The Bygdelag in America.* New York: Twayne Publishers in collaboration with the Norwegian-American Historical Association, 1975.

————. *Norwegians on the Prairie: Ethnicity and the Development of the Country Town.* St. Paul: Minnesota Historical Society Press, 2006.

————. *The Promise of America: A History of the Norwegian-American People.* Minneapolis: University of Minnesota Press, 1999.

Mancini, J. M. "Discovering Viking America." *Critical Inquiry* 28, no. 4 (summer 2002): 868–907.

Marling, Karal Ann. *The Colossus of Roads: Myth and Symbol along the American Highway.* Minneapolis: University of Minnesota Press, 1984.

Marsh, Dawn. "Penn's Peaceable Kingdom: Shangri-La Revisited." *Ethnohistory* 56, no. 4 (2009): 651–67.

Marvin, Carolyn, and David Ingle. *Blood Sacrifice and the Nation: Totem Rituals and the American Flag.* New York: Cambridge University Press, 1999.

Matsen, William E. "The Battle for Sugar Point: A Re-Examination." *Minnesota History* 50, no. 7 (fall 1987): 269–75.

McCloud, Sean. *Divine Hierarchies: Class in American Religion and Religious Studies.* Chapel Hill: University of North Carolina Press, 2007.

McDannell, Colleen. *Material Christianity: Religion and Popular Culture in America.* New Haven, Conn.: Yale University Press, 1995.

McGreevey, John T. *Parish Boundaries: The Catholic Encounter with Race in the Twentieth Century Urban North.* Chicago: University of Chicago Press, 1996.

McKeig, Cecelia, and Renee Geving. *The 1898 Battle of Sugar Point: The Last Encounter between the U.S. Army and the Indians of North America.* Walker, Minn.: Cass County Historical Society, 2011.

Mealey, Jenny Ann. "Qualitative Research in Anthropology: The Kensington Runestone Controversy." M.A. thesis, University of Minnesota, 2003.

Means, Philip Ainsworth. *Newport Tower.* New York: Henry Holt and Company, 1942.

Meinberg, Carl H. "The Norse Church in Medieval America." *Catholic Historical Review* 11, no. 2 (July 1925): 179–216.

Merling, Bert. *The Runestone Pageant Play: An Out-of-Doors Drama-Pageant* (1962). Minnesota Historical Society Archives.

Michlovic, Michael G. "Folk Archaeology in Anthropological Perspective." *Current Anthropology* 31, no. 1 (1990): 103–7.

———. "On Archaeology and Folk Archaeology: A Reply." *Current Anthropology* 32, no. 1 (1991): 321–22.

Michlovic, Michael G., and Michael W. Hughey. "Norse Blood and Indian Character: Content, Context and Transformation of Popular Mythology." *Journal of Ethnic Studies* 10, no. 3 (fall 1982): 79–94.

Morgan, David. *The Sacred Gaze: Religious Visual Culture in Theory and Practice.* Berkeley: University of California Press, 2005.

Morris, Lucy Leavenworth Wilder. *Old Rail Fence Corners: Frontier Tales Told by Minnesota Pioneers.* 1914. St. Paul: Minnesota Historical Society Press, 1976.

Mulder, William. "Mormons from Scandinavia, 1850–1900: A Shepherded Migration." *Pacific Historical Review* 23, no. 3 (August 1954): 227–46.

Nelson, Marion John, ed. *Material Culture and People's Art among the Norwegians in America.* Northfield, Minn.: Norwegian-American Historical Association, 1994.

Nielson, Richard, and Scott Wolter. *The Kensington Rune Stone: Compelling New Evidence.* Duluth, Minn.: Lake Superior Agate Publishing, 2006.

Nilsestuen, Rolf M. *The Kensington Runestone Vindicated.* Lanham, Md.: University Press of America, 1994.

"Notes and Comments." *Catholic Historical Review* 1, no. 4 (January 1916): 476–87.

O'Connell, Marvin R. *John Ireland and the American Catholic Church.* St. Paul: Minnesota Historical Society Press, 1988.

Orsi, Robert. The Madonna of 115th Street: Faith and Community in Italian Harlem. 2d ed. New Haven, Conn.: Yale University Press, 2001.

———. "U.S. Catholics between Memory and Modernity." In *Catholics in the American Century: Recasting Narratives of U.S. History,* ed. R. Scott Appleby and Kathleen Sprows Cummings, 11–42. Ithaca, N.Y.: Cornell University Press, 2012.

Orvell, Miles. *The Death and Life of Main Street: Small Towns in American Memory, Space, and Community.* Chapel Hill: University of North Carolina Press, 2012.

Øverland, Orm. *Immigrant Minds, American Identities: Making the United States Home, 1870–1930*. Urbana: University of Illinois Press, 2000.

Pahl, Jon. *Empire of Sacrifice: The Religious Origins of American Violence*. New York: New York University Press, 2010.

———. *Shopping Malls and Other Sacred Spaces*. Grand Rapids, Mich.: Brazos Press, 2003.

Penick, Steven. "A Test of Duty: Stearns County Volunteers in the Spanish-American War." *Minnesota History* 61, no. 7 (fall 2009): 292–305.

Price, Nelson. *Indianapolis Then and Now*. San Diego: Thunder Bay Press, 2004.

Reardon, James M. *The Catholic Church in the Diocese of St. Paul: From Earliest Origin to Centennial Achievement*. St. Paul: North Central Publishing Co., 1952.

Regan, Ann. "The Irish." In *They Chose Minnesota: A Survey of the State's Ethnic Groups*, 130–52. St. Paul: Minnesota Historical Society Press, 1981.

Reiersgord, Thomas E. *The Kensington Runestone and Its Place in History*. St. Paul: Pogo Press, 2001.

Remillard, Arthur. *Southern Civil Religions: Imaging the Good Society in the Post-Reconstruction Era*. Athens: University of Georgia Press, 2011.

Rey, Terry. *Bourdieu on Religion: Imposing Faith and Identity*. London: Equinox, 2007.

Richards, Carmen Nelson, ed. *Minnesota Skyline: Anthology of Poems about Minnesota*. St. Paul: League of Minnesota Poets, 1944.

Rogers, Elwin E. *Labyrinths of Speculation: The Kensington Rune Stone, 1898–1998*. Freeman, S.D.: Pine Hill Press, 1998.

Rølvaag, Ole. *Giants in the Earth: A Saga of the Prairie*. Trans. Lincoln Colcord. New York: Harper and Brothers, 1927. Reprinted with introduction by Lincoln Colcord. New York: HarperCollins, 1999.

Ruether, Rosemary Radford. *America, Amerikka: Elect Nation and Imperial Violence*. London: Equinox, 2007.

Salverson, Laura Goodman. *Immortal Rock: The Saga of the Kensington Stone*. Toronto: Ryerson Press, 1954.

Samuel, Lawrence R. *The End of Innocence: The 1964–1965 New York World's Fair*. Syracuse, N.Y.: Syracuse University Press, 2007.

Sawyer, Birgit. *The Viking-Age Rune-Stones: Custom and Commemoration in Early Medieval Scandinavia*. New York: Oxford University Press, 2000.

Schaefer, Francis J. "The Kensington Rune Stone." *Acta et Dicta* 2, no. 2 (July 1910): 26–210.

Schultz, April. "'The Pride of the Race Had Been Touched': The 1925 Norse-American Immigration Centennial and Ethnic Identity." *Journal of American History* 77, no. 4 (March 1991): 1265–95.

Selmela, Jack. *Of Vikings and Voyageurs*. St. Cloud, Minn.: North Star Press of St. Cloud, 2008.

Sevareid, Eric. *Canoeing with the Cree*. 1935. St. Paul: Borealis Books and the Minnesota Historical Society Press, 2004.

————. *Not So Wild a Dream.* 2d ed. 1946. Reprinted with introduction by author. Columbia: University of Missouri Press, 1976.

Skog, Carl. *The Kensington Runestone.* Evansville, Minn.: Enterprise Printery, 1928.

Sletto, Kathryn A. *Douglas County's Immigrants: From Europe to America.* Alexandria, Minn.: Explorer, 1992.

Slotkin, Richard. *Gunfighter Nation: The Myth of the Frontier in Twentieth-Century America.* Norman: University of Oklahoma Press, 1998.

Smith, Jonathan Z. *To Take Place: Toward Theory in Ritual.* Chicago: University of Chicago Press, 1987.

————. "The Wobbling Pivot." *Journal of Religion* 52, no. 2 (April 1972): 134–39.

Smith, Matthew Wilson. "American Valkyries: Richard Wagner, D. W. Griffith, and the Birth of the Classical Cinema." *Modernism/Modernity* 15, no. 2 (April 2008): 221–42

Solomon, Sheldon, Jeff Greenberg, and Tom Pyszczynski. "The Cultural Animal: Twenty Years of Terror Management Theory and Research." In *Handbook of Experimental and Existential Psychology,* ed. Jeff Greenberg, Sander L. Koole, and Tom Pyszczynski, 13–34. New York: Guilford Press, 2004.

Southwick, Sally J. *Building on a Borrowed Past: Place and Identity in Pipestone, Minnesota.* Athens: Ohio University Press, 2005.

Sprunger, David A. "Mystery and Obsession: J. A. Holvik and the Kensington Runestone." *Minnesota History* 57, no. 3 (fall 2000): 140–54.

Susag, Chris, and Peter Susag. "Scandinavian Group Identity: The Kensington Runestone and the Ole Oppe Festival." *Swedish-American Historical Quarterly* 51, no. 1 (January 2000): 30–51.

Thalbitzer, William. "Two Runic Stones from Greenland and Minnesota." *Smithsonian Miscellaneous Collections* 116, no. 3 (1951): 1–71.

Treuer, Anton. *Ojibwe in Minnesota.* St. Paul: Minnesota Historical Society Press, 2010.

Trow, Tom. "Small Holes in Large Rocks: The 'Mooring Stones' of Kensington." *Minnesota History* 56, no. 3 (fall 1998): 120–28.

Turner, Frederick Jackson. "The Significance of the Frontier in American History." *Annual Report of the American Historical Association for the Year 1893.* Washington, D.C.: Government Printing Office (1894): 199–227.

Tweed, Thomas. *Crossing and Dwelling: A Theory of Religion.* Cambridge, Mass.: Harvard University Press, 2006.

————. *Our Lady of the Exile: Diasporic Religion at a Cuban Catholic Shrine in Miami.* New York: Oxford University Press, 1997.

Upham, Warren. *Minnesota Place Names: A Geographical Encyclopedia.* 3d ed. St. Paul: Minnesota Historical Society Press, 2001.

Vidich, Arthur J., and Joseph Bensman. *Small Town in Mass Society: Class, Power, and Religion in a Rural Community.* Rev. ed. Champaign: University of Illinois Press, 2000.

Wahlgren, Erik. *The Kensington Stone: A Mystery Solved.* Madison: University of Wisconsin Press, 1958.

—. "Reflections around a Rune Stone." *Swedish Pioneer Historical Quarterly* 19 (January 1968): 37–49.

—. *The Vikings and America.* New York: Thames and Hudson, 1986.

Walker, Randi Jones. "Liberators for Colonial Anáhuac: A Rumination on North American Civil Religions." *Religion and American Culture* 9, no. 2 (1999): 183–203.

Wallace, Birgitta Linderoth. "Viking Hoaxes." In *Vikings in the West: Papers Presented at a Symposium Sponsored by the Archaeological Institute of America, Chicago Society, and the Museum of Science and Industry on April 3, 1982,* ed, Eleanor Guralnick, 53–76. Chicago: Archaeological Institute of America, 1982.

Ward, Elisabeth. "Reflection on an Icon: Vikings in American Culture." In *Vikings: The North Atlantic Saga,* ed. William W. Fitzhugh and Elisabeth I. Ward, 365–73. Washington, D.C.: Smithsonian Institution Press, 2000.

Warner, R. Stephen. "Work in Progress toward a New Paradigm for the Sociological Study of Religion in the United States." *American Journal of Sociology* 98, no. 5 (March 1993): 1044–93.

Warren, Louis S. *Buffalo Bill's America: William Cody and the Wild West Show.* New York: Alfred A. Knopf, 2005.

Weber, Max. *The Sociology of Religion.* Trans. Ephraim Fischoff. 1922. Boston: Beacon Press, 1963.

Welles, Albert. *The Pedigree and History of the Washington Family Derived from Odin, the Founder of Scandinavia. B.C. 70, Involving a Period of Eighteen Centuries, and including Fifty-five Generations, Down to General George Washington, First President of the United States.* New York: Society Library, 1879.

Westerman, Gwen, and Bruce White. *Mni Sota Makoce: The Land of the Dakota.* St. Paul: Minnesota Historical Society Press, 2012.

Williams, Henrik. "The Kensington Runestone: Fact and Faction." *Swedish-American Historical Quarterly* 63, no. 1 (January 2012): 3–22.

Williams, Stephen. *Fantastic Archaeology: The Wild Side of North American Prehistory.* Philadelphia: University of Pennsylvania Press, 1991.

Wingerd, Mary Lethert. *North Country: The Making of Minnesota.* Minneapolis: University of Minnesota Press, 2010.

Winsboro, Irvin D. S., and Michael Epple. "Religion, Culture, and the Cold War: Bishop Fulton J. Sheen and America's Anti-Communist Crusade of the 1950s." *Historian* 71, no. 2 (summer 2009): 209–33.

Wolfe, Audra J. *Competing with the Soviets: Science, Technology, and the State in Cold War America.* Baltimore: Johns Hopkins University Press, 2013.

Wolter, Scott. *The Hooked X: Key to the Secret History of North America.* St. Cloud, Minn.: North Star Press of St. Cloud, 2009.

Wuthnow, Robert. *Producing the Sacred: An Essay on Public Religion.* Urbana: University of Illinois Press, 1994.

Van Sertima, Ivan. *They Came before Columbus: The African Presence in Ancient America.* New York: Random House, 1976.

Yzermans, Vincent A. "Special Title of Bl. Mother Is Our Lady of the Runestone: History Pages Turned Back to 1898 Reveal Title's Vague Origin." *St. Cloud Register,* May 21, 1954, 1–2.

———. *The Spirit in Central Minnesota: A Centennial Narrative of the Church of St. Cloud, 1889–1989.* Vol. I, *The Bishops and Their Times.* St. Cloud, Minn.: Diocese of St. Cloud, 1989.

———. *The Spirit in Central Minnesota: A Centennial Narrative of the Church of St. Cloud, 1889–1989.* Vol. 2, *Parish, Priests and People.* St. Cloud, Minn.: Diocese of St. Cloud, 1989.

Zeidel, Robert F. "Knute Nelson and the Immigration Question: A Political Dilemma." *Minnesota History* 56, no. 6 (summer 1999): 328–44.

Zimmerman, Larry J., "Unusual or 'Extreme' Beliefs about the Past, Community Identity, and Dealing with the Fringe." In *Collaboration in Archaeological Practice: Engaging Descendent Communities,* ed. John Stephen Colwell-Chanthaphonh, Chip Colwell-Chanthaphonh, and T. J. Ferguson, 55–86. Lanham, Md.: Alta Mira Press, 2007.

INDEX

American civil religion, 10–13, 72, 76,
116, 119–20, 149, 163n31, 164n32,
165n42, 186n52, 188n4, 190n34,
192n84. *See also* religion
Anderson, Rasmus B., 18–21, 22, 24,
26, 29, 31, 35, 38–39, 43, 94, 96,
166n12, 170n70, 171n80
anti-Catholicism, 94, 96, 99–100;
coming from Lutherans, 94, 96,
107–9, 116, 185n19, 188n87,
188n88
anti-intellectualism, 3–4, 92, 130, 154
Atwater, Caleb, 44, 154

Bartholome, Bishop Peter W., 104–7,
109, 111, 114, 117
Bjorklund, Edwin, 37, 72–73, 76, 78
Blegen, Theodore, 26, 38, 144–45,
152, 165n4
Bourdieu, Pierre, 165n45, 185n25,
189n13
Breda, Olaus, 16
Bronsted, Johannes, 83–85
Buffalo Bill's Wild West, 57, 177n89

Catholicism: claims to American
space, 5, 93, 106, 109–13, 185n31,
186n53, 188n82; efforts to construct denominational history, 93,
96, 100–102; efforts to convert
Protestants, 5, 98–99, 111, 114;
notions of sacrifice, 102–6; social

history in Minnesota, 98, 100,
184n13, 185nn20–21, 187n65. *See
also* anti-Catholicism
Catlin, George, 35, 170n65
Christianity: fear of decline, 133,
134–35, 144; Vikings as exemplars
of, 123, 125, 130–33, 134
class conflict, 6, 184n102. *See also*
anti-intellectualism; Midwestern
identity
collective effervescence. *See* Durkheim,
Émile
collective memory, 5, 100, 161n6,
163n29, 167n27
Columbus, Christopher, ix, 1, 3, 5, 7,
9, 18, 25, 40, 43, 60, 65, 77, 94,
96, 101, 112, 130, 154, 166nn9–10
Coolidge, President Calvin, 40,
171n85
Curme, George, 16

Dahm, Marion, 55, 111–13, 147–48,
187n74, 190n32, 192n77
Dakota (people), ix, 7, 13, 44–51,
55, 57–58, 61–63, 66, 98, 155,
172n22, 172n27, 173n38, 177n84,
178n100, 194n22
Dakota War of 1862, 7, 13, 44–51, 57,
59, 62, 69, 155, 172n27, 173n38;
commemorations, 48–51, 173n38;
Mankato execution, 47
Dighton Rock, 18, 22, 166n13

David M. Krueger has a Ph.D. in religion from Temple University and a master's degree in theology from Princeton Theological Seminary. He is an ordained deacon in the United Methodist Church. His areas of specialization include American sacred spaces, religion and violence, U.S. religious history, and the sociology of religion. He grew up on a farm near Alexandria, Minnesota, and now lives in Philadelphia.